The Garland Library
of Medieval Literature

General Editors
James J. Wilhelm, Rutgers University
Lowry Nelson, Jr., Yale University

Literary Advisors
Ingeborg Glier, Yale University
William W. Kibler, University of Texas
Norris J. Lacy, University of Kansas
Fred C. Robinson, Yale University
Aldo Scaglione, University of North Carolina

Art Advisor
Elizabeth Parker McLachlan, Rutgers University

Music Advisor
Hendrik van der Werf, Eastman School of Music

London, British Library, Reg. 16. F. ii, fol. 73r. Reproduced by permission of the British Library.

The French Chansons of Charles D'Orleans

with the corresponding
Middle English chansons

edited and translated by
SARAH SPENCE

Volume 46
Series A
GARLAND LIBRARY OF MEDIEVAL LITERATURE

Garland Publishing, Inc.
New York & London
1986

Library of Congress Cataloging-in-Publication Data

Charles, d'Orléans, 1394–1465.
    The French chansons.

    (The Garland library of medieval literature ; 46, A)
    Originally Middle French text, with translation into
English.
    Includes indexes.
        1. Charles, d'Orleans, 1394–1465—Translations,
English.   I. Spence, Sarah, 1954–   .   II. Title.
III. Series: Garland library of medieval literature ;
v. 46.
PQ1553.C5A27   1986   841'.2   86-2012
ISBN 0-8240-8826-3 (alk. paper)

Printed on acid-free, 250-year-life paper
Manufactured in the United States of America

For W.T.H. JACKSON

Pour le don que m'avez donné
Dont tresgrant gré vous doy savoir

The Garland Library
of Medieval Literature

Series A (Texts and Translations); Series B (Translations Only)

Preface of the General Editors

The Garland Library of Medieval Literature was established to make available to the general reader modern translations of texts in editions that conform to the highest academic standards. All of the translations are original, and were created especially for this series. The translations attempt to render the foreign works in a natural idiom that remains faithful to the originals.

The Library is divided into two sections: Series A, texts and translations; and Series B, translations alone. Those volumes containing texts have been prepared after consultation of the major previous editions and manuscripts. The aim in the editing has been to offer a reliable text with a minimum of editorial intervention. Significant variants accompany the original, and important problems are discussed in the Textual Notes. Volumes without texts contain translations based on the most scholarly texts available, which have been updated in terms of recent scholarship.

Most volumes contain Introductions with the following features: (1) a biography of the author or a discussion of the problem of authorship, with any pertinent historical or legendary information; (2) an objective discussion of the literary style of the original, emphasizing any individual features; (3) a consideration of sources for the work and its influence; and (4) a statement of the editorial policy for each edition and translation. There is also a Select Bibliography, which emphasizes recent criticism on the works. Critical writings are often accompanied by brief descriptions of their importance. Selective glossaries, indices, and footnotes are included where appropriate.

The Library covers a broad range of linguistic areas, including all of the major European languages. All of the important literary forms and genres are considered, sometimes in anthologies or selections.

The General Editors hope that these volumes will bring the general reader a closer awareness of a richly diversified area that has for too long been closed to everyone except those with precise academic training, an area that is well worth study and reflection.

James J. Wilhelm
Rutgers University

Lowry Nelson, Jr.
Yale University

Contents

Introduction

Life of the Author

A great deal is known about the life of Charles d'Orléans, since he was nephew of one king of France, father of another, and the most famous and important of the hostages taken by the British at Agincourt in 1415. Two major biographical works exist (one in French, one in English), and both, supported by virtually the same evidence, depict the common picture of a man who was as interested in the arts as in politics. His parents are in part to thank for this: his father, Louis, brother of Charles VI, started a large and handsome library which, so far as we can tell, was developed for content as much as looks, and was so important to Charles that it was the last belonging he parted with when forced to sell to pay his debts; his mother, Valentine of Milan, who was Italian by birth, was well-educated and seemed to have instilled similar interests in her eldest son.

But life and politics constantly interfered with Charles's love and talent for poetry. Born at the Hôtel St.-Pol in Paris on November 24, 1394, he was forced to leave there two years later when his mother was accused of having interfered with the king's mental health. (The king's mental health was chronically bad; the exile was more probably due to Queen Isabeau's jealousy over attentions paid Valentine by the king.) Charles was raised in the idyllic Chateaudun, where he was surrounded by friends and admirers of his mother, including the poet Eustache Deschamps. Yet this paradise was rudely lost to him when his father was murdered brutally by men of John the Fearless, an action which, on the large scale, led France into a horrendous civil war between the Orleanists, supporters of Charles's father, Louis, and the Burgundians, those supporting his assassin; this weakened the realm to such a degree that the victory of the British at Agincourt was made more than possible and, on a small scale, forced Charles to recognize the frailty of such a paradise through the new responsibilities thrust upon him as prince, and the anger and pain that the loss caused his mother.

In fact, it is hard to imagine how Charles kept his

interests in the arts alive through all this turmoil. His
mother tried in vain to avenge the death of his father, a task
Charles took over when his mother died in 1408. In addition,
following the custom of the day, Charles married early, first
Isabelle, once a queen of England married to Richard II, then
on her death during childbirth, Bonne d'Armagnac, daughter of
an ally in the civil war. She too died (while Charles was in
prison) and soon after he was released, he married a third
time, Marie de Clèves. Moreover, in addition to his own chil-
dren, he cared for his brothers, sisters, and a stepbrother,
and seems to have been a generous and caring protector to all,
sending food and money whenever possible even when he was in
England. He was forced at one time to send his own brother
John Angoulême to England as one of seven hostages exchanged
for English strength to help fight the Burgundians, and though
the ransom was high--so high he was never able to meet it--
Charles constantly sent as much money as possible toward free-
ing his brother.

Ironically, what would appear to be the greatest inter-
ference of all--his being taken hostage at Agincourt--proved
to be the most fortunate event of Charles's life for his poetry, both because few were allowed the privilege of remaining
alive (the number of hostages taken was so great that Henry V
had most of them killed), and because his terms of imprisonment
were very favorable to writing. Legend has it that it was the
thought of Charles as a long-time prisoner of the British that
led Joan of Arc to undertake her mission, and later to exclaim
at her trial that "Dieu aime bien le duc d'Orléans, et qu'elle
avoit en plus de révélations de lui que d'homme de France,
excepté de son roy" (God favors the duke of Orléans, and she
had more visions of him than of any other Frenchman, except
the king). God must indeed have looked favorably upon Charles,
for during his twenty-five years in England he was moved from
castle to castle and guardian to guardian, one more solicitous
of his welfare than the next. It was during this time that
Charles wrote all but 38 of his ballades and the first half
of the chansons translated in this edition, the 52 which he
also wrote in English. Although there has been much debate
through the years over the attribution of the English chansons
--a point we will return to later--it seems logical in this
context to think that he might have tried his hand at writing
English poetry "when in Rome."

In fact, Charles's life in England seems to have been
well-suited to meditation and study. We know he was allowed
to take a sizeable library with him, a fair sampling of the
books he owned at Blois. It is interesting to note that though
his love of poetry and his talent for writing were apparent
from a very early age, his sources, judging from the books he

Battle of Agincourt. Paris, B.N. fr. 2880, fol. 208 Reproduced by permission of the Bibliothèque Nationale.

had in his library, were by and large extra-literary. Works
of St. Augustine and other religious writers and copies of
the Bible far outnumber strictly literary works; such works
of literature as there are, are not the most important of a
given author: he owns no copy of Petrarch's *Canzoniere*, for
example, though he does have Petrarch's *Epistole*, and perhaps
more surprisingly, owns no Dante whatsoever. Frequently kept
in isolation because of his assumed danger as a spy and rebel,
he would have had plenty of time and solitude to spend thinking
and writing; moreover there is evidence of his associating
with the religious association of the Grey Friars, a Franciscan
sect. His poetry from this twenty-five year period exhibits
a growing interest in making complex poetic comparisons, both
metaphoric and allegorical, of real originality and strength.
Given a life such as his, so full of changes of fortune and
differing styles of life, it is tempting to suggest that such
a metaphoric process could have developed as a psychological
defense; in coming to terms with his lonely situation of the
moment a comparison with the past would surface and lend itself
to the kind of strict allegorical systems so characteristic
of his writing of this period.

Because of a scarcity of historical information about
Charles's personal life during his exile (though we know everything about his whereabouts) much has been made of the histo-
ricity of the poems written during this period. While some
of them, such as Ballade 75, "En regardant vers le pais de
France," or Chanson 50, "Au besoing congnoist on l'amy," presumably addressed to Philippe le Bon in thanks for his support,
do indeed reflect an awareness of his situation of the moment,
the lyrics, by and large, are not about his life in England.
Rather they transcend the day-to-day realities of his existence
and dwell instead on the universal truths suggested by the
particulars of his unusual life. Whatever reference to his
exile might be ferreted out of his poems is better understood
and interpreted as a metaphor for the condition of every man;
so, for example, Chanson 38, "Ma seule amour, ma joye et ma
maistresse." Rather than explain this chanson in a historical
context as written to his wife Bonne about their unfortunate
separation, one should set this poem in a literary context and
compare it to the courtly lyrics of the troubadours; exile and
separation, whatever their source for Charles, provided him
with fruitful metaphors of great literary tradition and impact.
Charles was able to use his surroundings to his poetic advantage, drawing on his experience as an exile or prisoner (situ-
ations used frequently as metaphors for psychological states
by authors whose books he owned, such as Augustine and Aquinas)
to create a powerful and believable metaphoric matrix of his
own devising.

Such also is the truth of the lady addressed in his poems. From time to time sensible critics have suggested that this lady was a fiction--an allegorical representation of a concept such as France, a psychological projection, or, most sensibly I think, a formal requirement of the poems: Charles needed his *Dame* as Dante needed his Beatrice, Petrarch his Laura. But, unfortunately, much critical energy has been spent determining who this lady actually was, particularly in those poems written after Charles's second wife Bonne died and before he met and married his third, Marie de Clèves. Since the bulk of the poems written in this period were those with English counterparts, an English mistress was hypothesized and several names put forward, most notably that of Anne Moleyns, an anagram of whose name can be found in the poem, "Alas mercy wher shal myn hert yow fynd." Other suggestions include Alice Chaucer, daughter of the poet and wife of the Duke of Suffolk, one of Charles's wardens, and Maud Arundel, a countess who moved in the same circles as Charles. Given that there is no substantial proof for such an attachment, and that even if there were, it would tell us little of worth about the poetry, such information is irrelevant. Moreover, the poems Charles wrote after his exile are of a piece with those written during (compare the first 52 chansons with the remaining 35), suggesting a unity of purpose that postdates his supposed affair, and they are all such polished pieces of formal poetry that the referent is much less important than the intent of the metaphor or allegory. Finally, we know that his third wife Marie possessed a copy of the first 52 chansons (minus Nos. 30 and 31); it seems unlikely that she would have wanted to own such a thing if the poems had been written for someone else.

The chansons translated in this edition represent, then, both the period of Charles's exile and the time after his return to France. When he was finally released in 1440--"allowed to travel without safe-conduct," as he says--he returned to his chateau in Blois where he spent a much more peaceful, social, and uninterrupted time than had previously been afforded him. He entered little into politics--times and kings had changed sufficiently to allow him this indulgence--though he was present at the signing of the Treaty of Tours that marked the beginning of a five-year peace in the war between England and France which he had fought and suffered so hard to end. It was during this period following his exile that Charles's now-famous court of Blois existed, a poetic circle including such eminences as Villon, Meschinot, René d'Anjou, to name but a few. This poetic court consisted of courtly games and competitions including poetic debates or contests, with each poet writing in a given form, such as a rondeau, on a given line, or a proverb.

But mostly this was a time for Charles to try to recoup
the good life, to rebuild the paradise he had known so long
before and to continue his interest in writing. In addition
to the 35 chansons he wrote during this period, he composed
over 400 rondeaux, many of which reflect an even greater awareness of the privilege granted the poet to refer to the world
without being bound by it. While references to actualities
become in fact more frequent in these later poems, so does
the playfulness with which he uses them as metaphors of ab-
stract, often psychological, realities, as, for example, in
Chanson 76, "En gibessant."

One trip that we know Charles did take during this time
shows that he was never allowed to retire fully from the public
eye. As a part of her dowry, his mother had brought to her
marriage the fiefdom of Asti in Lombardy, which Charles had
then inherited. During his absence, however, he had been
forced to deed its rule to Filippo Maria Visconti, Duke of
Milan. Upon the Duke's death Charles, having returned from
England, tried to reassert his claim to the territory by going
to Asti and fighting for it, only to lose it to the new Duke
of Milan, Francesco Sforza. Aside from the insight into
Charles's continuing importance as a public figure that this
incident gives us, this event was important for his literary
fortunes, for it is during this sojourn that he met an Astesan
named Antonio who, in addition to fighting valiantly for
Charles's cause, elected to become Charles's amanuensis. He
copied the French manuscript Charles composed in part in England and for whatever reason, translated all the poems into
Latin. Beyond being a historical curiosity that suggests the
influence of Italian humanism on Antonio, if not on Charles,
this effort proved extremely useful to later scholars, for in
copying Charles's poems directly from the autograph manuscript,
Antonio preserved the order of the poems. This order would
no doubt otherwise have been destroyed along with the true
corpus of Charles's work, for it was composed in a curious
way: rather than filling the folios from top to bottom, left
to right, Charles wrote only on the bottom half of each folio,
leaving the top blank for accompanying music. Whatever the
intended purpose of these blank spaces, they were later filled
in with poems of his contemporaries, a fact which no editor
before Champion was insightful enough to figure out. Using
the Astesan's Latin manuscript in conjunction with Charles's
own, Champion was able to decipher this complex puzzle, and
to establish, finally, which poems were by Charles, and the
order in which he preserved them.

These lands in Italy also played a large part in the last
event of Charles's life. The French king at the time, Louis
XII, was Charles's nephew, and was apparently threatened by

Charles, or more accurately, by Charles's potential heirs, to
the degree that he tried to strip Charles of his holdings.
One of the areas of dispute was the land in Asti which the
king helped return to its Italian usurper. At an assembly in
Tours called by the king in 1465 Charles tried to suggest the
error of Louis's ways, only to be rebuffed by the king and
publicly humiliated in spite of the fact that he was old, fee-
ble, and barely able to speak. Heading home to Blois after
this assembly Charles was forced by his worsened health to
stop en route at Amboise. Here in the night of January 4-5,
1465, Charles d'Orléans died at the age of 71 of an unknown
illness.

Artistic Achievement

The artistic achievement of Charles d'Orléans is difficult
to chart. It would be both facile and true to say that he
was one of the pivotal figures in the development from medieval
to Renaissance lyric: facile because he was so much out of the
mainstream of what was happening in the lyric traditions of
his day, true because his poetry does indeed show traces of
both medieval and Renaissance style, and did, to some degree
at least, influence the later poets.

It is perhaps safer to say that the poetry of Charles
d'Orléans provided a significant link in the chain of the
French poetic tradition, for while, like Dante, Charles develops out of the troubadour tradition, he does so indirectly,
through the *trouvères*, picking up more on the style of the
lyrics--the highly stylized codes, the extremely rigorous rhyme
schemes--than on the metaphysical concepts the troubadours
were so influential in re-introducing into western literary
thought. It is his focus on style that links Charles most
clearly with the French lyric tradition, since style was cen-
tral to the *trouvères* who preceded him and the *rhetoriqueurs*
who were to follow.

Charles's stylistic achievements lie in two major areas:
his skill with the short fixed form (*ballade, chanson, rondeau*)
and his use of allegory. Both of these features recur throughout his poetry and both show a similar course of development
and refinement. The earliest poem of his we know of is the
Retenue d'Amours, a long allegorical work in the manner of the
Roman de la Rose. Like the *Roman* it is rhymed in couplets and
tells the tale of a youth confronting the trials and tribula-
tions of his first love, all presented in very pedestrian per-
sonification allegory. Charles's first major group of poems
shows significant development from this early work: a series
of ballades written mostly while he is first in exile show

him working in what many consider to be his most successful
medium, the fixed form. Here within the restrictions of the
ballade form (ABABBCBC ...) Charles is able to manipulate rhyme
and allegory to produce several extraordinary statements in
very few lines.

The ballades seem to be important largely as developmental
material: frequently the rhymes are forced and the ideas con-
torted or oversimplified to such a degree that his poems come
across as flighty and insignificant. But as a means to an
end, they play an extremely important role; one cannot help
but think that through experimenting with the ballade form he
became able to handle the even more rigorous forms of the chanson and rondeau. Both these shorter fixed forms, the chanson
and rondeau, have the same structure: the first strophe has
four lines; the second strophe, two lines plus the two first
lines of the first strophe; and the final strophe has four
lines plus the first line of the first, or 4 + 4(2+2) + 5(4+1);
the rhyme scheme is ABba abAB abbaA. (There is also a longer
version, but it is only a variant of the above form.) For a
long time it was thought that the difference between the two
forms was formal, the rondeau having a one-line refrain, the
chanson a two-line refrain, but that has been shown to be un-
true, and the difference is now assumed to be a matter of intent not form; the chanson, it is suggested, was to be set to
music, the rondeau not. This particular theory has gained
credence through Champion's discovery that the chansons in the
authoritative MS were written at the bottom of the page, the
top blank large enough for a musical setting to be added later.
As none of the chansons is, in fact, set to music, however,
it seems highly possible that the difference between chanson
and rondeau is more one of content than intent. Perhaps the
chansons were meant as the counterparts to the song-cycle or
canzoniere. They are, after all, about a single lady, and
though they show little Petrarchan neoplatonism, they do demonstrate the unity of the *Canzoniere* or later English song-
cycle.

There is one major reason why the boundary line between
these two bodies of poems remains so hazy, and that is that
the later rubricator of Charles's autograph manuscript marked
the poems indiscriminately as rondeau or chanson, a mistake
all the early editions of the French poems, copying the rubric,
reproduced. Champion's sorting out of the manuscript has al-
leviated this problem, and starting with his edition, the order
of which is repeated here, the chansons are clearly set apart
from the rondeaux.

The critic who has succeeded in differentiating these
two groups of poems most successfully is Sergio Cigada. In
his work, *L'Opera Poetica di Charles d'Orléans*, Cigada charts

Charles's development in terms of three styles. The first, the "metaforizzazione della maniera cortese" (metaphorisization of the courtly style), Cigada sees as developmental; the second (from 1444-1445), as "naturalismo prezioso" (manneristic naturalism); the third "realismo psicologico" (psychological realism), which, in many ways, reflects a spiraling return to elements of his first style as Charles reincorporates allegorical vocabulary to accommodate his familiar and psychologically realistic subject matter. Because the second period is so brief, Cigada is really talking about two styles, one courtly, the other realistic. To my mind this corresponds in a real way to the development one can sense within the chansons, and can help to distinguish the essence of the chanson from that of the rondeau. For while the chansons, ranging as they did over a number of years, show traces of all three styles, they cluster around the courtly in both subject and treatment: the majority is about love for an absent lady; that love is often threatened by such figures as *Dangier* (Suspicion), who corresponds to the Provençal figure of the *gilos*; and the language in the early chansons has fewer allegorical figures than it does metaphors, and few of the early chansons develop a single conceit through the course of the poem. The later chansons, like the rondeaux, show less of the courtly influence in their choice of subject matter and, most notably, in their treatment of allegory; in contrast to the early chansons, the rondeaux often do play out an allegorical conceit as the focus of the lyric.

This difference can be seen by a brief comparison of the two most well-known of Charles's poems, Chanson 6, "Dieu, qu'il la fait bon regarder," and Rondeau 31, "Le temps a laissié son manteau." The first is remarkable more for its musical qualities than its metaphoric ones. About a lady, "la gracieuse, bonne et belle," who is beyond compare and description, the poem reads like a testimony of her incomparable beauty. The second, by contrast, methodically develops the image of time, or weather, as a courtly figure who leaves off his winter mantle of wind, cold, and rain to show his garment of spring embroidered with (or by) the sun. In the final strophe, "his" attributes are assumed by all of Nature, as river, fountain, and rivulet wear drops of silver filigree as their new spring outfits. This difference between a song of little metaphoric complexity and a piece whose metaphoric system is highly worked, and worked out, can be felt within the chansons as well. If one were to graph the relative metaphoricity of the chansons, the odds are that the earlier ones, 1-52, would have fewer systematic allegories than the later ones; the early ones being more like Chanson 6, the later like Rondeau 31. Yet even among the later chansons, amid such pre-rondeaux as

"En gibessant," one finds a poem such as "Encore lui fait il
grant bien," which, devoid of all metaphors, is highly reminiscent of the earlier chansons, and suggests that this simple
musical quality is in fact an important distinguishing characteristic of the chansons after all.

One other index of the difference between the two groups
of poems is *Nonchaloir*, the conceptualization of Lack. This
figure is without a doubt the most influential and insightful
of Charles's chest of allegorical figures, important both
within his own corpus and within the French literary tradition
as a whole, for it corresponds at least in a rough way to
Baudelaire's *Ennui*. While *Nonchaloir* appears only rarely in
the chansons, and then mostly in the later ones, it becomes
Charles's constant companion in the rondeaux, replacing to a
large degree the Lady of the chansons. This change in the
poems' addressee indicates a shift in viewpoint that is extremely significant. While the chansons are really modified
courtly lyrics, focused either on the absent lady or on the
emotional and psychological effects of her absence on the poet,
the rondeaux adopt this courtly mode to address issues which
are both larger, in their universality, and smaller, in their
introspection. At the risk of over-generalizing, it seems
fair to place the work of Charles d'Orléans in the context of
Dante on the one hand and Montaigne on the other. While the
first is driven by a desire to attain the unattainable other
who exists even if she is always beyond reach; the second,
spurred on by a desire to know himself, is constantly led further inward until forced to confront the abyss within, where
the spectres of change and mortality loom all the larger.
Further, while Dante reaches his goal and returns to tell the
tale, Montaigne discovers that it is impossible to define himself; the best he can do is to etch a frame around where he
was, around the blank space that he is. That blank space corresponds to Charles's understanding of *Nonchaloir*, and his
later rondeaux, like Montaigne's later essays, are tinged with
fear and desperation. Yet often at his most desperate Charles
saves his poetry in a way that Montaigne does not: through
humor, as in Rondeau 19.

In sum, Charles's artistic achievement consisted of moving
from lyrics which showed the heavy influence of the foregoing
courtly lyric tradition, complete with its oral, musical aspect, to poems that, through their skillful use of metaphor
and allegory, enabled the poet to probe universal concerns,
such as defining the self or confronting death, in a very help-
ful and perceptive way. As his poetry makes this transition
from the courtly to the psychological realms, it bridges the
more general movement from medieval to Renaissance lyric.

Sources and Influences

It is difficult to know what to call Charles's sources.
Coming from a family that was both well-situated and also interested in books--his father both had a great library and
cared enough about the material to have many of the works
translated into French--Charles would presumably have known
about, if not known personally, all available texts of his day.
It is apparent from his writings and the inventory of his library that he knew four literatures: Latin, Italian, English,
and French, yet the books he seemed to have been most interested in were philosophical and religious, not literary.

In fact, given his social and political position in history, he seems amazingly free of influences. He was clearly
taken with earlier allegorical texts like the *Roman de la Rose*,
which his *Retenue d'Amours* is clearly modeled on, and he seems
to have been influenced by the poetry of Jean de Garencières
(1370?-1415?), a contemporary who may have fallen at the battle
of Agincourt, as well as the works of his mother's friends,
Eustache Deschamps and Christine de Pisan. A more distant
influence seems equally probable: his use of allegory is often
reminiscent of that of Guillaume de Machaut and Alain Chartier;
I feel a strong strain of troubadour influence, both in his
courtly subject matter and his interest in complex forms; he
may have known them through reading their works directly or
indirectly through the Italian poets, whose proto-humanism
informs his later poems. His English poems, some feel, show
the influence of Chaucer and Gower.

Charles's influence on the later tradition is equally
elusive. While taken seriously as a poet while alive, enough
so that Martin le Franc praised him in no uncertain terms in
his *Le Champion des Dames*, and many manuscripts exist of his
poems, by the sixteenth century Charles's name was practically
forgotten. Francis I, Charles's nephew, asked Clément Marot
to edit the works of Villon, not Charles, thus starting a trend
that has never ended of viewing Villon as the first great
French poet of all time. It is to Charles's credit that a
majority of his works was published in three different editions
during the sixteenth century, yet as the editors of those texts
chose not to identify Charles as the author, his name was
quickly forgotten, and whatever influence his poetry had on
the now-famous poets of the Pléiade was never duly acknowl-
edged. Given the hindsight granted us it seems possible that
he fell between two stools: too introspective to conform to
the medieval lyric around him, he was considered too medieval
in his use of allegory to be useful for the Renaissance.

It was the Abbé Sallier who, in 1874, finally mentioned
him in an article and thus resurrected his name from a long

and undue oblivion. Since then numerous artists, visual and musical as well as literary, have been influenced by him directly, and countless others, critics speculate, indirectly. It seems fair to suggest that his being forgotten for so long made him even more influential when rediscovered than he perhaps would have otherwise been: the added impact of being new and fresh made people stand up and take notice when contemporaries such as Villon or Deschamps were considered passé.

Note on the English Chansons

The attribution of all the pieces in MS Harley 682 is still a matter of great debate. Long assumed by British and French alike to be poor imitations by an inferior poet, or translations by an equally poor translator, most people are now convinced that Charles did in fact write the poems that comprise this manuscript. By way of adding fuel to the fire, not in an attempt to extinguish it, I have here provided the English chansons that have corresponding French chansons. Not being a specialist of Middle English poetry I do not feel qualified to settle the dispute, but from comparing the two versions of the 52 chansons it seems to me that the English ones were written after the French ones (and I think by a Frenchman), either as translations or separate renditions.

For the most part the English versions are good poems in their own right, though one would be hard-pressed to call them translations. The basic conceit is usually the same in both the English and the French, as is the rhyme scheme and the number of lines in the strophes; the major differences can be ascribed to the shift in language: whereas the French have eight beats per line, the English have an extra two, a meter borrowed, some have suggested, from Chaucer. This change in meter seems necessary to accommodate the French ideas to English, even though from time to time it is clear that Charles is struggling to fill out the line, as in No. 35 which begins: "Take, take this cosse atonys, atonys my hert."

The other major difficulty in changing languages—both gratifying and frustrating to this translator—comes in translating idioms, images, and puns. Often Charles seems to find that such a transfer just cannot be done, and resorts to a complete change of image, as in Chanson 17 where the implicit metaphor of the Ship of Hope that appears in the French version is replaced by an entirely different metaphor, Death in his shirt-sleeves, in the English.

It is possible that the English poems were written under a different set of circumstances, a suggestion that would explain changes that are otherwise difficult to explain, such

as the fact that No. 50 is written to a woman in English, to
a man in French, yet it seems most likely that Charles chose
to write in English as an exercise during his twenty-five years
there, and such non-linguistic changes should be ascribed to
a change of mood, aesthetic, or mind.

Editorial Policy of This Text and Translation

The editing of the chansons was a relatively easy task,
since the English is contained in a single manuscript (MS C,
Harley 682), and Champion has proven that MS O (B.N. fr.25458)
is the diplomatic one since it is in part autograph. Because
there exist diplomatic texts, then, for both the English and
the French poems there is no *apparatus criticus* except in the
rare case where I have emended. Since other, non-diplomatic
manuscripts served as the base for some of the earlier editions, indications of the differences among these editions
and, by extension, among the manuscripts, can be found in the
Textual Notes. I had intended to reproduce the poems as they
appear in those manuscripts, but have since decided to emend
to aid the reader. I have therefore, reluctantly, added punctuation and accents, spelled out all abbreviations, standard-
ized spelling to conform to modern pronunciation, and capitalized words that are always capitalized in modern spelling,
such as Dieu and France. But, on the whole, I have tried, to
the best of my ability, to leave the French and English texts
as close to the original as is possible. The reader will
therefore find incomplete lines; and few substantives are capitalized.
I decided on this policy after using Champion's text
which, while a landmark edition that enabled scholarship on
Charles d'Orléans essentially to begin, I found often blocked
possible readings, particularly New Critical ones, with its
often intrusive editorial policy. As I was editing the chansons I was struck over and over again by the semantic possi-
bilities that opened up in reading a text as it stood in the
manuscript. It is my hope that new interpretations will be
made possible if the reader is not led so carefully through
the text, that the increased difficulty the reader encounters
in gaining access to these poems will pay off in renewed understanding of Charles's merit as a poet.
The English edition is equally faithful to the manuscript;
as with the French I have emended where I found it essential.
In addition to the editorial changes listed above I have supplied and underlined final e's, abbreviated in the manuscript,
that aren't to be counted metrically.
Choosing to leave the originals rough made me feel I

should--or perhaps could--edit the translations, and so these
will appear much more highly emended. I have added capitals,
finished lines, and on the whole reshaped the poems to suggest
what I feel is their meaning. As a translation is already an
edition if not an analysis, I felt additional editorial intru-
sion was not out of line.

And, finally, since this work is primarily the text and
translation of Charles's French chansons I have omitted any
English chanson for which there exists no French counterpart.

Grateful acknowledgment is made to the following for per-
mission to use their materials: to the Bibliothèque Nationale
for the folios from B.N. fr. 25458 and B.N. fr. 2680; to the
British Library for the folios from Harley 682 and Reg. 16.
F.ii; and to the Archives Nationales for the reproduction of
Charles's letter of release.

I would like to thank the General Editor, James J.
Wilhelm, whose interest in this project stayed alive throughout
its entire preparation; Joan M. Ferrante who, in addition to
her continuing presence as my Muse of Encouragement, introduced
me to the General Editor; Pamela Chergotis, managing editor,
who patiently answered all my letters and phone calls; Janet
Rodriguez who gave legible life to my primordial scribble, and
Lynette Reed who turned the frog into a Prince; and the anonymous readers without whom this work would not have its present
shape. I would also like to thank Dean Karl Anatol and the
Professional Opportunities Program at California State University, Long Beach, for funding and much-needed release time
from teaching in which I could begin this project, and the
Mellon Faculty Fellow program at Harvard University where I
finished it; and finally, to JM who listened with interest to
every turn of phrase I proudly came up with, read each draft
with a wonderfully critical eye, and provided constant and
necessary moral support across the months and miles.

Seal Beach, California   S.S.

Select Bibliography

I. Major Editions and Transcriptions of Manuscripts

N.B.: Only the chansons included in the following editions
are listed here.

Barthélemy, Imbert, ed. *Annales poétiques.* In the *Almanach
des Muses.* Paris: Delalain, 1778. Contains 2, 4, 20, 37,
43, 47, 48, 58.

Bernard, Jean-Marc, ed. *Charles d'Orléans: Rondeaux choisis.*
Paris, 1913. Contains 4, 6, 10, 22, 37, 38, 41, 43, 46,
51, 59, 67, 71, 73, 74, 84.

Bruneau, C.G.E.M. *Charles d'Orléans et la poésie aristocra-
tique.* (Bibliothèque du bibliophile.) London: Lardanchet,
1924. Contains 2, 4, 6, 8, 15, 19, 20, 33, 37, 39, 41, 46,
47, 51, 52, 55, 60, 63, 73, 78, 84.

Chalvet, Pierre Vincent, ed. *Poésies de Charles d'Orléans,
père de Louis XII et oncle de François Ier, rois de France.*
Grenoble: Giroud, 1803. Based on MS G. Contains majority
of chansons: see Textual Notes.

Champion, Pierre, ed. *Charles d'Orléans. Poésies.* (Les
Classiques français du Moyen Age, 34, 56.) 2 vols. (1923-
1927); rpt. Paris: H. Champion, 1956. Based on MS O. Standard edition. Chansons contained in Vol. I with notes in
second volume. Excellent Introduction.

Champollion-Figeac, Aimé Louis, ed. *Les Poésies du duc Charles
d'Orléans publiées sur le manuscrit original de la Bibliothèque de Grenoble conféré avec ceux de Paris et de Londres.*
Paris: Belin-Leprieur, 1842. Based primarily on MS G sup-
plemented by MS O. Complete edition; see Textual Notes.

————. *Notice historique et littéraire sur Charles, duc
d'Orléans, sur ses poésies, les Manuscrits qui nous les
ont conservées, et sur cette première édition complète de
ses ouvrages.* Paris: Belin-Leprieur, 1842. *Apparatus
criticus* for above edition.

Charpier, Jacques, ed. *Vie et oeuvres de Charles d'Orléans.*
    (Ecrivains d'hier et d'aujourd'hui.) 2nd ed. Paris:
    Seghers, 1970 (1st ed., 1958). Contains 1, 8, 23, 38, 46,
    73, 86.

Coke, John, ed. *Le débat des hérauts d'armes de France et
    d'Angleterre,* suivi de *The Debate between the Heralds of
    England and France.* Edition commencée par Léopold Pannier
    et achevée par Paul Meyer. SATF. Paris: Didot, 1877.
    Fifteenth-century French work ascribed by some to CdO.
    Meyer here refutes such a claim.

Dufy, Raoul, illus. *Charles d'Orléans: Poésies.* Lausanne:
    Mermod, 1958.

Fox, John Howard, ed. *Charles d'Orléans. Choix de poésies.*
    Editées d'après le MS Royal 16 F II du British Museum
    (Textes littéraires. IX). Exeter: Univ. of Exeter Press,
    1973. Includes 51 and 52. Interesting for base MS.

Frélaut, Jean, ed. *Charles d'Orléans: Ballades, rondeaux et
    complaintes.* Paris: Lacourière, 1949.

Guichard, J.M., ed. *Poésies de Charles d'Orléans publiées
    avec l'autorisation de M. le ministre de l'Instruction Pub-
    lique, d'après les manuscrits des Bibliothèques du Roi et
    de l'Arsenal.* Paris: Gosselin, 1842. Earliest complete
    edition, appearing six days before that of Champollion-
    Figeac. See Textual Notes.

Hausknecht, E. "Vier Gedichte von Charles d'Orléans." *Anglia;
    Zeitschrift für Englische Philologie,* 17 (1895), 445-47.
    Contains English chansons 9, 10, 17, 18.

Héricault, Charles d', ed. *Poésies complètes de Charles
    d'Orléans revues sur les mss.* 2 vols. (1874); rpt. Paris:
    Flammarion, 1896. Based on MS O. Complete edition. See
    Textual Notes for chansons.

Janot, Denis and Simon, eds. *Le Triomphe de l'Amant Vert.*
    Paris, 1535.

Matisse, Henri, illus. *Poèmes de Charles d'Orléans*; manuscrits
    et illustrés par Henri Matisse. [Paris]: Tériade, 1950.
    Contains 6, 7, 8, 15, 37, 43, 48, 73. Hand-written and
    illustrated in multi-colored pastel by Matisse. The Spencer
    Collection of the New York Public Library has a copy, as
    does the Boston Public Library.

Montagna, Gianni, ed. *Carlo d'Orléans. Antologia di Ballate,
    Canzoni, Compianti, Carole e Rondò.* (Coll. Studi e Testi.)
    Pisa: Libreria Goliardica, 1957.

Ouy, Gilbert, ed. *Un Poème mystique de Charles d'Orléans, le 'Canticum Amoris.'* Milan: Società Editrice Internazionale, 1959. Standard edition of the "Canticum Amoris" often ascribed to CdO.

Pauphilet, Albert, ed. *Charles d'Orléans: Poésies.* Illustrated by Pierre Courtois. Paris, 1926, 1952, 1956.

Sallier, Abbé, ed. "Observations sur un recueil manuscrit de poésies de Charles d'Orléans." In *Mémoires de l'Académie Royale des Inscriptions et Belles-Lettres*, 13 (1740), 580-92. Article responsible for reviving interest in CdO.

Seché, Alphonse, ed. *Charles d'Orléans: Poèmes, ballades, caroles, chansons, complaints, rondeaux.* ("Bibliothèque des poètes français et étrangers.") Paris: Michaud, 1909. Includes 1, 4, 6, 7, 8, 9, 16, 19, 22, 23, 27, 30, 33, 36, 37, 38, 41, 42, 43, 46, 47, 50, 51, 57, 59, 62, 63, 70, 72, 74, 78.

Steele, Robert, and Mabel Day, eds. *The English poems of Charles of Orleans.* Edited from the manuscript, British Museum, Harleian 682. EETS OS Nos. 215 and 220. 2 vols. Oxford: Oxford Univ. Press, 1941-1946. Standard edition of the English poems. Chansons 1-52 found in Vol. I; notes and Introduction in Vol. II.

Taylor, George Watson, ed. *Poems, written in English, by Charles duke of Orleans, during his Captivity in England after the Battle of Azincourt.* London: The Roxburghe Club, 1827. First edition of the English poems, of which Taylor believes CdO to be author.

Tardieu, Jean, ed. *Charles d'Orléans: Choix de Rondeaux.* (Le Cri de la France.) Freiburg: Egloff, 1947.

Tournoux, G., ed. *Charles d'Orléans: Poésies.* Haarlem: Enschede en Zonen, 1914. 300 copies; Princeton University has No. 9. Includes: 1, 2, 6, 8, 10, 13, 14, 15, 16, 17, 18, 19, 20, 22, 25, 26, 33, 35, 36, 37, 39, 41, 45, 46, 47, 48, 49, 52, 57, 59, 72, 73, 75, 78, 82.

Valkhoff, V., ed. *Chansons: Charles d'Orléans.* Rotterdam, 1932. Contains all French chansons except 52, 72a.

Vérard, Antoine, ed. *La Chasse et le Départ d'amours faict et composé par ... Octavien de Sainct Gelais ... et par ... Blaise d'Auriol.* Paris, 1509. Contains numerous poems by CdO. The so-called "Edition Gothique" of CdO, these poems were published by the "authors" as their own works. Contains: 1-8, 18-52, 56, 58-72, 74-85.

————. *Le Jardin de Plaisance et fleur de Rhétorique nou-
vellement imprimé à Paris.* (c. 1501.) Includes 11, 16,
30, 48, 49, and rewritten version of 16 and 74.

Vulpesco, Romulus, ed. *Charles d'Orléans. Ballades, chansons,
caroles, complaints, rondeaux.* Bucuresti: Univers, 1975.

II. English Translations and Major Anthologies

Auguis, Pierre. *Les Poètes François depuis le XIIe siècle
jusqu'à Malherbe.* 6 vols. Paris: Crapelet, 1824. Vol. 2,
pp. 185-99. Includes 2, 37.

Balmas, Enea, and Diego Valeri. *L'Età del Rinascimento in
Francia* (Letteratura e storia). Milano: Sansoni, 1969,
pp. 38-44.

Banville, T. de. *Petit traité de poésie française.* Paris:
Charpentier, 1881. Mentions CdO in chapter 9: "Poèmes
traditionnels à forme fixe."

Belloc, Hilaire. *Avril, being Essays on the Poetry of the
French Renaissance.* (Essay Index Reprint Series.) 1904;
rpt. Freeport, N.Y.: Books for Libraries Press, 1969. Includes 6.

Canfield, Arthur Graves, ed. *French Lyrics.* With Introduction
and Notes. New York: Henry Holt, 1928. Includes 6, 58.

Carey, H. *London Magazine*, Sept. 1823, pp. 301-06. Trans.
of 27.

Champagnac, J.-B.-J. *Poètes français ou choix de poésies des
auteurs du seconde et du troisième ordre des XVe, XVIe,
XVIIe, et XVIIIe siècles.* 6 vols. Paris: Menard et
Desenue, 1825. Vol. 1, pp. 2-7.

Currey, Ralph Nixon, ed. *Formal spring: French Renaissance
Poems of Charles d'Orléans and others.* Oxford Univ. Press:
1950; rpt. Freeport, N.Y.: Books for Libraries Press, 1969.
Facing-page trans. of 10, 74.

Davies, R.T., ed. *Medieval English Lyrics: A Critical Anthology.* With Introduction and Notes. Northwestern Univ.
Press, 1964.

Fowlie, Wallace. *French Literature: Its History and Its Meaning.* Englewood Cliffs, N.J.: Prentice-Hall, Inc., 1973,
pp. 25-26.

Giese, William Frederic, ed. *French Lyrics in English Verse.*
Foreword by Frederick Manchester. Madison: Univ. of Wisconsin Press, 1942, p. 18. Trans. of 6.

Hammond, Eleanor Prescot. *English Verse between Chaucer and Surrey*. Cambridge Univ. Press, 1927, pp. 214-32. Includes 20-23 in both French and English versions.

Lang, Andrew. *Ballads and Lyrics of Old France*. London: Longmans, Green & Co., 1872. Trans. of 14.

Lanson, Gustave. *Histoire de la littérature française*. 12th ed. Paris, 1912, p. 170.

Lenormant, A. *Livre de poésies à l'usage des jeunes filles chrétiennes*. Paris: Leleux, 1840, pp. 403-409.

Mary, André, ed. *Le Fleur de la poésie française, depuis les origines jusqu'à la fin du XVe siècle*. 2 vols. Paris: Garnier, 1951. Vol. 2, pp. 544-67.

Nardis, Luigi de. "Charles d'Orléans, Chansons" *Marsia*, I, 24-27. Italian trans. of 33, 35, 37, 39, 43, 48, 56. Reviewed by G.A. Brunelli, *Studi Francesi*, 2 (1958), 266-69.

The Oxford Book of French Verse: XIIth Century-XXth Century. Chosen by St. John Lucas. Oxford: The Clarendon Press, 1926, pp. 20-27. Includes 6, 58.

Paris, Gaston. *Medieval French Literature*. 1903; rpt. Freeport, N.Y.: Books for Libraries Press, 1971, pp. 128-29.

————, and E. Langlois. *Chrestomathie du Moyen Age*. Paris: Hachette, 1897, pp. 303-306.

Pauphilet, Albert. *Poètes et Romanciers du Moyen Age*. (Bibliothèque de la Pléiade. No. 52.) Paris: Gallimard, 1952, pp. 519-592.

Perier, A., ed. *Charles d'Orléans et François Villon: Poésies choisies*. (Les Classiques pour tous, no. 129.) Paris: Hatier, 1932.

Pound, Ezra. *Ripostes*. London: Swift and Co., 1912. Trans. of 6.

Purcell, Sally, trans. and ed. *The Poems of Charles d'Orléans*. Cheshire: Carcanet, 1973. A selection of poems, with an Introduction. Includes 15. Useful notes on English poems, allegory, comparative table of French and English.

Raynaud, Gaston, ed. *Rondeaux et autres poésies du XVe siècle*. (Publications V, 31.) Paris: Firmin Didot, 1889. Based on MS R.

Schwob, Marcel. *Le Parnasse satyrique du XVe siècle*. Paris, 1905. Study of MS S. Includes 37.

Wallis, Cedric, ed. *Charles d'Orléans: A Selection of Poems*.
    London: Caravel Press, 1951. Includes trans. of 6, 46,
    58, 74.

Wilhelm, James J. *Medieval Song: An Anthology of Hymns and
    Lyrics*. New York: Dutton, 1971; London: Allen and Unwin,
    1972.

Wilkins, Nigel, ed. *One Hundred Ballades, Rondeaux and Vire-
    lais from the Late Middle Ages*. Cambridge: Cambridge Univ.
    Press, 1969.

Woledge, Brian, ed. *The Penguin Book of French Verse: Twelfth
    to Fifteenth Centuries*. With Introduction and Notes. 2
    vols. Hammondsworth, England, 1961, 1966. Vol. 1, pp.
    106-114. Includes 4, 37.

III.   Critical Writings and Related Works

Agada, S. "Studi su Charles d'Orléans e François Villon."
    Studi Francesi, 2 (1960), 201-19. One of a series of arti-
    cles on the phrase "boire ses hontes."

Arn, Mary-Jo. "The English Poetry of Charles of Orleans."
    Dutch Quarterly Review of Anglo-American Letters, 8 (1978),
    [108]-21. Argues CdO as author of both English and French.
    Sees them of a piece. Notes influence of both Chaucer on
    French and French tradition on English. By overlooking
    irony and humor we have misunderstood CdO.

————. "The Structure of the English Poems of Charles
    of Orleans." *Fifteenth-Century Studies*, 4 (1981), 17-23.
    English poems to be read as single work with continuity
    and plot. Two ballade sequences discussed.

————. "'Fortunes Stabilnes': The English Poems of Charles
    of Orleans in their English Context." *Fifteenth-Century
    Studies*, 7 (1983), 1-18.

Aubry, Pierre. "Iter Hispanicum: notices et extraits de
    manuscrits de musique ancienne conservés dans les biblio-
    thèques d'Espagne." *Sammelbände der internationallen Musik
    Gesellschaft*. July, 1907 (517-534). On two chansonniers
    in the Escorial, one of which contains sixteenth-century
    settings for 37 and 45.

Barroux, Marius. "La forme des rondeaux et chansons de Charles
    d'Orléans." *Moyen Age*, 49 (1939), 186-91.

Beaufils, Constant. *Etude sur la vie et les poésies de Charles d'Orléans*. Diss., Paris. Coutances: Durand, 1861. Blames lack of critical attention on CdO's simplicity and purity; ignored because different.

Bernard, Jean-Marc. "Charles d'Orléans: Prince et poète." *La Revue Critique des Idées et des livres*, 18 (1912), [689]-705. Summary and review of Poirion, *Le Poète et le Prince*, q.v.

Böhmer, Helga. "Claude Debussy, 'Yver, vous n'estes qu'un vilain' für vierstimmigen Chor a cappella (aus der 'Trois chansons de Charles d'Orléans')." *Romania Cantat* (Lieder in alten und neuen Chorsätzen mit sprachlichen, literarischen und musikwissenschaftlichen Interpretationen. Gerhard Rohlfs zum 85). Tübingen: Narr, 1980. Bd II, pp. 453-454.

Bullrich, G. "Über Charles d'Orléans und die ihm zugeschriebene englische Übersetzung seiner Gedichte." In *Wissenschaftliche Beilage zu Programm der 2. städtischer Realschule zu Berlin*. Programm Berlin, 1893. Against CdO as author of English poems in part because rhymes are too clever.

Burgoyne, L., and R. Gelinas. "Christine de Pisan, Alain Chartier, and Charles d'Orléans. Cinq ans d'études (1976-1980)." *Le Moyen français*, 8-9 (1983), 291-308. Useful bibliographic source and statistical study of interest in CdO, among others.

Cary, Henry. "Poems, Written in English, by Charles Duke of Orleans, during his Captivity in England, after the Battle of Agincourt." *Gentlemen's Magazine* (May 1842), 459-72. Argues for CdO as author of English "translations."

Cellini, B. "Le poesie inglesi di Charles d'Orléans." In *Studi in onore di Italo Siciliano*. Florence, 1966, pp. 225-39. Argues for CdO as author of English poems, noting they are less refined than French; more spontaneous and realistic than well expressed.

Champion, Pierre. "A Propos de Charles d'Orléans. I. La Dame Anglaise de Charles d'Orléans. II. Recueils imprimés contenant des poésies de Charles d'Orléans." *Romania*, 49 (1923), 580-87. I. Identifies Chaucer's granddaughter, Alice, as addressee of poems. II. Proposes emendation of poem in *Livre du cuer d'amours espris* to make it refer to CdO.

————. *Charles d'Orléans, joueur d'échecs*. (Bibliothèque du XVe siècle.) Paris: Champion, 1908; rpt. Geneva: Slatkine, 1975. Attempt to reconstruct Charles's intellectual atmosphere.

————. "Du succès de l'oeuvre de Charles d'Orléans et de ses imitateurs jusqu'au XVIe siècle." In *Mélanges ... Emile Picot.* 1913; rpt. Geneva: Slatkine, 1969. Vol. 1, pp. [410]-20. Large number of MSS and imitations indicate success.

————. *La Librairie de Charles d'Orléans, avec un album de facsimiles.* (Bibliothèque du XVe siècle, 11.) Paris: Champion, 1910; rpt. Geneva: Slatkine, 1975.

————. *Le Manuscrit autographe des poésies de Charles d'Orléans.* (Bibliothèque du XVe siècle, 3.) Paris: Champion, 1907; rpt. Geneva: Slatkine, 1975. Landmark study of MS O.

————. "Remarques sur un recueil de poésies du milieu du XVe siècle (BN fr. 9223)." *Romania,* 48 (1922), [106]-14. Poems by CdO and circle.

————. *Vie de Charles d'Orléans (1394-1465).* (Bibliothèque du XVe siècle, 13.) Paris: Champion, 1911. Definitive life. Useful chronological charts at end.

Champollion-Figeac, Aimé Louis. *Reponse à une critique littéraire.* Paris: Belin-Leprieur, 1842. Argues that even though his edition appeared six days after that of Guichard his is really the first.

Choffel, Jacques. *Le Duc Charles d'Orléans (1394-1465): Chronique d'un prince des fleurs de lys.* Paris, 1968. Short biography.

Cholakian, R. "The Poetic 'Persona' in the Ballades of Charles d'Orléans." *Fifteenth-Century Studies,* 6 (1983), 41-58.

Cigada, Sergio. "Christine de Pisan e la traduzione inglese delle poesie di Charles d'Orléans." *Aevum,* 32 (1958), 509-16. About "Alone am y and wille to be alone" as possible translation of Christine de Pisan's "Seulete suy...."

————. *L'Opera poetica di Charles d'Orléans.* Milan: Società Editrice Vita e Pensiero, 1960. Best general study of CdO. Intelligently argued with nice balance of poetry and biography.

————. "Studi su Charles d'Orléans e François Villon relativi al MS B.N. fr. 25458." *Studi Francesi,* anno 4 (1960), 201-19. On ballades.

Clark, Cecily. "Charles d'Orléans: Some English Perspectives." *Medium Aevum,* 40 (1971), 254-61. Critique of McLeod; questions attribution of English poems.

Cocco, Mia. "The Italian Inspiration in the Poetry of Charles d'Orléans." *Mid-Hudson Language Studies*, 2 (1979), 46-60. Traces of Petrarchism.

Croft, Sir Thomas. "Early English Poetry." *Retrospective Review and Historical and Antiquarian Magazine*, 2nd Series, 1 (1827), 147-56. For Charles as author of English poems.

Darby, George O.S. "Observations on the Chronology of Charles d'Orléans's Rondeaux." *Romanic Review*, 34 (1943), [3]-17.

Daunt, Marjorie. "A Study of the Rhymes Used by Charles d'Orléans in his English Poems." *Transactions of the Philological Society*, 16 (1949), 135-54. Rhymes as key to English Charles spoke.

Dédéyan, Christian. "Les cris d'amour de Charles d'Orléans." *Nouvelles Littéraires* (December 23, 1965), 6. Historical overview to commemorate 500th anniversary of CdO's death.

Deschères, T. "Charles d'Orléans." *Le plutarque français*. Paris: Crapelet, 1838, pp. 1-6.

Droz, E., and G. Thibault. *Poètes et musiciens du XVe siècle*, I. Paris, 1924. Contains transcriptions of sixteenth-century settings of 37 and 45.

Dufaux, Gérard. "Charles d'Orléans ou la poétique du secret: A propos du rondeau XXXIII de l'édition Champion." *Romania*, 93 (1972), 194-243. Excellent article on function of internal refrain in rondeaux and chansons.

Dwyer, R.A. "'Je meurs de soif auprès de la fontaine.'" *French Studies*, 23 (1969), 225-28.

Fein, David A. *Charles d'Orléans*. (TWAS, No. 699.) Boston: Twayne, 1983. Straightforward study of CdO and his poetry. Divided into periods. Sections on orientation, humor, diversification of language, stylistic similarities with Villon.

—————. "Verb Usage in a Ballade of Charles d'Orléans." *Romance Philology*, 35 (1981), 343-47.

Foffano, Tino. "Charles d'Orléans e un gruppo di umanisti lombardi in Normandia." *Aevum*, 41 (1967), 452-73. Epistolary evidence of contact between CdO and group of Italian humanists during his last years of imprisonment.

Fox, John Howard. "Charles d'Orléans, poète anglais." *Romania*, 86 (1965), 433-62. Careful study of English poems. Suggests they weren't written by an Englishman (non-idiomatic usage, mistakes, etc.) and so concludes they were written by CdO.

————. *The Lyric Poetry of Charles d'Orléans*. Oxford: The
Clarendon Press, 1969. Historically grounded study with
good Introduction. Blames history for style and subject
matter; CdO as worst of Middle Ages and Renaissance.

Françon, Marcel. "Note sur les rondeaux et les chansons de
Charles d'Orléans." *Studi Francesi*, 11 (1967), 76-77. On
rondeaux.

————. "Notes de littérature, de musique et d'histoire. I.
Jean de Meun, Charles d'Orléans, Clément Marot, Ronsard."
Francia, 19 (1976), 52. Use of *Faulx Dangier* in 14.

————. "Les Refrains des rondeaux de Charles d'Orléans."
Modern Philology, 39 (1941-42), 259-63. This and the following article distinguish between chansons and rondeaux
on the basis of refrain.

————. "La Structure du rondeau." *Medium Aevum*, 44 (1975),
54-59.

Frank, Grace. "Villon at the Court of Charles d'Orléans."
Modern Language Notes, 47 (1932), 498-505. "Les gaiges
ravoir" translated as "to redeem pledges;" connected here
to the *Epître à Marie* by Villon.

Friedman, W.F., and E.S. Friedman. *Medium Aevum*, 27 (1958),
194-98. Review of Seaton article, q.v.

Garey, Howard B. "The Variable Structure of the Fifteenth-
century Rondeau." *The Sixth LACUS Forum* (1979). Ed. H.J.
Izzo. Columbia, S.C.: Hornbeam, 1980, pp. 494-501. Struc-
tural stylistic approach to rondeaux of Alain Chartier,
Christine de Pisan, CdO.

Godefroy, F. *Dictionnaire de l'ancienne langue française et
de tous ses dialectes du IXe siècle*. 10 vols. Paris:
Bouillon, 1880-1902.

Goodrich, Norma Lorre. *Charles, duke of Orleans: A Literary
Biography*. New York: Macmillan, 1963. Good biography in-
terspersed throughout with translations of many texts on
and by CdO.

————. *Charles d'Orléans: A Study of Themes in his French
and in his English poetry*. (Histoire des idées et critique
littéraire.) Geneva: Droz, 1967. Attributes English poems
to CdO on basis of thematic continuity.

————. "Concerning Research in the Fifteenth Century."
Coranto 6 (1970), 28-37. For attribution, however tenta-
tive.

Hammond, Eleanor Prescot. "Charles d'Orléans et Anne
  Molyneux." *Modern Philology*, 22 (1924), 215-16. A now-
  classic article that argues for attribution on basis of
  anagram Anne Molins in "Alas mercy." Attempts identifica-
  tion.

Harrison, Ann Tukey. *Charles d'Orléans and the Allegorical
  Mode*. Univ. of North Carolina Studies in Romance Languages
  and Literature, 150.) Chapel Hill: Univ. of North Carolina
  Press, 1975. Important study of CdO's innovative use of
  allegory.

Horrent, Jacques. "Un rondeau de Charles d'Orléans." *Cahiers
  d'analyse textuelle*, no. 9 (1967), 88-97. On *Rondeau 24*,
  "Dedens la maison de Doleur."

Jordan, Nicole Amon. "Des couleurs et des signes: essai sur
  la symbolique des couleurs chez quelques auteurs du Moyen
  Age et de la Renaissance." Diss. California (Berkeley),
  1975. (*DAI*, 37, p. 361-A, 1976.) Notes CdO's non-formulaic
  use of color symbolism, e.g., black is not color of desperation.

Kelly, Douglas. "Imagination in the poetry of Charles
  d'Orléans and René d'Anjou." In *Medieval Imagination: Rhet-
  oric and the Poetry of Courtly Love*. Madison: Univ. of
  Wisconsin Press, 1978, pp. 204-29.

Kühl, Ferdinand. *Die Allegorie bei Charles d'Orléans*. Diss.
  Marburg, 1886. Predecessor of Poirion *Lexique*.

Leroux, Normand. "Charles d'Orléans." *Cahiers de l'Académie
  Canadienne-Française*, No. 11--*Reconnaissances littéraires*.
  Montreal, 1967, pp. 7-15. Feels that the poetry of CdO
  "n'est pas autre chose que le commentaire rhythmé de son
  existence quotidienne" (p. 7).

MacCracken, Henry Noble. "An English Friend of Charles
  d'Orléans." *PMLA*, NS 26, 19 (1911), 142-80. The friend
  is William de la Pole, one of Charles's wardens and husband
  of Alice Chaucer, maybe CdO's Lady.

Margolis, Nadia. "The Human Prison: The Metamorphoses of Mis-
  ery in the Poetry of Christine de Pizan, Charles d'Orléans,
  and François Villon." *Fifteenth-Century Studies*, I (1978),
  185-92.

McLeod, Enid. *Charles of Orleans: Prince and Poet*. London:
  Chatto and Windus, 1969; Viking, 1970. Engaging biography,
  well-illustrated by his lyrics.

Ménard, Philippe. "'Je Meurs de Soif Auprès de la Fontaine': D'un mythe antique à une image lyrique." *Romania*, 87 (1966), 394-400. Posits myth of Tantalus as source of image.

Mera Cisternino, Concetta. *Charles d'Orléans, il Petrarca francese*. Bari: Resta, 1969.

Michel, Francisque. "Manuscrit du Musée Britannique, Bibliothèque Harléienne, No. 682." In *Collection des Documents Inédits sur l'Histoire de France, publiés par ordre du roi* (Rapports au roi et pièces; also, Rapports au ministre). Paris, 1835, pp. 274-85. Catalogue description of MS C. Gives first lines of poems and some full poems as examples. Says English translations are by contemporary.

Monreal-Wickert, I. "Zu Charles d'Orléans, 'Yver, vous n'estes qu'un vilain.'" *Romania Cantat* (Lieder in alten und neuen Chorsätzen mit sprachlichen literarischen und musikwissenschaftlichen Interpretationen. Gerhard Rohlfs zum 85). Tübingen: Narr, 1980. Bd II, pp. 447-452.

Montagna, Gianni. "En relisant Charles d'Orléans." *Les Lettres Romanes*, 8 (1954), 303-28. Criticizes biographical approach to poems--leads to exaggeration.

Nardis, L. De. "Charles d'Orléans (Divagazioni e spunti critici)." *Marsia*, 2 (1958), 96-111.

Neal, Y.A. *Recherches sur la vie du Chevalier poète Jehan de Garencières*.... Paris, 1903. Vol. I, pp. 195-215. Standard work on fellow poet and source of inspiration.

Newman, Karen. "The Mind's Castle: Containment in the Poetry of Charles d'Orléans." *Romance Philology*, 33 (1979), 317-28. Good study of metaphors of "containment."

Nordström, Th. *Étude grammaticale sur les poésies de Charles d'Orléans*. Carlsbad, 1878.

Ouy, Gilbert. "Recherches sur la librairie de Charles d'Orléans et de Jean d'Angoulême pendant leur captivité en Angleterre, et étude de deux manuscrits autographes de Charles d'Orléans récemment identifiés." In *Compte-rendus de l'Académie des Inscriptions et Belles-Lettres* (1955), 273-87.

Paris, G. "Un poème inédit de Martin le Franc." *Romania*, 16 (1887), 383-437. Discussion and edition of *Le Champion des Dames* by Martin le Franc, which contains praise of CdO as poet.

Pasquali, Costanza. "Charles d'Orléans ed il suo *Nonchaloir*."
Studi Angelo Monteverdi, 2 (1959), 551-70. CdO's *Nonchaloir*
as predecessor of Baudelaire's *Spleen*.

Perreau, A. "La véritable édition originale des poésies de
Charles d'Orléans." *Bulletin du Bibliophile et du Biblio-
thécaire*, NS 2 (1923), 144-50. Argues that the "Choix des
Poésies" (1778) was first edition.

Petit de Julleville, L. "La vie et l'oeuvre de Charles
d'Orléans." *Bulletin hebdomadaire des Cours et Conférences*,
I (1894-95), 129-31, 145-48, 161-64, 177-82, 209-213. Biographical approach, outdated yet valid.

Piaget, Arthur. "Une édition gothique de Charles d'Orléans."
Romania, 20 (1892), 580-96. Points out that Vérard's 1509
La Chasse et le Depart d'Amours is little more than a flori-
legium of CdO's poems.

Picot, E. "Une supercherie d'Antoine Vérard. Les 'Regnars
Traversans' de Jehan Bouchet," *Romania*, 22 (1893), 244-54;
followed by a commentary by A. Piaget, pp. 254-260. It
was Vérard who brought out CdO's poem under the name of
Sainct-Gelais.

Planche, Alice. "Approches de la conscience de soi dans
l'oeuvre de Charles d'Orléans." In *Mélanges ... Pierre
Jonin*. (Senefiance No. 7.) Aix-en-Provence, 1979, pp.
[527]-41. Proto-Renaissance sense of self.

———. "Charles d'Orléans et la musique du silence." *Musique, littérature et société au moyen-âge*. Actes du co-
lloque, 24-29 mars 1980. Paris: Champion, 1981, pp. 437-
49. Fascinating paper suggesting CdO left blanks in MS
not out of laziness, economy, or autonomy but because he
didn't like the music of his day.

———. "Charles d'Orléans et le théâtre allégorique de la
conscience." In *Actes du groupe de recherches sur la
conscience de soi ... Les Belles-Lettres* (1980), 51-64.
CdO seizes moments but does not unify them; "conscience à
soi non de soi."

———. "Charles d'Orléans: L'Exclusion et ses métaphores."
In *Exclus et systèmes d'exclusion dans la littérature et
la civilisation médiévales*. (Senefiance No. 5.) Aix-en-
Provence, 1978, pp. 401-18.

———. *Charles d'Orléans ou la recherche d'un langage*. (Bibliothèque du XVe siècle, 38.) Paris: Champion, 1975.
Evocative study suggesting correlation between *forme* and
fond of CdO's poems, e.g., *rondeau* and metaphors of containment.

————. "Le gris de l'espoir." *Romania*, 94 (1973), 289-302. CdO's use of grey as metaphor and symbol.

————. "'Petit mercier, petit panier ...' Le débat du grand et du menu." In *Mélanges Pierre Le Gentil*. Ed. Jean Dufournet and Daniel Poirion. Paris, 1973, pp. 661-71. On Rondeau 330.

Poirion, Daniel. "Charles d'Orléans et l'Angleterre: un secret désir." In *Mélanges ... Jeanne Wathelet-Willem*. [Liège], 1978, pp. 505-27.

————. "Création poétique et composition romanesque dans les premiers poèmes de Charles d'Orléans." *Revue des Sciences Humaines*, 90 (1958), 185-211. First-rate study of CdO's poems. Uses literary tradition, not biography as context.

————. "La Nef d'Espérance: Symbole et allégorie chez Charles d'Orléans." In *Mélanges ... Jean Frappier*. (Publications romanes et françaises, 92.) Geneva: Droz, 1970. Vol. II, pp. 913-28. CdO's sense and use of Espérance.

————. "Le fol et le sage 'auprès de la fontaine': La recontre de François Villon et Charles d'Orléans." *Travaux de linguistique et de littérature*. (Etudes littéraires.) Université de Strasbourg: Le Centre de philologie et de littératures romanes, 6 (1968), [53]-68. On "Je meurs de soif."

————. *Le Lexique de Charles d'Orléans dans les Ballades*. (*Publications romanes et françaises*, 91.) Geneva: Droz, 1967. Very useful as lexicon; somewhat dated study of the poetry and its semantic fields.

————. *Le Poète et le Prince: L'évolution du lyrisme courtois de Guillaume de Machaut à Charles d'Orléans*. Paris: Presses Universitaires de France, 1965. Useful literary and historical survey of French lyric poetry of the fourteenth and fifteenth centuries.

Rickard, Peter. *Chrestomathie de la langue française au quinzième siècle*. Cambridge: Univ. Press, 1976. Indispensable for its glossary.

Robbins, Rossell Hope. "Some Charles d'Orléans Fragments." *MLN*, 66 (1951), 501-05.

Sasaki, Shigemi. "Fontaine et Forêt." *Etudes de langue et littérature françaises*, 22 (March 1973), 11-35.

————. "L'émergence des temps dans la poésie de Charles d'Orléans." *Medioevo romanzo*, 30 (1980), 255-265.

————. "'Nonchaloir' et 'amoreux-prisonnier.' Mutations de la vie intérieure de Charles d'Orléans." *Etudes de langue et littérature françaises*, 16 (1970), n.p.

————. *Sur le thème de Nonchaloir dans la poésie de Charles d'Orléans*. Paris: Nizet, 1974. Background of concept of Nonchaloir including Epicurus' *ataraxia*, Stoic's *otium*.

Sauerstein, P. *Charles d'Orléans und die Englische Übersetzung seiner Dichtungen*. Halle, 1899. Could not have been written by a French poet. Includes useful table comparing English and French.

Seaton, Mary Ethel. *Studies in Villon, Vaillant and Charles d'Orléans*. Oxford: Blackwell, 1957, pp. 20-48. Three chapters on CdO's use of anagrams. Impressive if true.

Simmons, Autumn. "A Contribution to the *Middle English Dictionary*: Citations from the English Poems of Charles, duc d'Orléans." *Journal of English Linguistics*, 2 (1968), 43-56.

Starobinski, Jean. "L'encre de la mélancolie." *Nouvelle revue française*, 123 (1963), 410-23. Comparative study of melancholy and Nonchaloir in CdO and others.

Stemmler, Theo. "Zur Verfasserfrage der Charles d'Orléans zugeschriebenen Englischen Gedichte." *Anglia, Zeitschrift für Englische Philologie*, 82 (1964), 458-73. Argues for anonymous English translator.

Stevenson, Robert Louis. *Familiar Studies of Man and Books*. In *The Works of Robert Louis Stevenson*. London: Cassel, 1906. Vol. III. Breezy essay about CdO, the man and the poet. Important for attention it drew to him.

Sturm-Maddox, Sara. "Charles d'Orléans devant la critique: Vers une poétique de l'allégorie." *Oeuvres Critiques: Revue Internationale de la Réception Critique des Oeuvres Littéraires de Langue Française*, 5 (1980), 9-24.

Tardieu, Jean. "*Charles d'Orléans.*" *les cahiers de la pléiade* 1 (1946), 117-26. Provocative overview arguing for studying CdO for magical power of his language.

Thom, Michel. "'Ce sont amourettes tremblans,'" *Mélanges ... Carl Theodor Gossen*. Ed. Colon and Kopp. Bern: Francke; Liège: Marche Romane, 1976, T. 2, pp. 897-904. Identifies *amourettes tremblans* in 49 as flower. See Textual Notes.

Thomas, Antoine. "Les Premiers Vers de Charles d'Orléans." *Romania*, 32 (1893), 128-33. On CdO's work, *Le Livre contre tout Pechié*.

Thorndike, L. "An Anonymous Work on Poisons Addressed to
    Charles of Orléans." *Romanic Review*, 31 (1940), 239-41.

Tucci, Patrizio. *Charles d'Orléans. L'uomo e l'opera*. Uni-
    versità di Padova. Collana dell'Istituto di lingue stra-
    niere. 2^a serie. Milan: Editrice Viscontea, 1970.

Urwin, Kenneth. "The 59th English Ballade of Charles of Or-
    leans." *Modern Language Review*, 38 (1943), 129-32.

Vallet de Viriville. "Charles, duc d'Orléans." *Nouvelle bio-
    graphie générale*. Paris: Didot, 1862. Vol. 38, col. 805-
    817.

Vigneron, L. "Charles d'Orléans poète anglais." *Les Humani-
    tés*, classe de lettres, sect. classiques, 35e année (1958-
    59), 22-25.

Viollet-le-Duc. *Bibliothèque poétique*. Paris: Hachette, 1843,
    pp. 77-79. Argues that Chalvet's edition is first.

V. P(lace). "Noble jeu, jeu de nobles." *La Strategie. Jour-
    nal d'échecs* (mai 1911), 157-61. Companion to Champion's
    article.

Watson, Harold. "Charles d'Orléans: 1394-1465." *Romanic Re-
    view*, 56 (1965), 3-11. Summary article, points to Non-
    chaloir as key concept and index of change.

Winter, John F. "Considerations on the Medieval and Renais-
    sance Concept of Space." In *Jean Misrahi Memorial Volume:
    Studies in Medieval Literature*. Ed. Hans R. Runte, Henri
    Niedzielski, and William L. Hendrickson. Columbia, S.C.:
    French Literature Publications Co., 1977, pp. 344-58. On
    Ronsard and CdO (Rondeau 24). Static vs. dynamic; medieval
    vs. Renaissance.

Wolfzettel, Friedrich. "La poésie lyrique en France comme
    mode d'appréhension de la réalité: remarques sur l'invention
    du sens visuel chez Machaut, Froissart, Deschamps et Charles
    d'Orleans." In *Mélanges ... Charles Foulon*. Rennes:
    Institut de français, Université de Haute-Bretagne, 1980,
    Vol. 1, pp. [409]-19.

Yenal, Edith. *Charles d'Orléans: A Bibliography of Primary
    and Secondary Sources*. New York: AMS Press, 1984. First
    book-length bibliography. Very useful.

Zumthor, Paul. "Charles d'Orléans et le langage de l'allé-
    gorie." In *Mélanges ... Rita Lejeune*. Ed. J. Ducolot.
    Gembloux: 1969. Vol. II, pp. 1481-1502. Significance of
    allegory to CdO's importance as innovative poet.

The French Chansons of
Charles D'Orleans

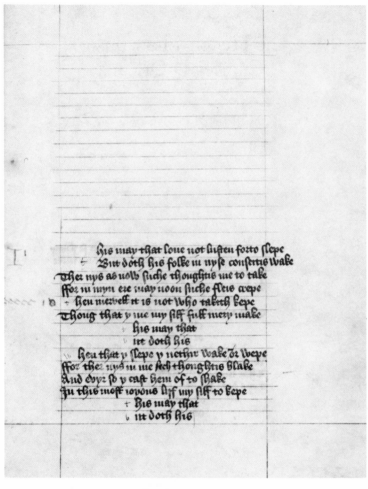

ſhis may that ſoue not liſten forto ſlepe
Butt dotħ ħis folke in nyſe conſertis wake
Ther nys as now ſuche thoughtis me to take
ffor in myn ere may noon ſuche fleis crepe
ħen merveft it is not who takith kepe
Though that y me my ſiff ſitt mery make
    ħis may that
    itt doth ħis
ħeu that y ſlepe y nerthir wake or weye
ffor ther nys in me ſich thoughtis ſlake
And chyr ſo y caſt hem of to ſhake
ju this moſt iopous liff my ſiff to kepe
    ħis may that
    itt doth ħis

London, British Library, MS Harley 682, fol. 61r Reproduced by permission of the British Library.

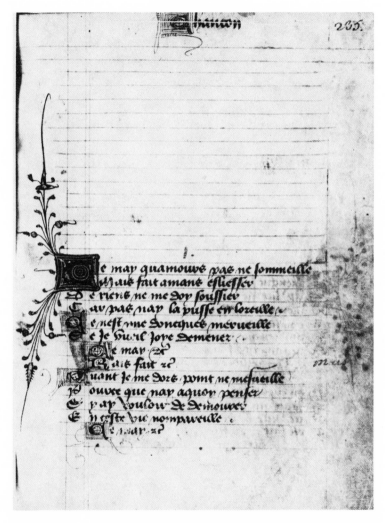

E may quamouve pas ne sommeille
M aus fait amant esliesser
D e riens ne me doy soussier
G au pas may la puisse en loreille
e nest que doneques mervueille
e Je vuel Joye demener
E may &c
B uit fait &c
Q uant Je me dors point ne mesvueille
f ouvre que may aguov penser
C y ap voulou de demouver
E n ceste vie nonpareille
Q e may &c

1. CE MAY QU'AMOURS PAS NE SOMMEILLE

Ce May qu'amours pas ne sommeille,
Mais fait amans esliesser,
De riens ne me doy soussier,
Car pas n'ay la pusse en l'oreille.
Ce n'est mie doncques merveille   5
Se je vueil joye demener,
     Ce May . . .
     Mais fait . . .
Quant je me dors, point ne m'esveille,
Pource que n'ay a quoy penser;   10
Sy ay vouloir de demourer
En ceste vie nompareille,
     Ce May . . .

Rejected readings of O: 1. may   7. may   8. Rais   13. may

I. THIS MAY THAT LOVE NOT LUSTEN FORTO SLEPE*

This May that love not *lusten*[1] forto slepe
But doth his folke in nyse *consertis*[2] wake,
Ther nys as now suche thoughtis me to take
For in myn ere may noon suche fleis crepe.[3]
Then mervell it is not *who takith kepe*   5
Thoug that[4] y me my silf full<u>e</u> mery make
     This May that . . .
     But doth his . . .
When that y slepe y nethir wake nor wepe
For[5] ther nys in me sech thoughtis *blake*[6]   10
And evyr so *y cast hem of to shake.*[7]
     This May that . . .
     But doth his . . .

Rejected readings of C: 1. may   7. may   13. may

*Notes opposite.

2

1

This May when love doesn't sleep,
But instead inspires[8] all lovers,
I needn't worry about a thing,
For I don't have [that] flea in my ear;
And so it is not the least surprising   5
If I wish to express[9] [some] joy
      This May when love doesn't sleep,
      But instead inspires all lovers.
When I sleep, nothing wakes me,
For I have nothing to brood about;[10]   10
And so I wish to remain
In this unparalleled life,
      This May when love doesn't sleep.

[8]Lit.: "makes happy."
[9]Here following Chalvet who glosses as *démontrer*. Else-
where glossed as "pursue," "track down," "follow up."
[10]Lit.: "think."

I. (Notes)

[1]Closest to Modern English "please": "when it doesn't
please love to sleep."
[2]"musical consorts."
[3]An unusual metaphor. Translated from the French where
more common. See, e.g., Rabelais, *Gargantua and Pantagruel*,
Book 3, Chapter 7: "Comment Panurge avoit la pusse en
l'aureille...."
[4]"Who notices that, even so."
[5]*that* may have been omitted.
[6]"wicked," "evil."
[7]"I try to shake them off."

2. TIENGNE SOY D'AMER QUI POURRA

Tiengne soy d'amer qui pourra,
Plus ne m'en pourroye tenir,
Amoureux me fault devenir;
Je ne sçay qu'il m'en avendra.
Combien que j'ay oy, pieça,   5
Qu'en amours fault mains maulx souffrir,
    Tiengne soy . . .
    Plus ne . . .
Mon cueur devant yer accointa
Beauté qui tant le scet chierir   10
Que d'elle ne veult departir;
C'est fait; il est sien et sera.
    Tiengne soy d'amer . . .

II. NOW HOLDE HIM SILF FROM LOVE LET SE THAT MAY

Now holde him silf from love *let se that may*[1]
For as for me, *y may kepe me no more,*[2]
I nede must love for any greef or sore[3]
And yet y not what happe wol to me way.[4]
For *whi*[5] oft tyme y haue herd folkis say   5
That *trowbille*[6] gret is ther in lovis *lore,*[7]
    Now hold . . .
    For as for . . .
My hert *gan him acquaynt*[8] the tothir day
With bewte which so *cherid*[9] him therfore   10
That hir to serve he hath him silf yswore;
Teys doon,[10] he *here*[11] is, and wol be *to he day.*[12]
    Now hold . . .
    For as for . . .

2

Let him keep from loving, he who can;
No longer can I hold myself from it,
I must become a lover;
I don't know what will come of it.
Even though I heard some time ago   5
That when in love one must suffer much pain,
    Let him keep from loving, he who can;
    No longer can I hold myself from it.
My heart the other day became acquainted with
Beauty, who knows how to treat[13] it[14] so right   10
That it never wishes to leave her.
It's done; it's hers and ever will be.
    Let him keep from loving, he who can.

[13]Or: "caress," "cheer up."
[14]"it": the heart; "her": Beauty.

II. (Notes)

[1]"let's see who can."
[2]"I can no longer keep myself from it."
[3]"I must love even if it brings grief or pain."
[4]"And though I don't know what fortune will come my way";
Taylor reads "y may not," an interpolation that emphasizes
the lack of control.
[5]"while."
[6]"trouble," "difficulty."
[7]"teaching," "behavior."
[8]"did acquaint."
[9]"cheered up," "made cheerful."
[10]"It's done."
[11]"hers."
[12]"until he dies."

3. QUELQUE CHOSE QUE JE DYE

Quelque chose que je dye
D'amour ne de son povoir,
Toutesfois, pour dire voir,
J'ay une dame choisie,
La mieulx, en bien acomplie,   5
Que l'en puist jamais veoir,
  Quelque chose . . .
  D'amour ne . . .
Mais a elle ne puis mie
Parler selon mon vouloir,   10
Combien que, sans decevoir,
Je suis sien toute ma vie,
  Quelque chose . . .

III. WHAT SO BE THAT Y SAY PARDE

What so be that y say, parde,
Of love or of his gret *rigure*,[1]
Yet this for trouthe, y yow ensure,
A lady have y chosen me,
Fulfillid of grace and gret bounte   5
Surmountyng[2] every creature
  What so . . .
  Of love . . .
But nevirtheles yet am y he
That dar not out his hert *discure*;[3]   10
Yet alsolong as that y lijf endure
I hiris am and evir so wolle be.
  What for . . .
  Of love . . .

3

Whatever I might say
Of love or of its power,[4]
Nevertheless, to tell the truth,
I have found a lady--[5]
The best, blessed with every virtue,[6]   5
That one might ever see,
    Whatever I might say
    Of love or of its power.
But to her I can not at all
Speak as I would wish,   10
Even though, with no deception,
I'm hers as long as I [may] live,
    Whatever I might say.

[4]All other editions personify love and thus translate
son povoir as "his power."
[5]Lit.: "chosen."
[6]"virtue," "grace," see Textual Notes and Glossary

III. (Notes)

[1]"discipline," "rigor."
[2]"Surpassing."
[3]"make known," "reveal"; "Nevertheless I'm still at the
stage where I dare not reveal my desires."

4. N'EST ELLE DE TOUS BIENS GARNIE

N'est elle de tous biens garnie,
Celle que j'ayme loyaument?
Il m'est advis, par mon serement,
Que sa pareille n'a en vie.
Qu'en dittes vous, je vous en prie,　　　　　　　　5
Que vous en semble vrayement?
　　　N'est elle . . .
　　　Celle que . . .
Soit qu'elle dance, chante, ou rie,
Ou face quelque esbatement;　　　　　　　　　　10
Faictes en loyal jugement,
Sans faveur ou sans flaterie,
　　　N'est elle . . .

IV. IS SHE NOT FULLE OF ALLE GOODLY MANERE

Is she not fulle of alle goodly manere
The which y love in my most feithful wise?
God helpe me so as when y hir *avise*[1]
In alle this world me thynkith not hir pere.[2]
Ye lovers now, how say yow, lete us here:　　　　5
What is she worth? *Let se sett to a prise.*[3]
　　　Is she not . . .
　　　The which . . .
In daunce or song, laughtir or *sobir chere,*[4]
Or what she doo *in ought that to hir lise;*[5]　　10
Say yowre verdit, let trowthe be justice,
And flatir not, *on trouthe, y yow requere:*[6]
　　　Is she not . . .
　　　The whiche . . .

Rejected reading of C: **6.** let

4

Isn't she blessed[7] with every virtue,
She whom I faithfully love?
It's my opinion, on my oath,
That no one alive's her rival.
What do you say, I ask you,
How does she really seem to you?
    Isn't she blessed with every virtue,
    She whom I faithfully love?
Whether she dances, sings, or laughs,
Or engages in some diversion;[8]
Make a true judgment of this,
Without any bias or flattery,[9]
    Isn't she blessed with every virtue?

                              5

                              10

[7]Or: "fortified," "prepared," "provided."
[8]Or: "pleasantry," "light conversation."
[9]Lit.: "without favoritism."

IV. (Notes)

[1]"consider."
[2]"In the whole world I don't think she has an equal."
[3]"Let a price be set."
[4]"serious expression."
[5]"whatever pertains."
[6]"in truth I ask you."

5. QUANT J'AY NOMPAREILLE MAISTRESSE

Quant j'ay nompareille maistresse
Qui a mon cueur entierement,
Tenir me vueil joyeusement
En servant sa gente jeunesse.
Car certes je suis en l'adresse   5
D'avoir de tous biens largement,
    Quant j'ay . . .
    Qui a mon . . .
Or en ayent dueil ou tristesse,
Envieux, sans allegement,   10
Il ne m'en chault, par mon serement,
Car leur desplaisir m'est liesse.
    Quant j'ay . . .

V. SYN THAT Y HAVE A NOUNPARALLE MAYSTRES

Syn that y have a nounparalle maystres
The which hath hool my service and myn hert[1]
I shall<u>e</u> be glad for any greef or smert
To serve hir in hir goodly *lustynes*.[2]
For now y trust to have dowtles   5
More ioy then ther be stichis in my shert.
    Syn that . . .
    The whiche . . .
Though to envyous hit be hevynes
And sorow gret to don hem prike and stert,[3]   10
Yet bi my trouthe when that y *me advert*[4]
Ther displesere hit is my gret gladnes.
    Syn that . . .
    The whiche . . .

Since I have an unrivaled lady,[5]
Who owns my heart completely,
I happily stay where I am,
Serving her attractive youthfulness.[6]
For indeed I'm on the right path[7]   5
Toward having much of it all,[8]
    Since I have an unrivaled lady,
    Who owns my heart completely.
Now may it cause them pain[9] or sorrow,
The envious, without relief;   10
It doesn't bother me, by my oath,
For their distress is happiness to me,
    Since I have an unrivaled lady.

[5]No connotation of adultery in French *maistresse*.
[6]The quality that his mistress and the month of May share.
[7]Or: "on the right path," "headed in the right direction."
[8]Lit.: "To have a great share of every bounty."
[9]Lit.: "pining."

V. (Notes)

[1]"Who has my entire service and my heart."
[2]As the equivalent of French *jeunesse*, the meaning is perhaps best rendered by Modern English "freshness" or "youthfulness." Cf. Ballade 10.1: *Fresche Beauté, tres riche de jeunesse*.
[3]"Even though it cause pining and great sorrow for the envious to make them prance and start."
[4]"realize" (reflexive).

6. DIEU QU'IL LA FAIT BON REGARDER

Dieu, qu'il la fait bon regarder
La gracieuse, bonne, et belle!
Pour les grans biens qui sont en elle,
Chascun est prest de la louer.
Qui se pourroit d'elle lasser? 5
Tousjours sa beauté renouvelle.
     Dieu, qu'i . . .
     La grac . . .
Par deça, ne delà, la mer
Ne sçay dame, ne damoiselle 10
Qui soit en tous biens parfais telle;
C'est un songe que d'y penser.
     Dieu, qu'i . . .

VI. O GOD HOW THAT SHE LOKITH VERRY FAYRE

O God, how that she lokith verry fayre
The goodly swete, my very hertis blis,
That for the grace the which that in hir is[1]
To everi *wight*[2] hir prays doth *newe repayre.*[3]
Who is it he that kouthe hit, loo, contrayre?[4] 5
For hir bewte renewith *ay ywis.*[5]
     O god how . . .
     The goodly . . .
She hath no peere, she lyvith *withouten eyre,*[6]
Of alle the fayre y *except noon as this*[7] 10
For in hir, loo, ther *nys oon poynt amys,*[8]
Tis a dere hert worth a thousand *payre.*[9]
     O God how . . .
     The goodly . . .

6

God, what a vision she is,[10]
The gracious[11] one, true and beautiful!
For all the virtues that are hers
Everyone is quick to praise her.
Who could tire of her?   5
Her beauty constantly renews itself;
        God, what a vision she is,
        The gracious one, true and beautiful.
On neither side of the ocean[12]
Do I know any girl or woman   10
Who is in all virtues so perfect;[13]
It's a dream even to think of her;
        God, what a vision she is.

[10]Lit.: "God, it does one good to look at her!" Or, as
Ezra Pound translates, "God! that mad'st her well regard her."
[11]Difficult to translate, as English "gracious" has more
to do with manners and demeanor than French *gracieuse* which
implies being imbued with the grace of God.
[12]Lit.: "Neither this nor that."
[13]Or: "complete," "finished."

VI. (Notes)

[1]"for the grace that is in her."
[2]"fellow."
[3]EETS paraphrases: "To everyone continually her merit is
present, is obvious."
[4]"Who could possibly contradict it?"
[5]"always, indeed."
[6]"without an heir."
[7]I.e., I leave no one out.
[8]"not one point amiss."
[9]Coin.

7. PAR DIEU MON PLAISANT BIEN JOYEUX

Par Dieu, mon plaisant bien joyeux,
Mon cueur est si plain de leese
Quant je voy la doulce jeunesse
De vostre gent corps gracieux.
Pour le regard de voz beaulx yeux   5
Qui me met tout hors de tristesse,
    Par Dieu . . .
    Mon cueur . . .
Combien que parler envieux
Souventes fois moult fort me blesse,   10
Mais ne vous chaille, ma maistresse;
Je n'en feray pourtant que mieulx,
    Par Dieu . . .

Rejected readings of O: 7. Pardieu   10. Souventesfois

VII. BI GOD BUT OON MY VERRY PLEASAUNT JAY

Bi God but oon, my verry pleasaunt *jay*,[1]
Myn hert *even*[2] full_e is of gladnes,
When y biholde the yowthe and *lustynes*[3]
Of yowre body with long streight *sidis tay*.[4]
For whi the lookis of yowre eyen gray   5
Thei putt me out of all_e hevynes.
    Bi God but . . .
    Myn hert . . .
Albe[5] that cursid speche--*yville mote they day*[6]
Full often tyme han doon me gret dures,   10
But care ye not, lady maystres,
Forwhi[7] the more y love yow, lo, alway,
    Bi God but . . .
    Myn hert . . .

7.

By God, my delightful, joyous treasure,
My heart is full of delight
Whenever I see the sweet suppleness
Of your attractive, lovely form.
For a look from your beautiful eyes   5
Puts me completely out of sorrow;
  By God, my delightful, joyous treasure,
  My heart is full of delight.
Although the talk of the jealous
Often wounds me very badly,   10
Don't let that worry you, my love;
I wouldn't change a thing,[8]
  By God, my delightful, joyous treasure.

 [8]Here following all but Chalvet, who reads: "I wouldn't
be anyone else."

VII. (Notes)

[1]Following Taylor who prints *Jay*: "joy."
[2]"equally," "completely."
[3]See 5.2.
[4]"two sides."
[5]"although."
[6]"may the evil [ones] drop dead."
[7]"because of this," "for this reason."

8. QUE ME CONSEILLIEZ VOUS MON CUEUR

Que me conseilliez vous, mon cueur?
Iray je par devers la belle,
Luy dire la peine mortelle
Que souffrez pour elle en doleur?
Pour vostre bien et son honneur,   5
C'est droit que vostre conseil celle.
    Que me . . .
    Iray je . . .
Si plaine la sçay de doulceur
Que trouveray mercy en elle;   10
Tost en aurez bonne nouvelle.
G'y vois; n'est ce pour le meilleur?
    Que me . . .

Rejected reading of O: 2. pardevers.

VIII. NOW SAY ME LO MYN HERT WHAT IS THI REED

Now say me, lo, myn hert, what is thi *reed*?[1]
Ne is hit best y to my lady goo,
And telle hir of my dedly greef and woo
That y endure thorugh hir *goodlihed*?[2]
Loo, for thi *wele*[3] and for hir womanhed,   5
Reson wol not she uttir hit, no, no.[4]
    Now say . . .
    Ne is hit . . .
For whi y *wot*[5] she is so good in dede
That harme it were and mercy were hir fro.[6]   10
How thenkist thou, nyst best that y do so?
O comfort me that am so full of drede.
    Now say . . .
    Ne is hit . . .

8

What do you advise me, my heart?
Should I go straight to my love
To tell her of the deadly pain
That you suffer for her in anguish?
For your well-being and her honor[7]   5
It's right that your advice remain secret;[8]
    What do you advise me, my heart,
    Should I go straight to my love?
I know that she is so full of sweetness
That I will find her merciful;   10
You will soon have some good news from her.
I'll go to her; isn't that for the best?[9]
    What do you advise me, my heart?

[7]Or: "its honor."

[8]D'Hericault glosses as: "It's right that I keep your advice secret." Bruneau glosses: "for your happiness, my heart, and for your lady-friend's young man it is better for me to hide your advice." But comparison with English would suggest that it's she who will keep the lover's confessions secret.

[9]Guichard reads "I see that's for the best."

VIII. (Notes)

[1]"advice."
[2]"goodness."
[3]"well-being."
[4]"It's right she won't speak aloud, no, no."
[5]"know."
[6]"That she'd take it badly and show no mercy."

9. OU REGARD DE VOZ BEAULX DOULX YEULX

Ou regard de voz beaulx doulx yeulx
(Dont loing suis par les envieux)
Me souhaide si tressouvent,
Que mon penser est seulement
En vostre gent corps gracieux.   5
Savez pourquoy, mon bien joyeux,
Celle du monde qu'ayme mieulx
De loyal cueur, sans changement?
        Ou regard . . .
        Dont loing . . .
        Me souhaide . . .   10
Pource que vers moy, en tous lieux,
J'ay trouvé plaisir ennuieux--
Trop fort--puis le departement
Que de vous fis derrainement,   15
A regret merencolieux
        Ou regard . . .

IX. AS OON SWETE LOOK OF YOWRE EYEN TAYNE

As oon swete look of yowre eyen tayne,[1]
Which wikkid speche doth *fro me refrayne,*[2]
As wisshith hit me[3] at lest as often, loo,
As[4] y have thoughtis on yow where y goo,
Of yowre fayre body and streight sidis playne.   5
Wot ye wherfore, my verry ioy soverayne,
Whom y most love (god wot y do not *fayne*[5])
As for my trouthe if cause ye fynde no moo
        As oon swete . . .
        Which wikkid . . .   10
        As wisshe hit . . .
For whi[6] y best may say this (dar y seyne)
That all plesere y take hit of disdayne[7]
For this, madame, (ye kan not thenke hit, noo)
When y departid last, ye did me soo   15
Werthefully yowre look forto refrayne,[8]
        As oon swete . . .
        Which wikkid . . .
        As wisshe hit . . .

Rejected reading of C: 16. Werthe fully

18

9

Whenever I see your beautiful, sweet eyes
(From which the jealous keep me distant)
I wish for them so very often
That my dreams[9] are only
Of your attractive, lovely body.   5
Do you know why, my joyful treasure,
The one whom I love most in all the world,
With a loyal, unchanging heart?
    Whenever I see your beautiful, sweet eyes
    (From which the jealous keep me distant)   10
    I wish for them so very often.
Because around me, everywhere,
I've found delights tedious--
All too much--since the departure[10]
I most recently[11] made from you   15
With melancholic regret,
    Whenever I see your beautiful, sweet eyes.

[9]Or: "thoughts," "hopes," "reveries." See Textual Notes.
[10]*puis* to be understood with *que* from line 15.
[11]In the sense of the last one done.

IX. (Notes)

[1]"One sweet look from your two eyes." *As* is used pleo-
nastically.
  [2]"keep from me."
  [3]"I desire." EETS notes the impersonal form is not usually used in English. Perhaps suggested by reflexive in
French.
  [4]"as often as."
  [5]"pretend."
  [6]"For this reason."
  [7]"That I am disdainful of all pleasure."
  [8]EETS paraphrases: "for this reason madame (though you
cannot believe it possible!) namely, that when I went away,
you in all your honour withheld your eyes from me."

10. QUI LA REGARDE DE MES YEULX

Qui la regarde de mes yeulx,
Ma dame, ma seule maistresse,
En elle voit, a grant largesse,
Plaisirs croissans de bien en mieulx.
Son parler et maintien sont tieulx   5
Qu'ilz mettent un cueur en liesse,
    Qui la . . .
    Ma dame . . .
Tous la suient, jeunes et vieulx,
Dieu scet qu'elle n'est pas sans presse;   10
Chascun dit: "C'est une deesse
Qui est descendue des cieulx."
    Qui la . . .

Rejected readings of O: 3. agrant   5. Lon   9. lasuient
11. cest   13. ui

X. WHO SO BIHOLDITH WEL AS WITH MY EYE

Who so biholdith wel as with my eye,
Mi *verry*[1] lady and my *sul*[2] maystres,
In hir shalle see so gret and *hvug larges*[3]
Of *plesaunt*[4] spryngyng from gret to more goodly.
Hir speche is such and hir demene trewly   5
That hit wol brynge any hert into gladnes
    Who so . . .
    My verry . . .
For yong and oold *that lokith here, wisly,*[5]
To preysen hir hardily they nevir cesse;   10
But sayne *echon*[6] that his is a goddes
Which is descendid downe from heven on hy.
    Who so . . .
    My verry . . .

10.

Whoever would look at her with my eyes,
My lady, my only love,
Would see in her, in great abundance,
Pleasures[7] that grow from better to best.[8]
Her speech and bearing are such   5
That they put a heart in joy,[9]
  Whoever would look at her with my eyes,
  My lady, my only love.
All pursue her, young and old;
God knows she is not without a following;   10
Everyone says: "It's a goddess
Who has descended from heaven!"
  Whoever would look at her with my eyes.

[7]Another loaded word that, like Modern French *plaisir*,
implies sexual connotations.
 [8]Lit.: "from good to better."
 [9]Lit.: "That they put a heart in happiness."

X. (Notes)

[1]"true."
[2]"sole."
[3]"huge abundance."
[4]EETS suggests this is a scribal error for *plesaunce*.
[5]"that look at her, certainly."
[6]"each one."

11. CE MOIS DE MAY NOMPAREILLE PRINCESSE

Ce mois de May, nompareille princesse,
Le seul plaisir de mon joyeulx espoir,
Mon cueur avez et quanque puis avoir,
Ordonnez en, comme dame et maistresse.
Pour ce requier vostre doulce jeunesse,   5
Qu'en gré vueille mon present recevoir
  Ce mois . . .
  Le seul . . .
Et vous supply, pour me tollir tristesse,
(Tres humblement et de tout mon povoir)   10
Qu'a m'esmayer ayez vostre vouloir
D'un reconfort bien garny de liesse,
  Ce mois . . .

Rejected readings of O: 1. may 5. Pource 6. Quengre
10. povair 11. Quamesmayer

XI. THIS MONTHE OF MAY WITHOUTEN PERE PRINCESSE

This monthe of *May*,[1] withouten pere princesse,
The soul plesere of all myn hope and thought,
Ye have myn hert *yn al ye may or ought*,[2]
So ordeyne me a lady and maystres.
Wherfore that y biseche yowre *gantiles*[3]   5
To take *in gree*[4] this *bille*[5] here to yow *wrofft*[6]
  This monthe . . .
  The soul plesere . . .
And that ye so *lust to lesse*[7] myn hevynes,
I yow biseche that ye *forslouthe*[8] it nought,   10
But in yowre silf, that ye ben ay bithought,
Sum recomfort to geve me or gladnes,[9]
  This monthe . . .
  The soul plesere . . .

Rejected readings of C: 1. may 3. ye

22

This month of May, unrivaled princess,
The only delight of my joyous hope,
You have my heart and whatever else you want;[10]
Order it, as my lady and love.
For this reason I ask your sweet youthfulness   5
That it gladly agree to accept my offering:[11]
    This month of May, unrivaled princess,
    The only delight of my joyous hope.
I beg you, so as to take away my sadness,
Humbly and with all my strength,[12]
That your desire be to garland[13] me
With solace well supplied with happiness,
    This month of May, unrivaled princess.

[10]Lit.: "and all that you can have."
[11]The present here refers to the poem and the request it makes.
[12]"strength," "power," "ability."
[13]"reinforce," "replenish." The term means literally to crown with green branches.

XI. (Notes)

[1]Pun intended; see Textual Notes.
[2]"for all you would or should."
[3]French *gentilesse*: "courtesy."
[4]"willingly."
[5]I.e., the poem.
[6]"wrought," "made."
[7]"wish to lessen."
[8]"delay."
[9]"But in your capacity, as you've been ever disposed, to give me some solace or happiness."

12. COMMANDEZ VOSTRE BON VOULOIR

Commandez vostre bon vouloir,
A vostre treshumble servant;
Il vous sera obeissant
D'entier cueur et loyal povoir.
Prest est de faire son devoir;   5
Ne l'espargnés ne tant ne quant:
      Commandez . . .
      A vostre . . .
Mettez le tout a nonchaloir,
Sans lui estre jamais aydant;   10
S'en riens le trouvez refusant,
Essaiez se je vous dy voir:
      Commandez . . .

Rejected reading of O: 4. povair

XII. COMAUNDE ME WHAT YE WILLE IN EVERI WISE

Comaunde me what ye wille in everi wise,
To me that am yowre *sely*[T] poore servaunt,
And evir more unto yow obeyshaunt,
With myn hool hert with power and servise.
I redy am in what that in me *lise*,[2]   5
Out spayng[3] this or that, *y dar avaunt*,[4]
      Comaunde me . . .
      To me that . . .
Cast all*e consait*[5] away that doth yow *grise*,[6]
Asay me where that y be suffisaunt[7]   10
To doon for yow *as y have made yow graunt*,[8]
And if y fayle take nevir of me prise:[9]
      Comaunde me . . .
      To me that . . .

12

Order your every good wish
Of your humble servant;
He will be obedient to you
With his whole heart and loyal power.
He's ready to carry out his duty;   5
Don't spare him at all, whatever it may be:
    Order your every good wish
    Of your humble servant.
Put all your cares aside;[10]
Don't help him in any way;   10
And if you find him refusing anything,
Try to see if what I say is true:
    Order your every good wish.

   [10]A loaded term, especially for Charles. See Introduction.

XII. (Notes)

[1]"innocent," "simple."
[2]"lies."
[3]"Without sparing."
[4]"I dare to boast."
[5]"concern."
[6]"trouble."
[7]"Try me to see whether I am satisfactory."
[8]"as I have promised."
[9]"And if I fail, consider me worthless."

13. BELLE SE C'EST VOSTRE PLAISIR

Belle, se c'est vostre plaisir,
De me vouloir tant enrichir
De reconfort et de liesse,
Je vous requier, comme maistresse,
Ne me laissiez du tout mourir.   5
Car je n'ay vouloir ne desir,
Fors de vous loyaument servir,
Sans espargnier dueil ne tristesse,
      Belle . . .
      De me . . .   10
      De reconfort . . .
Et s'il vous plaist a l'acomplir,
Vueilliez tant seulement bannir
D'avec vostre doulce jeunesse
Dolent refus qui trop me blesse;   15
Dont bien vous me povez guerir, Belle . . .

XIII. MOST GOODLY FAYRE IF HIT WERE YOWRE PLESERE

Most goodly fayre, if hit were yowre plesere
So moche forto enriche yowre servaunt here
Of recomfort of ioy and of gladnes,
I wolde biseche yow lady and maystres
Nor lete me dye *as all*[1] in displesere.   5
Syn that in me there nys wele nor desere,
Save trewly serve yow unto my powere,
Without eschewyng payne or hevynes,
      Most goodly fayre . . .
      So moche forto . . .   10
      Of recomfort . . .
And if ye lust so doon, my lady dere,
Ye banysshe must [*now*][2] yowre *straungely chere*[3]
Which is not *sittyng*[4] to yowre lustynes,
And *fowle refuse*[5] that doth me such dures;   15
This is my payne, this mowe ye hele me clere,[6]
      Most goodly fayre . . .
      So moche forto . . .
      Of recomfort . . .

13

Beauty, if it's your desire
To see me so enriched
With solace and happiness,
Then I ask you, as my lady,
Don't let me completely die[7]   5
For I have no wish or desire
Except to serve you loyally,
Avoiding neither pining nor sorrow;
    Beauty, if it's your desire
    To see me so enriched   10
    With solace and happiness.
And if you wish to carry this out,
With your sweet youthfulness,
Be only so good as to banish
The painful refusal[8] that wounds me so;   15
Thereby you can heal me well,
    Beauty, if it's your desire.

---

[7]Chalvet reads "I ask you as a lady to let me die." This seems to make little sense in the context.

[8]Champollion-Figeac personifies as *Dolent-refus*; Champion, exceptionally, does not.

XIII. (Notes)

[1]"entirely."

[2]*now* supplied *metri causa*, following Taylor.

[3]"unfriendly expression."

[4]"becoming"; Taylor reads *fitting* which works equally well.

[5]I.e., your unpleasant habit of turning me down.

[6]"This is my pain, this [is what] you may heal me of entirely."

14. RAFRESCHISSEZ LE CHASTEL DE MON CUEUR

Rafreschissez le chastel de mon cueur
D'aucuns vivres de joyeuse plaisance;
Car faulx dangier, avec son aliance,
L'a assegié, tout entour, de doleur.
Se ne voulez le siege sans longueur   5
Tantost lever ou rompre par puissance,
    Rafreschissez . . .
    D'aucuns . . .
Ne souffrez pas que dangier soit seigneur,
En conquestant soubz son obeissance   10
Ce que tenez en vostre gouvernance;
Avancez vous et gardez votre honneur.
    Rafreschissez . . .

Rejected reading of O: 5. Fe ne

XIV. REFRESSHE THE CASTELLE OF MY POORE HERT

Refresshe the castelle of my poore hert
With sum *lyvyng*[1] of ioy or of plesaunce,
For false daunger, with his allyaunce,
Asegith his with woo and grevous smert.
That it may not longe holde ye may advert   5
Which woo *forbetith*[2] so with ordenaunce
    Refresshe the . . .
    With sum . . .
Not suffir him to lorde this fals coward,
In conqueryng unto his obeyshaunce   10
Which that ye have undir yowre governaunce;
Avaunce yow now and kepe yow, lo, covert.
    Refresshe the . . .
    With sum . . .

14.

Replenish the castle of my heart
With some victuals of joyous pleasure,
For false Suspicion, with his allies,
Has assieged it all around with sorrow.[3]
If you want a short siege[4]   5
Soon ended or broken by force,
        Replenish the castle of my heart
        With some victuals of joyous pleasure.
Don't put up with[5] Suspicion as lord,
Conquering under his rule   10
What you hold in your domain;
Set forth, and watch out for your honor:
        Replenish the castle of my heart.

[3]Chalvet and Champollion-Figeac read: "Have assieged it
in the tower of sorrow."
[4]Here same meaning as English "siege."
[5]Or: "allow," "permit."

XIV.   (Notes)

[1]"victuals"; i.e., things to live on.
[2]"batters."

29

15. SE MA DOLEUR VOUS SAVIES

Se ma doleur vous saviés,
Mon seul joyeux pensement,
Je sçay bien certainement
Que mercy de moy auriés.
Du tout refus banniriés   5
Qui me tient en ce tourment,
    Se ma . . .
    Mon seul . . .
Et le don me donneriés
Que vous ay requis souvent,   10
(Pour avoir allegement)
Ja ne m'en escondiriés,
    Se ma . . .

XV. IF SO WERE THAT YE KNOWE MY WOO TREWLY

If so were[1] that ye knowe my woo trewly,
Mi verri gladdist remembraunce,
This *knowe*[2] y welle, withouten doutaunce,
That ye wolde shewe unto me sum mercy.
Allas, madame, banysshe yowre refuse, fy!   5
That cowardly me holdith in penaunce,
    If so were . . .
    My verry . . .
Ye graunten wolde my *bone*[3] *that for cry*[4]
Syn that y hool am yowris in substaunce   10
What *vaylith*[5] yow to doon me this grevaunce?
Whi lustith yow forto geynsay me, why?
    If so were . . .
    My verry . . .

30

15.

If [only] you knew my pain,[6]
My one joyful reflection,
I know for a certainty
That you would have pity on me;
You would entirely banish refusal   5
Which keeps me in this torment,
     If [only] you knew my pain,
     My one joyful reflection.
And you'd give me the gift
I've often requested of you--   10
Namely, to have relief--
You would never deny me that,
     If [only] you knew my pain.

[6]Lit.: "preoccupation." See Textual Notes for additional
connotations.

              XV.   (Notes)

[1]"If it so happened." See Textual Notes.
[2]EETS suggests this should probably read *knewe*.
[3]"boon," "gift."
[4]*y* omitted after *that*: "that I ask for."
[5]"avails," "helps."

16. MA SEULE PLAISANT DOULCE JOYE

Ma seule, plaisant, doulce joye,
La maistresse de mon vouloir,
J'ay tel desir de vous veoir,
Que mander ne le vous sauroye.
Helas, pensez que ne pourroye   5
Aucun bien, sans vous, recevoir,
      Ma seule . . .
      La maistresse . . .
Car, quant desplaisir me guerroye,
Souventesfois, de son povoir,   10
Et je vueil reconfort avoir,
Esperance vers vous m'envoye,
      Ma seule . . .

Rejected reading of O: 10. povair

XVI. MI VERRY IOY AND MOST PARFIT PLESERE

Mi verry ioy and most parfit plesere,
Whiche are of me and alle y have maystres,
So willith me to se yow, lo, dowtles,
That half how moche y kan not say yow here.
For wot ye this, myn owyn lady dere,   5
That without yow nave y good nor gladnes
      My verry ioy . . .
      Whiche are of . . .
For when y *werid*[1] am with displesere,
Whos power oft hath brought me in distres,   10
Me to requere to comfort, more or lesse,
Nis there save hope as sone to se yow here.[2]
      My verry ioy . . .
      Whiche are of . . .

My only, gracious, sweet joy,
The mistress of my desire,
I have such a yearning to see you
That I don't know how to tell you.[3]
Alas! Please know that I cannot   5
Enjoy anything without you,[4]
  My only, gracious, sweet joy,
  The mistress of my desire.
For when displeasure wars against me
Often, with its forces,   10
And I want to have solace,
Hope sends me towards you,
  My only, gracious, sweet joy.

[3]"declare," "articulate."
[4]Lit.: "receive."

XVI. (Notes)

[1]"weary."
[2]"There is nothing to invite me to be comforted, more or less, except the hope that soon I'll see you here."

17. JE NE VUEIL PLUS RIENS QUE LA MORT

Je ne vueil plus riens que la mort,
Pource que voy que reconfort
Ne peut mon cueur eslyesser;
Au meins me pourray je vanter
Que je seuffre douleur a tort.   5
Car puis que n'ay d'espoir le port,
D'amours ne puis souffrir l'effort;
Ne doy je donc joye laisser,
  Je ne . . .
  Pource . . .   10
  Ne peut . . .
Au dieu d'amour je m'en rapport
Qu'en peine suis bouté si fort
Que povair n'ay plus d'endurer;
S'en ce point me fault demourer.   15
Quant est de moy, je m'y accort,
  Je ne . . .

Rejected reading of O: 4. Aumeins

XVII. MORE THEN THE DETH NYS THYNG UNTO ME LEEF

More then the deth nys thyng unto me leef,
Syn recomfort unto my *karfulle*[1] greef
May noon be found to ioy my woofulle hert.[2]
But as a wrecche *avaunt y may of smert*[3]
That wrongfully my payne is to *[me]*[4] geef.   5
Fare welle hope, for noon may me releef;
Thorugh love fortune hath cast me to myschef
Which shapen had my deth tofore my shert.[5]
  More then the . . .
  Syn recomfort . . .   10
  May noon ben . . .
O god of love, thou wost y am no theef,
Nor falsyng of my trouthe thou kan not preef!
Whi shall y dey then wolde y fayne *advert*,[6]
Although from deth y kepe not now *astert*,[7]   15
Though that he stood right even here at my sleve.
  More then the . . .
  Syn recomfort . . .
  May noon ben . . .

I want nothing more than death,
Because I see that solace
Cannot relieve my heart.
At least I could boast
That I suffer pain wrongfully.   5
For since I don't have the port for hope,[8]
I cannot suffer love's onslaught;[9]
And so should I not abandon joy?
    I want nothing more than death,
    Because I see that solace   10
    Cannot relieve my heart.
To the god of love I wish to report
That in pain I am pushed so far[10]
That I don't have the power to last any longer.
If at this pass I must remain,   15
As far as I'm concerned I'm ready for it,
    I want nothing more than death.[11]

[8]For the Ship of Hope.
[9]The effort, force, harm of love.
[10]I.e., pushed to the limit.
[11]The meaning of this is the following: "If I must stay at this painful point (of being pushed to the limit by love) then I'm ready for it, that is, I'm ready to die."

XVII. (Notes)

[1]"full of woe," "care-filled."
[2]"May not be found to revivify my woeful heart."
[3]"I may boast of pain."
[4]*me* supplied *metri causa*, following Taylor.
[5]I.e., death appears at his elbow. EETS cites another use of this in Chaucer, *Canterbury Tales*, "The Knight's Tale," A 1566: "That shapen was my deeth erst than my sherte."
[6]"attend to," "learn of."
[7]"escaped."

18. BELLE QUE JE CHERIS ET CRAINS

Belle que je cheris et crains,
En cest estat suis ordonné
Que dangier m'a emprisonné
De vostre grant beauté loingtains;
N'il ne m'a, de tous biens mondains,   5
Qu'un souvenir abandonné,
    Belle . . . En cest . . .
Mais de nulle riens ne me plains
Fors qu'il ne m'a tost raençonné;
Car bien lui seroit guerdonné   10
Se j'estoie hors de ses mains, Belle . . .

Rejected reading of O: 6. Qun

XVIII. O GOODLY FAYRE WHICH Y MOST LOVE AND DREDE

O goodly fayre, which y most love and drede,
Such is myn *happe*,[1] suche grace is me ordeynyd,
That yowre *daunger*[2] hath me enprisonyd
Longe in[3] the bewte of yowre goodlihed.
But, welaway, that pite, loo, is deed,   5
For were she qukke longe nar y this bandonyd[4]
    O goodly fayre . . .
    Suche is myn . . .
But and ye helpe wolde of yowre womanhed
That onys y myght ben out raunsonyd   10
A shulde ben, lo, right well gardonyd.[5]
If ones at large y myght bere yp myn hed!
    O goodly fayre . . .
    Suche is myn . . .

Rejected reading of C: 2. Yn seche hape and grace as have y
wonyd (written in margin; used by Taylor). 4. longe

36

18

Beauty whom I cherish and fear,
In this situation where I'm ordered [to stay].
Namely, where Suspicion has imprisoned[6] me,
Far away from your great beauty.
There are no earthly pleasures here for me,   5
Except an abandoned memory,
     Beauty whom I cherish and fear,
     In this situation where I'm ordered [to stay]
But I complain of nothing at all
Except that he[7] should ransom me soon;   10
For well he would be rewarded
If I were out of his hands,
     Beauty whom I cherish and fear.

[6]Extended metaphor is that of capture and imprisonment
by the jealous and suspicious.
[7]Personified Suspicion.

XVIII. (Notes)

[1]"fortune."
[2]French *daunger*: "Suspicion."
[3]"far from."
[4]"For if she [Pity] were alive I would not be so long
abandoned."
[5]"But if you would help by using your womanly ways so
that I might soon be ransomed, he [Suspicion] would be, indeed,
very well rewarded."

19. MA DAME TANT QU'IL VOUS PLAIRA

Ma dame, tant qu'il vous plaira
De me faire mal endurer,
Mon cueur est prest de le porter,
Jamais ne le refusera.
En esperant qu'il guerira,   5
En cest estat veult demourer,
     Ma dame . . .
     De me . . .
Une fois pitié vous prandra,
Quant seulement vouldrez penser   10
Que c'est pour loyaument amer
Vostre beauté qu'il servira,
     Ma dame . . .

XIX. MADAME AS LONGE AS HIT DOTH PLESE YOW AY

Madame, as longe as hit doth plese yow ay
To doon me lyve in this paynfulle manere,
Myn hert is redy forto bere it here,
Without *grucchyng*,[1] and shalle *to that y day*;[2]
Only in trust yet of a bettir day   5
Endewre y shalle, syn hit is yowre plesere.
     Madame as . . .
     To doon me . . .
For onys ye wolle have pite, dar y say,
When ye have welle bithought, yow lady dere,   10
That alle is for the love y to yow bere
That wrongfully doth holde me this away,
     Madame . . .
     To doon me . . .

19

My lady, as much as it would please you
To make me endure hard times,
My heart is ready to suffer,[3]
And never will it refuse.
Hoping that things will improve,   5
In this condition it wishes to remain,
    My lady, as much as it would please you
    To make me endure hard times.
Pity will take hold of you once
You stop to think long enough[4]   10
That it's for faithfully loving
Your beauty that it continues to serve,
    My lady, as much as it would please you.

[3]"ready to support it," "ready to take it."
[4]Loose translation of a difficult phrase. More literally
the phrase means: "Pity would take hold of you at the time
when (une fois) you would choose (vouldrez) to remember only
the following."

XIX. (Notes)

[1]"complaining."
[2]"until I die."

39

20. DE LA REGARDER VOUS GARDEZ

De la regarder vous gardez,
La belle que sers ligement,
Car vous perdrés soudainement
Vostre cueur, se la regardez.
Se donner ne le lui voulés,   5
Clignez les yeulx hastivement,
    De la . . .
    La belle . . .
Les biens que Dieu lui a donnez
Emblent un cueur soubtilement,   10
Sur ce, prenez avisement,
Quant devant elle vous vendrés.
    De la . . .

Rejected readings of O: 9. dieu 11. Surce

XX. BEWAR Y REDE YOW LOKE HERE NOT UPON

Bewar, y *rede*,[1] yow loke here not upon
The goodly fayre that y love feithfully,
For ye shalle *lese*[2] yowre hert even sodaynly
If so be that ye cast her lokyng on.[3]
Wherfore but ye lust gefe yowre hert anoon,[4]   5
Shette up yowre eyen and close hem wel surely,
    Bewar y . . .
    The goodly . . .
For the bewte she hath, bi god, alon,
Hit stelith, lo, an hert so *pratily*[5]   10
That but ye bet abowt yowre silf aspy,
Or ye be war, yowre hert shalle be goon.[6]
    Bewar y . . .
    The goodly . . .

20

Keep yourself from watching her,
The beauty whom I serve as liege,
For you will suddenly lose
Your heart if you look at her.
If you don't wish to give it to her,   5
Blink your eyes hastily,
    Keep yourself from watching her,
    The beauty whom I serve as liege.
The treasures[7] which God has given her
Subtly steal away[8] a heart,   10
So do watch out for this
Whenever you come upon her:
    Keep yourself from watching her.

[7]See Glossary; here the sense seems to be more physical
than purely virtuous.
   [8]"steal," "rob," "take."

XX. (Notes)

   [1]"advise."
   [2]"lose."
   [3]EETS paraphrases: "If you cast your sight on her."
   [4]"Therefore unless you want to give your heart right now."
   [5]"cleverly."
   [6]"That you better watch out for yourself, or beware, your
heart will be gone."

21. PUIS QUE JE NE PUIS ESCHAPPER

Puis que je ne puis eschapper
De vous, courrous, dueil, et tristesse,
Il me couvient suïr l'adresse
Telle que me vouldrés donner.
Povoir n'ay pas de l'amender,
Car doleur est de moy maistresse.
     Puis . . .
     De vous . . .
Si manderay par un penser
A mon las cueur, vuit de liesse,
Qu'il prangne en gré sa grant destresse,   10
Car il lui fault tout endurer.
     Puis . . .

XXI. SYN Y MAY NOT ASKAPE ME FER NOR NERE

Syn y may not *askape me*,[1] fer nor nere,
As from the wrath of kare and hevynes,
I nedis must abiden the redres
That they me geve of payne or displesere.
It to amende y have noon ellis powere,[2]   5
For sorowe is bicomen my maystres.
     Syn y may . . .
     As from the . . .
Yet with this thought y shalle my silf *achere*:[3]
To pray myn hert, to take it for gladnes   10
The enduring of so gret distres,
Syn it is had for myn owen lady dere,
     Syn y may . . .
     As from the . . .

21.

Since I can't escape
From you, anger, pining, and sorrow,
It's good for me to follow the path,[4]
The one you'd have me take.[5]
I don't have the strength to improve things[6]   5
For pain is my mistress
        Since I can't escape
From you, anger, mourning, and sorrow.
And so I'll send on a thought
To my weary heart, empty of joy,   10
Namely, for it to suffer[7] gladly its great distress
Since it must endure all that comes
        Since I can't escape.

[4]Or: "go directly."
[5]Or: "whatever you wish to dole out to me."
[6]Lit.: "to change," "to amend."
[7]Lit.: "take." Here I follow Chalvet, but Poirion also
glosses as "être pris par un sentiment."

XXI. (Notes)

[1]EETS notes that this is not usually reflexive in English;
perhaps another calque from the French.
[2]"I have no additional power to alter it."
[3]"cheer up."

22. C'EST FAIT IL N'EN FAULT PLUS PARLER

C'est fait; il n'en fault plus parler,
Mon cueur s'est de moy departy;
Pour tenir l'amoureux party,
Il m'a voulu abandonner.
Riens ne vault m'en desconforter,   5
Ne d'estre dolent ou marry,
    C'est fait . . .
    Mon cueur . . .
De moy ne se fait que mocquer:
Quant piteusement je lui dy   10
Que je ne puis vivre sans luy,
A peine me veult escouter,
    C'est fait . . .

XXII. HIT IS DOON THER IS NO MORE TO SAY

Hit is doon; ther is no more to say,
Myn hert departid is fro me,
To holde with love and his parte.
That in bandone y lyve must to y day[1]
To wrethe my silf hit were me but fole,   5
Nor yet forto discomfort me, ma fay,[2]
    Hit is doon . . .
    Myn hert . . .
He doth not ellis but mokke with me and play
When y him say in myn adversite   10
I may not lyve withouten him, parde,
But saith me *"tewche!"*,[3] and turneth me away.
    Hit is doon . . .
    Myn hert . . .

22

It's done; there is no more to say.[4]
My heart is gone from me.
To play the role of lover,
It decided to abandon me.
It's pointless to make myself uncomfortable over this,   5
By being sad or pained,
  It's done, there is no more to say,
  My heart is gone from me.
It does nothing but mock me:
When pitifully I tell it   10
That I can't live without it
It hardly hears me.[5]
  It's done; there is no more to say.

[4]Or: "Nothing more needs be said about it."
[5]Lit.: "He hardly cares to listen to me."

XXII. (Notes)

[1]"That I must live in exile until I die,"
[2]"It would only be foolish for me to get angry; it would
only cause me discomfort, by my faith."
[3]"tut!"

23. PUIS QU'AMOUR VEULT QUE BANNY SOYE

Puis qu'amour veult que banny soye
De son hostel, sans revenir,
Je voy bien qu'il m'en fault partir,
Effacé du livre de joye.
Plus demourer je n'y pourroye,   5
Car pas ne doy ce mois servir,
     Puis . . .
     De son . . .
De confort ay perdu la voye,
Et ne me veult on plus ouvrir   10
La barriere de doulx plaisir
Par desespoir qui me guerroye
     Puis . . .

XXIII. SYN LOVE HATH CAST ME BANYSSHE EVERYDELLE

Syn love hath *cast me, banysshe everydelle*,[1]
Out of his hous, for now and evermore,
I must depart unto my grevous sore,
With face delyverid from alle ioy and *wele*.[2]
This se y, that y may no lengir dwelle,   5
Nor can aright deserven, lo, wherfore,
     Syn love . . .
     Out of . . .
For of comfort the wey hit fro me felle[3]
Thorugh mysfortune that hath me so *fortore*[4]   10
That my lady hath my deth yswore,
With *dubbil sorow*[5] thus y *entirmelle*[6]
     Syn love . . .
     Out of . . .

23

Since love wishes I be banished
From his hostel, with no hope of return,
I see that I must go,
Erased from the book of joy.
I can delay there no longer,   5
For this month is not to be served,
 Since love wishes I be banished
 From his hostel with no hope of return.
I've lost the path of comfort,
And it's no longer wished that I open   10
The barrier to sweet pleasure,
(On behalf of despair who fights me)
 Since love wishes I be banished.

XXIII. (Notes)

[1]"cast me out, banished altogether."
[2]"health."
[3]"For the way of comfort fell from me."
[4]"torn up."
[5]EETS glosses as 1) his misfortune, 2) his lady's consequent estrangement from him.
[6]"mix together," though EETS suggests that here it means "contend."

24. POUR LE DON QUE M'AVEZ DONNE

Pour le don que m'avez donné,
Dont tresgrant gré vous doy savoir,
J'ay congneu vostre bon vouloir
Qui vous sera bien guerdonné.
Raison l'a ainsi ordonné: 5
Bien fait doit plaisir recevoir,
      Pour . . .
      Dont . . .
Mon cueur se tient emprisonné
Et obligié, pour dire voir,   10
Jusqu'a tant qu'ait fait son devoir
Vers vous et se soit raençonné
      Pour . . .

XXIV. AS FOR THE GYFT YE HAVE UNTO ME GEVE

As for the gyft ye have unto me geve,
I thanke yow, lo, *in alle*[1] that in me is,
Forwhi y knowe now that ye love me this,
Which shalle be *quyt*[2] to yow, if so y lyve.
For resoun wolle hit so (this may y preve)   5
For goode doon good, wherfore myn hertis blis.
      As for the . . .
      I thanke . . .
Myn hert wol evir thynke him silf *in greve*[3]
To that *desert*[4] hit ben to yow *ywis*[5]   10
Of which that long y trust ye shalle not mys
Parcas[6] sumwhat to raunsom yow *or eve*[7]
      As for the . . .
      I thanke . . .

24

For the gift you've given me,
The great desirability of which I would make known to you,
I recognized your good will,
For which you'll be well-rewarded.
Reason has thus ordered it: 5
Good deeds must receive rewards[8]
    For the gift you've given me,
    The great desirability of which I would make known to you,
My heart is held imprisoned
And is legally bound, to tell the truth,   10
Until it has done its duty
Toward you and may be ransomed
    For the gift you've given me.

[8]Or: "delights," "pleasures."

XXIV.   (Notes)

[1]"with all."
[2]"requited."
[3]"imprisoned."
[4]"deserved."
[5]"indeed."
[6]"Per chance."
[7]"before nightfall"; i.e., as soon as possible.

25. SE J'EUSSE MA PART DE TOUS BIENS

Se j'eusse ma part de tous biens
Autant que j'ay de loyauté,
J'en auroye si grant planté
Qu'il ne me fauldroit jamais riens.
Et si gaingneroye des miens,   5
Ma dame, vostre voulenté,
    Se j'eusse . . .
      Autant . . .
Car pour asseuré je me tiens
Que vostre tresplaisant beauté   10
De s'amour me feroit renté,
Maugré dangier et tous les siens,
    Se j'eusse . . .

XXV. HAD Y AS MOCHE OF WORLDLY GOODIS

Had y as moche of worldly goodis
As ther is trouthe of love in me,
I had therof so gret plente
That ricches shulde y *neuyr*[1] mys.
Als[2] bettir myght y gete, ywis,   5
The good will_e_, lo, of my lady,
    Had y as . . .
    As ther is . . .
Forwhi[3] my trust, madame, is this:
That yowre most plesaunt fresshe bewte   10
So der, I wolde *arent*[4] it, shulde ye se,
That daungere shulde not *lette*[5] me, *nor al his.*[6]
    Had y as . . .
    As ther is . . .

25

If I had of all good things
As much as I have of loyalty,
I would have such a number of them
That nothing would be lacking me.
And I would also gain as mine,   5
My lady, your will,
    If I had of all good things
    As much as I have of loyalty.
For I hold myself assured
That the very delightful beauty   10
Of your love would pay me rent,
In spite of Suspicion and all his type,
    If I had of all good things.

XXV.   (Notes)

[1]"never."
[2]"and so."
[3]"Because."
[4]"pay rent for." See Textual Notes.
[5]"delay," "hinder."
[6]"nor any of his type." Cf. French: "et tous les siens."

26. POUR LES GRANS BIENS DE VOSTRE RENOMMEE

Pour les grans biens de vostre renommée
Dont j'oy parler a vostre grant honneur,
Je desire que vous aiez mon cueur,
Comme de moy tresloyaument amee.
Tresoriere, je vous voy ordonnee   5
A le garder en plaisance et doulceur,
  Pour les . . .
  Dont j'oy . . .
Recevez le, s'il vous plaist et agree,
Du mien ne puis vous donner don melleur;   10
C'est mon vaillant, c'est mon tresor greigneur,
A vous l'offre de loyalle pensee
  Pour . . .

XXVI. AS FOR YOWRE PRAYES YN FAME THAT IS UPBORE

As for yowre *prayes yn fame*[1] that is *upbore*,[2]
Ay growyng fresshe unto your gret honour,
That is the cause y do myn hert *soiowr*[3]
With yow to bide for now and evirmore.
But, y pray yow, y shulde have seid tofore,   5
In plesaunce forto kepe *him*[4] and favoure
  As for yowre . . .
  Ay growyng . . .
And him in gre take as yowre servaunt sowre
To gefe yow gift y nave of mor valowre,[5]   10
Tis my good wille, hit is my hool tresowre,
I offre yow with inward sighis sore.
  As for yowre . . .
  Ay growing . . .

As one of the great riches of your renown
Of which I've heard tell[6] to your great honor,
I want you to have my heart,
As by me, very loyally loved.
Treasurer[7] I'll see you ordered   5
To watch it in pleasure and sweetness.
    As one of the great riches of your renown
    Of which I've heard tell to your great honor.
Take it, if you wish and agree.
Of my things I can't give you a better gift;   10
It's my worth,[8] it's my greatest treasure,
I offer it to you with faithful intent.[9]
    As one of the great riches of your renown.

[6] In addition to the literal meaning, the word *joye*, written as it is in the MS, would introduce the concept of *joie* into the poem, subliminally reinforcing its already *joyeux* tone.

[7] Treasurer, especially of female parts: Cf. Deschamps, *Oeuvres*, SATF, Vol. 3, p. 102.

[8] Used substantively.

[9] See Textual Notes on use of this word.

XXVI.   (Notes)

[1] "praiseworthy merit."
[2] "borne aloft."
[3] "sojourn."
[4] I.e., the heart.
[5] "And willingly take him [my heart] as your sworn servant; I have nothing of greater value to give you as a gift."

27. EN SONGE SOUHAID ET PENSEE

En songe, souhaid, et pensee,
Vous voy chascun jour de sepmaine,
Combien qu'estes de moy loingtaine,
Belle, tresloyaument amee.
Pource qu'estes la mieulx paree   5
De toute plaisance mondaine,
    En songe . . .
    Vous voy . . .
Du tout vous ay m'amour donnee,
Vous en povez estre certaine,   10
Ma seule dame, souveraine,
De mon las cueur moult desiree
    En songe . . .

XXVII. IN THOUGHT IN WISSHIS AND IN DREMES SOFT

In thought, in wisshis, and in dremes soft,
God wot how that y se yow nyght and day,
Albe[1] that fer am y from yow away,
Whom that y love as feithfully y ought.
This say y me (not yow)[2] that ye are *wrought*[3]   5
The most pleasant that evir yet y *say.*[4]
    In thought . . .
    God wot . . .
My love is yowre, *for noon except y nought*
Be seid[5] (so thenke ye trouthe y to yow say),   10
But my soul lady are ye to y day,
Withouten choyse as of newfangille thought:[6]
    In thought . . .
    God wott . . .

27

In dream, wish, and reverie,
I see you every day of the week,
Even though you are far from me,
Beautiful one, you're very truly loved.
Since you are most blessed[7]   5
With every earthly pleasure.
    In dream, wish, and reverie,
    I see you every day of the week.
I have given you my love absolutely,
You can be certain of that,   10
My sole lady, queen,
Much desired by my tired heart,
    In dream, wish, and reverie.

[7]"decorated," "garnished."

XXVII. (Notes)

[1]"even though."

[2]EETS paraphrases: "Thus I say to myself, not to you (who are absent)." I would add the following secondary reading of the entire line: "Thus I saw, and you did not, that you are written about in the best way I can." See Textual Notes.

[3]"crafted," as both lady and poem.

[4]"saw."

[5]"beside." EETS paraphrases: "for I make no exception at all as compared to you."

[6]"But you are my only lady until I die, without choice such as sudden impulses."

28. DE LEAL CUEUR CONTENT DE JOYE

De leal cueur, content de joye,
Ma maistresse, mon seul desir,
Plus qu'oncques vous vueil servir,
En quelque place que je soye.
Tout prest en ce que je pourroye   5
Pour vostre vouloir adcomplir,
    De leal . . .
    Ma maistresse . . .
En desirant que je vous voye,
A vostre honneur et mon plaisir,   10
Qui seroit briefment, sans mentir,
S'il fust ce que souhaideroye
    De leal . . .

XXVIII. WITH MY TREWE HERT CONTENT OF IOY AND WELE

With my trewe hert, content of ioy and *wele*,[1]
Mi fayre maystres, myn hertis soul *desere*,[2]
Thenke how y serve yow, be y fer or nere,
What so me happe, in seeknes or in hele.
As redy ay to yow in every *dele*,[3]   5
Forto fulfille yowre wille, my lady dere.
    With my . . .
    My fayre . . .
Yowre presence were to me an *hertis melle*,[4]
With yowre honoure (and to my gret plesere),   10
Whiche shulde ben, lo, right sone (so trust me here),
If hit myght be as y koude wisshe hit felle[5]
    With my . . .
    My fayre . . .

28

With loyal heart, content with joy,
My mistress, my sole desire,
More than ever I wish to serve you
Wherever I may be.[6]
I'm as ready as I can be   5
To carry out your will,
    With loyal heart, content with joy,
    My mistress, my sole desire.
Desiring that I see you,
For your honor and my pleasure,   10
Which would be soon, it's no lie,
If it was the way I wanted it.[7]
    With loyal heart, content with joy.

[6]Lit: "In whatever place I may be."
[7]Guichet reads: "Desiring that I see you, for your honor,
and it would be my pleasure if soon, truthfully, it was the
way I wanted it."

XXVIII. (Notes)

[1]"well-being."
[2]"desire."
[3]"way," "aspect."
[4]"feast for the heart."
[5]"If it might turn out the way I want it to."

29. SE MON PROPOS VIENT A CONTRAIRE

Se mon propos vient a contraire,
Certes, je l'ay bien desservy,
Car je congnois que j'ay failly
Envers ce que devoye plaire.
Mais j'espoire que debonnaire   5
Trouveray sa grace et mercy,
      Se mon . . .
      Certes . . .
Je vueil endurer et me taire,
Quant cause sui de mon soussy;   10
Las, je me sens en tel party
Que je ne sçay que pourray faire,
      Se mon . . .

XXIX. AND SO BE NOW THAT Y MY PURPOS LESSE

And so be now that y my purpos *lesse*[1]
Certis, y have *desert*[2] hit *wil*[3] wherfore,
For well_e y wott y have my silf *mysbore,*[4]
As toward hir that y ought most to plese.
But what as, loo, *this doth myn hert an ese*[5]   5
That y have knowen hir mercy heretofore
      And so be . . .
      Certis y . . .
But what y shall_e endure and holde my pese,
Syn that y have my *steffen*[6] thus forswore,   10
The feere y have me grevith now so sore
That, by my lijf, y sett not here a pese.[7]
      And so be . . .
      Certis y . . .

29

If my wish finds disapproval,[8]
Indeed I have deserved it well,
For I recognize that I have failed
Where I should have pleased.
But I trust that I will find her   5
Pardon and pity noble;
    If my wish finds disapproval
    Indeed I have deserved it well.
I will endure and keep silent
Since I am the cause of my cares;   10
Alas! I feel I am at such a pass
That I don't know what I can do
    If my wish finds disapproval.

[8]Or: "is contrary to what it should be."

XXIX. (Notes)

[1]"leave off," "lessen."
[2]"deserved."
[3]"well."
[4]"misconducted."
[5]"this grants my heart some ease."
[6]Although this usually means "speech," perhaps here it
means "voice."
[7]"That, upon my word, I cannot remain calm." Or, "I don't
care a fig."

30. PAR LE POURCHAS DU REGARD DE MES YEULX

Par le pourchas du regard de mes yeulx,
En vous servant, ma tresbelle maistresse,
J'ay essayé qu'est plaisir et tristesse,
Dont j'ay trouvé maint penser ennuieux.
Mais de cellui que j'amoye le mieulx,   5
N'ay peu avoir qu'a petite largesse,
    Par le pourchas . . .
      En vous . . .
Car pour un jour qui m'a esté joyeux,
J'ay eu trois moys la fievre de destresse;   10
Mais bon espoir m'a guery de liesse
Qui m'a promis de ses biens gracieux
    Par le pourchas . . .

XXX. AS BY THE PURCHAS OF MYN EYEN TAYNE

As by the *purchas*[1] of myn eyen *tayne*[2]
In servyng yow, myn hertis fayre mastres,
I *seid*[3] have what is ioy and hevynes,
In which y founde have moche of thought and payne.
But ioyes[4] whiche y *faynyst*[5] wolde attayne,   5
I kan not gete *but passyng smalle larges*,[6]
    As bi the . . .
    In servyng . . .
For why as for oon ioyfulle day certayne,
I leve an hundrid wekys in distres;   10
But what good hope doth me moche gladnes:
To have a grace as onys, to be more fayne.[7]
    As bi the . . .
    In servyng . . .

30

Through the hard work[8] of my eyes' glance
In serving you, my beautiful lady,
I've tasted[9] both delight and sorrow
Which have given me many a troubled thought.[10]
But of that one I love the most   5
I could get only the smallest sampling[11]
    Through the hard work of my eyes' glance
    In serving you, my beautiful lady.
But for one day that finds me happy
I've had three months the fever of distress;   10
But good hope has healed me with happiness
And has promised me some of his gracious favors.
    Through the hard work of my eyes' glance.

[8]Action of pursuing, seeking, making an effort to obtain
something.
    [9]Lit.: "tried."
    [10]Lit.: "depressing frame of mind." Champollion-Figeac
reads "envious frame of mind."
    [11]Or: "small abundance;" play on usual form, *a grant
largesse.* Cf. 10.3.

XXX. (Notes)

[1]"endeavour."
[2]"two."
[3]"tried."
[4]EETS interpolates *of* between *But* and *ioyes.*
[5]"gladly."
[6]"but in very small doses."
[7]"To soon have a favor, to be more joyful."

31. POUR VOUS MOUSTRER QUE POINT NE VOUS OUBLIE

Pour vous moustrer que point ne vous oublie,
Comme vostre que suis ou que je soye,
Presentement ma chançon vous envoye,
Or la prenés en gré, je vous en prie.
En passant temps, plain de merencolie,   5
L'autr'ier la fis ainsi que je pensoye,
     Pour vous . . .
     Comme . . .
Mon cueur tousjours si vous tient compaignie;
Dieu doint que brief vous puisse veoir a joie,   10
Et, a briefz motz, en ce que je pourroye,
A vous m'offre du tout a chiere lye
     Pour vous . . .

XXXI. TO SHEWE THAT Y HAVE NOT FORGOTEN YOW

To shewe that y have not forgoten yow,
But redy am to serve yow, lady dere,
This poore song y sende it to yow here,
So takith hit *in gre*,[1] y pray yow now.
Forwhi *to dryve forth tyme*[2] (this wot ye how)   5
I made it when y wisshid yow to me nere.
     To shewe . . .
     But redy . . .
Myn hert hath yow, *albe*[3] that y *ne mowe*;[4]
But God me graunt as *onys*[5] to my plesere,   10
What that y mene, y nede not say yow here,
To yelde me yow, y kan not make it *tow*.[6]
     To shewe . . .
     But redy . . .

31

To show you[7] that I've not forgotten you at all,
As the yours that I am or may be,
I send you here my song;
Accept it now, please, willingly, I beg you.
To pass some time, full of loneliness[8]   5
I made it the other day, while I was brooding,
    To show you that I've not forgotten you at all,
    As the yours that I am or may be.
My heart thus always keeps you company;
God grant that soon I can see you joyfully,   10
And, in a few words, in as much as I am able,
I'll offer myself to you with a completely happy face.[9]
    To show you that I've not forgotten you at all.

[7]"demonstrate," "make plain."
[8]Cf. Poirion, *Lexique*, q.v.
[9]I.e., without putting up a front.

XXXI. (Notes)

[1]"without complaint," "willingly."
[2]Lit.: "to chase time away." Perhaps best rendered as
"to pass time."
[3]"even though."
[4]"may not."
[5]"once for all."
[6]"tough." The point is that he will all too willingly
yield himself to her.

32. LOINGTAIN DE JOYEUSE SENTE

Loingtain de joyeuse sente,
Ou l'en peut tous biens avoir,
Sans nul confort recevoir,
Mon cueur en tristesse s'ente.
Par quoy couvient que je sente   5
Mains griefz maulx, pour dire voir,
    Loingtain . . .
    Ou l'en peut . . .
En deuil a fait sa descente
De tous poins, sans s'en mouvoir;   10
Et s'il fault qu'a mon savoir,
Maugré mien, je m'y consente.
    Loingtain . . .

Rejected reading of O: 4. sente

XXXII. FORSEEK IN WOO AND FER FROM IOYOUS HELE

Forseek in woo and fer from ioyous *hele*[1]
Wherin all<u>e</u> welthe doth most (to me) habounde,
Myn hert, allas, y fele in sorow wounde,
Without rekever of comfort, lo, or wele.[2]
Thorugh which that y most fele this, wot y wele,   5
Of *paynys grete me caytijf to confounde.*[3]
    Forseek in . . .
    Wherin . . .
Thus am y falle in woo, and karis fele
Of all<u>e</u> the greef that goth here on the ground,   10
But syn ther can noon hele to me be found,
As, maugre me, y gre must eche a dele.[4]
    Forseek in . . .
    Wherin . . .

32

Far from the joyous path
(Where one can find all favors)
Without receiving any solace,
My heart is rooted in sorrow.
Why is it necessary that I feel   5
So many sorry ills, to be honest,[6]
    Far from the joyous path
    Where one can find all favors?
In mourning it has made its descent[7]
From every level, without even moving;[8]   10
And so it must be that this realization,
Whether I like it or not, I must face it,[9]
    Far from the joyous path.

[5]Chalvet and Champollion-Figeac read *sente*: "My heart
feels sorrow."

[6]Lit.: "to tell the truth."

[7]The heart has fallen to such depths.

[8]Refers to heart as plant whose roots descend without
the plant itself moving. (?)

[9]Difficult to render into English. The sense of the line
is: "and so, in spite of myself, I must consent to what I
know."

XXXII. (Notes)

[1]Taylor paraphrases: "For sick with sorrow and far from
joyous health;" EETS glosses the first word as "very sick."

[2]"Without the recovery of comfort, indeed, or well-being."

[3]"great pains to destroy me as a wretch."

[4]"Thus am I fallen into woe, and feel cares of all the
grief that resides here on earth. But since no one who can
heal me is to be found, in spite of myself, I must give in
entirely."

33. DEDENS MON SEIN PRES DE MON CUEUR

Dedens mon sein, pres de mon cueur,
J'ay mussié un privé baisier
Que j'ay emblé, maugré dangier,
Dont il meurt en peine et langueur.
Mais ne me chault de sa douleur,   5
Et en deust il vif enragier
    Dedens . . .
    J'ay . . .
Se ma dame, par sa doulceur,
Le veult souffrir, sans m'empeschier,   10
Je pense d'en plus pourchassier,
Et en feray tresor greigneur,
    Dedens . . .

XXXIII. RIGHT NY MYN HERT WITH MY BOSOM LO

Right ny myn hert, with my bosom, lo,
I have yputt a *cosse*[1] of gret plesere,
Which y have stolne, maugre false daungere,
So that he dieth welnygh for verry woo.
But wherfore shulde y care as for my foo,   5
Though that for payne he *maddid alle a yere*?[2]
    Right ny . . .
    I have y . . .
But and of grace hit lust my lady so,[3]
To suffre me, *withouten displesere,*[4]   10
To stele a nothir wold y go right nere;
To riche me with, to, y koude gedir moo.[5]
    Right ny . . .
    I have y . . .

33

Within my breast, near to my heart,
I've hidden a secret kiss
That I stole in spite of Suspicion,
And so he is mortified with pain and sickness.
But I don't care about his suffering,   5
Even if it causes him to go mad,[6]
    Within my breast, near to my heart,
    I've hidden a secret kiss.
If my lady, through her sweetness,
Will put up with it, without impeding me,   10
I think I'll pursue[7] it even further
And will make a greater treasure of it.
    Within my breast, near to my heart.

[6]Very difficult to translate. Perhaps a more literal
rendering would be: "And that he should be enmaddened from it."
   [7]A *pourchassier* is one who seeks; the verb thus means
"to seek out," "try."

XXXIII. (Notes)

[1]"kiss."
[2]"went mad for an entire year."
[3]"But if, by grace, my lady so desires."
[4]I.e., for him.
[5]"To make me rich, also, I would gather more."

34. DE VOSTRE BEAUTE REGARDER

De vostre beauté regarder,
Ma tresbelle, gente maistresse,
Ce m'est certes tant de lyesse
Que ne le sauriés penser.
Je ne m'en pourroye lasser,   5
Car j'oublie toute tristesse
    De vostre . . .
    Ma tresbelle . . .
Mais, pour mesdisans destourber,
De parler sus vostre jeunesse,   10
Il fault que souvent m'en delaisse,
Combien que ne m'en puis garder
    De vostre . . .

XXXIV. FORTO BIHOLDE THE BEWTE AND MANERE

Forto biholde the bewte and manere
Of yow, *myn hertis lady and maystres*,[1]
Hit is to me more verry gret gladnes
Then y kan thynke as now to say yow here.
God wolde *hit were me*[2] a thousand yere   5
Forwhi therwith y lesse all_e_ hevynes.
    Forto ben . . .
    Of yow . . .
But for ille speche, allas, my lady dere,
Unnethis[3] dar y speke of yowre goodnes,   10
But oft forbere hit, to my gret distres,
But alway, lo, to hard to me it were.[4]
    Forto ben . . .
    Of yow . . .

34

Looking at your beauty,
My pretty, appealing mistress,
Gives me indeed such joy
That you can't even imagine it.
I couldn't tire of it,   5
For I forget all sorrow
    Looking at your beauty,
    My pretty, appealing mistress.
But to confuse[5] the evil-sayers,
From speaking about your youthfulness   10
I must often refrain[6]
Even though I can't keep myself from
    Looking at your beauty.

[5]"vex," "perturb."
[6]"abandon," "leave off."

          XXXIV. (Notes)

[1]"lady and mistress of my heart."
[2]EETS paraphrases: "were with me."
[3]"scarcely."
[4]"But always, indeed, it was too hard for me."

35. PRENEZ TOST CE BAISIER MON CUEUR

Prenez tost ce baisier, mon cueur,
Que ma maistresse vous presente,
La belle, bonne, jeune, et gente,
Par sa tresgrant grace et doulceur.
Bon guet feray, sus mon honneur,   5
Afin que dangier riens n'en sente,
  Prenez . . .
  Que ma . . .
Dangier, toute nuit en labeur,
A fait guet; or gist en sa tente.   10
Accomplissez brief votre entente
Tantdis qu'il dort; c'est le meillieur,
  Prenez . . .

XXXV. TAKE TAKE THIS COSSE ATONYS ATONYS MY HERT

Take, take this cosse atonys, atonys, my hert,
That thee presentid is *of*[1] thi maystres
(The goodly fayre, so fulle of lustynes,
Only of grace) to lessen with thi smert.[2]
But to myn honoure loke thou welle, avert   5
That daunger not parseyve my sotilnes,[3]
  Take, take this . . .
  That the . . .
Daunger wacchith al nyght in his *shert*[4]
To spye me in a *gery currisshenes;*[5]   10
So to have doon attones let se thee *dresse,*[6]
While in a slepe his eyen ben covert.
  Take, take this . . .
  That thee . . .

Quickly take this kiss, my heart,
That my mistress presents to you,
The pretty, good, young, and attractive one,
By her great pardon and sweetness.
I'll make a good watchman, on my honor,   5
So that Suspicion doesn't suspect[7] any of this,
  Quickly take this kiss, my heart,
  That my mistress presents to you.
Suspicion, all night at work,
Stood the watch; now he lies in his tent.   10
Carry out your duty quickly
While he sleeps: that's best,[8]
  Quickly take this kiss.

[7]Lit.: "feel."
[8]D'Hericault omits this line.

XXXV. (Notes)

[1]"by."
[2]Paraphrased, the first four lines read: "Take this kiss at once, my heart, that is presented to you by my mistress-- that lovely lady, so full of life, made only of grace--with which to lessen your pain."
[3]"But for my honor, look out well, take heed that Suspicion does not perceive my subtle ways."
[4]"nightshirt." (?) Perhaps this links Suspicion with Death in the earlier chansons.
[5]"capricious ill-breeding."
[6]"right now," "at once."

36. COMMENT VOUS PUIS JE TANT AMER

Comment vous puis je tant amer,
Et mon cueur si tresfort haïr
Qu'il ne me chault de desplaisir,
Qu'il puisse pour vous endurer.
Son mal m'est joyeux a porter,   5
Mais qu'il vous puisse bien servir.
     Comment . . .
     Et mon cueur . . .
Las, or ne deusse je penser
Qu'a le garder et chier tenir,   10
Et non pour tant, mon seul desir,
Pour vous le vueil abandonner.
     Comment . . .

Rejected reading of O: 5. aporter

XXXVI. WHI LOVE Y YOW SO MOCHE HOW MAY THIS BE

Whi love y yow so moche, how may this be,
And hate so moche myn hert, this wold y lere,
Which *recchith*[1] not to doon me displesere,
Nor, of my dewryng, long adversite.[2]
His harme me grevid hit small̲e, parde,[3]   5
If that my service were to yowre plesere.
     Whi love y . . .
     And hate . . .
But what, allas, allas, wel may y se
That ye cherisshe to moche with you daungere;   10
But nevertheles, myn hertis soul desere,
To serve yow to my last, *y shall̲e ben he.*[4]
     Whi love y . . .
     And hate . . .

36

How can I love you so much
And hate my heart so strongly
That I don't care about the displeasure
That he must endure for you?
His ill is a joy for me to bear,   5
But only as long as he can serve you well;
    How can I love you so much
    And hate my heart so strongly?
Alas! now I must think only
Of watching out for him and holding him dear,   10
Even though, my sole desire,
I wish to abandon him for you.
    How can I love you so much?

XXXVI. (Notes)

[1]"cares."
[2]"Nor, in my experience, long adversity."
[3]"His discomfort wouldn't cause me much pain."
[3]"I'll be the one."

37. JE NE PRISE POINT TELZ BAISIERS

Je ne prise point telz baisiers
Qui sont donnez par contenance,
Ou par maniere d'acointance:
Trop de gens en sont parçonniers.
On en peut avoir par milliers,   5
A bon marchié, grant habondance:
     Je ne . . .
     Qui sont . . .
Mais savez vous lesquelz sont chiers?
Les privez, venans par plaisance;   10
Tous autres ne sont, sans doubtance,
Que pour festier estrangiers:
     Je ne prise . . .

XXXVII. I PRAYSE NO THING THESE COSSIS DOWCHE

I prayse no thing these cossis *dowche*[1]
Which geve are for a *countenaunce*[2]
And forto take with aqueyntaunce,
Though many folkis love to towche.
A man may bie out *crosse or crowche*,[3]   5
Ynowe of them, gret habundaunce.
     I prayse no . . .
     Which geve . . .
But wot ye which y cherisshe moche?
The prive cossis of plesaunce;   10
Alle othir whiche that come *askaunce*[4]
Ben goode to feste with straungeris soche.[5]
     I prayse no . . .
     Which geve . . .

Rejected reading of C: 6. ynowe

37

I don't value[6] such kisses
That are given just to save face,
Or for reasons of acquaintance:
Too many men partake of those.[7]
One can have them by the thousands,   5
At a good price, in great numbers,
    I don't value such kisses
    That are given just to save face.
But you know the ones that are valuable?
The secret ones, offered[8] for pleasure;   10
All others are, without a doubt,
Only for entertaining strangers.
    I don't value such kisses.

[6]Loan word from English: "prize," "praise."
[7]Lit.: "are participants."
[8]"coming," "being offered."

XXXVII. (Notes)

[1]Loan word from French *douce*: "sweet."
[2]"encouragement," "favor."
[3]Two kinds of coins.
[4]Refers perhaps to the direction of the eyes. EETS suggests it refers to a kiss on the cheek rather than on the lips.
[5]"Are good to entertain such strangers with."

38. MA SEULE AMOUR MA JOYE ET MA MAISTRESSE

Ma seule amour, ma joye, et ma maistresse,
Puisqu'il me fault loing de vous demorer,
Je n'ay plus riens, a me reconforter,
Qu'un souvenir pour retenir lyesse.
En allegant, par espoir, ma destresse,   5
Me couvendra le temps ainsi passer,
     Ma seule . . .
     Puisqu'il . . .
Car mon las cueur, bien garny de tristesse,
S'en est voulu avecques vous aler,   10
Ne je ne puis jamais le recouvrer,
Jusques verray vostre belle jeunesse,
     Ma seule . . .

Rejected readings of O: 2. Puis quil   3. ame   4. Qun

XXXVIII. MY LOVE ONLY MY IOY AND MY MAYSTRES

My love only, my ioy, and my maystres,
Syn y may not ben longe with yow present,[1]
With discomfort y must ben resident,
Save oon poore hope which doth to me gladnes,
That moche *alightith*[2] me myn hevynes   5
In abidyng the werre that is me sent,
     My love only . . .
     Syn y may . . .
That my faynt hert, forchargid with distres,
Went forth with yow anoon right as ye went,   10
And trust of metyng nar but tyme yspent[3]
To eft[4] y see yowre yowthe and goodlynes,
     My love only . . .
     Syn y may . . .

38

My only love, my joy and my mistress,
Since I must remain far from you,
I have nothing more for comfort
Than a memory to keep me happy.[5]
Relieving,[6] through hope, my distress,   5
I am thus forced to pass the time,
    My only love, my joy and my mistress,
    Since I must remain far from you.
For my sorry heart, well-furnished with sadness,
Thus decided to go with you,   10
Nor can I ever recover him
Until I see your pretty youthfulness,
    My only love, my joy and my mistress.

[5]Lit.: "To hold onto happiness."
[6]"alleviating," "lessening."

XXXVIII. (Notes)

[1]"Since I cannot be with you for long at this time."
[2]"alleviates."
[3]EETS glosses: "hope as prospect of future meeting if time of waiting were only past."
[4]"until."

39. SE DESPLAIRE NE VOUS DOUBTOYE

Se desplaire ne vous doubtoye,
Voulentiers je vous embleroye
Un doulx baisier, priveement,
Et garderoye, seurement,
Dedens le tresor de ma joye.   5
Mais que dangier soit hors de voye,
Et que, sans presse, je vous voye,
Belle, que j'ayme loyaument,
      Se desplaire . . .
      Voulentiers . . .   10
      Un doulx . . .
Jamais ne m'en confesseroye,
Ne pour larrecin le tendroye,
Mais grant aumosne vrayement;
Car a mon cueur joyeusement   15
De par vous le presenteroye,
      Se desplaire . . .

XXXIX. NAR THAT Y DREDE DISPLESEN YOW ONLY

Nar[1] that y drede displesen yow only,
I passyng fayne wold stele here verily
A pryvy cosse of yow, myn hertis swete,
Which y shalle kepe fulle clos to eft we mete,
In tresoure of my ioy right privyly.   5
So hit were there as daunger shuld not spy
Withouten *prese*[2] of mo, save yow and y;
O fayre, which y most love, y yow *bihete*.[3]
      Nar that y . . .
      I passyng . . .   10
      A prive cosse . . .
Confesse me nolde y therof to y dey,[4]
Forwhi y take it for no felony;
But *almes*[5] gret of yow, if so ye lete,
Me forto doon, and *alls this mow ye wete*,[6]   15
The poore to fede ye do a gret mercy.[7]
      Nar that y . . .
      I passyng . . .
      A prive cosse . . .

39

If I didn't fear displeasing you,
Gladly from you would I steal
A sweet kiss, secretly,
And guard it securely
In the treasure house of my joy.   5
If only Suspicion were out of my way,
And I could see you without a crowd,
Pretty one whom I love faithfully,
 If I didn't fear displeasing you,
 Gladly from you would I steal   10
 A sweet kiss, secretly.
I would never confess it
Nor view it as a robbery,
But rather as truly a great boon;[8]
For to my heart, joyfully,   15
I would present it from you,
 If I didn't fear displeasing you.

[8]"alm," "gift of charity."

XXXIX.   (Notes)

[1]"If it weren't."
[2]From French *presse*: "crowd."
[3]"promise."
[4]"I would not confess it before I died." Taylor omits *y*
between *nolde* and *thereof*, which makes no significant change
in meaning.
[5]"boon," "gift."
[6]"and otherwise you must wait this out."
[7]English extends the metaphor further than the corresponding French.

Malade de mal ennuieux,
Faisant la peneuse sepmaine,
Vous envoye, ma souveraine,
Un souspir merencolieux.
Par lui saurez, mon bien joyeux,   5
Comment desplaisir me demaine,
     Malade . . .
     Faisant . . .
Car aler ne peuent mes yeulx
Vers la beauté dont estes plaine,   10
Mais au fort, ma joye mondaine,
J'endureray pour avoir mieulx,
     Malade . . .

XL. THE GRET DISESE OF SEEKFULLE ANNOYAUNCE

The gret disese of *seekfulle*[1] anoyaunce
Which causith oft the *penaunt*[2] sore to playne,
Here sendith yow, my lady and soverayne,
A *seeklew*[3] seek of my long grevaunce.
Bi which ye may welle knowe the governaunce   5
Of displesere that rewlith me certayne,
     The gret disese . . .
     Which causith . . .
For syn yowre bewte of so gret plesaunce
May not ben with my derkid eyen *sayne*,[4]   10
I *lese*[5] therwith alle worldly plesere playne;
This doth me seeke, this is myn aturbance.[6]
     The gret disese . . .
     Which causith . . .

Sick with sickly fretfulness,[7]
During the Lenten season,[8]
I send you, my queen,
A lonely[9] sigh.
By it you will know, my joyous treasure,   5
How displeasure rules my life,
    Sick with sickly fretfulness,
    During the Lenten season.
For my eyes cannot go
Toward the beauty of which you've plenty.   10
But, in the end, my earthly joy,
I will stick it out to have better.
    Sick with sickly fretfulness.

[7]Or: "depression."
[8]Means both "painful" and "penitent", so the *peneuse sepmaine* would be a week of painful penitence such as during Lent.
[9]Following Poirion, *Lexique*, q.v.

XL. (Notes)

[1]As EETS points out, this is a translation of the French *mal*: "sick."
[2]"penitent."
[3]"sickly."
[4]"seen."
[5]"leave," "lose."
[6]"This makes me sigh, this is my cause of distraction."

41. S'IL VOUS PLAIST VENDRE VOZ BAISIERS

S'il vous plaist vendre voz baisiers,
J'en achatteray voulentiers,
(Et en aurés mon cueur en gage)
Pour les prandre par heritage,
Par douzaines, cens, ou milliers.   5
Ne les me vendez pas si chiers
Que vous feriés a estrangiers
En me recevant en hommage.
  S'il vous . . .
  J'en achat . . .   10
  Et en . . .
Mon vueil et mon desir entiers
Sont vostres, maugré tous dangiers;
Faittes, comme loyalle et sage,
Que pour mon guerdon et partage,   15
Je soye servy des premiers.
  S'il vous . . .

XLI. IF HIT PLESE YOW YOWRE COSSIS FORTO SELLE

If hit plese yow yowre cossis forto selle,
I redy am here forto bie hem welle,
Which geve yow shalle myn hert as in morgage,
Hit to dispende as yowre owen heritage,[1]
Mi love, and of plesaunce a thousand elle.   5
Beth not as hard with [me] to entirmelle[2]
As with a straunger which that bi yow dwelle,
That holde no *lyve*,[3] but of yow, in homage.
  If hit plese . . .
  I redy am . . .   10
  Which geve . . .
This bargeyne make, and fy on alle perelle,
Though daunger with for sorow him forswelle,[4]
And *worche*[5] wisly, though ye be yong of age,
That y may have a plesaunt hool *partage*,[6]   15
Thus serve me sone, or say me that ye *nelle*.[7]
  If hit plese . . .
  I redy am . . .
  Which geve . . .

Rejected reading of C: 15. portage

If you wish to sell your kisses,
I will gladly buy some,
And in return[8] you will have my heart as deposit.[9]
To use them as inheritance,
By the dozens, hundreds, or thousands.   5
Don't sell them to me at as high a price
As you would to a total stranger
For you are receiving me as your liegeman.
 If you wish to sell your kisses,
 I will gladly buy some.   10
 And in return you will have my heart as deposit.
My complete wish and desire[10]
Are yours in spite of all suspicion;
Allow, as a faithful and wise woman,
That for my reward and share   15
I may be among the first served,
 If you wish to sell your kisses.

[8]Lit.: "for them."
[9]Poirion glosses as "deposit left as guarantee."
[10]Chalvet reads "My wish and complete desire."

XLI. (Notes)

[1]Here English gives the heart, no strings attached, while French gives as pledge for payment. *Heritage* refers to a possession, especially an estate.
 [2]"Don't strike as hard a bargain with me"; *me* supplied *metri causa*.
 [3]"belief."
 [4]"Though Suspicion may swell up with disappointment."
 [5]"do."
 [6]"whole share." Emended following EETS suggestion.
 [7]"will not."

42. MA SEULE AMOUR QUE TANT DESIRE

Ma seule amour que tant desire,
Mon reconfort, mon doulx penser,
Belle, nompareille, sans per,
Il me desplaist de vous escrire.
Car j'aymasse mieulx a le dire   5
De bouche, sans le vous mander,
    Ma seule . . .
    Mon re . . .
Las, or n'y puis je contredire,
Mais espoir me fait endurer,   10
Qui m'a promis de retourner
En liesse mon grief martire,
    Ma seule . . .

XLII. MY LOVE AND LADY WHOM Y MOST DESERE

My love and lady whom y most desere,
Mi recomfort, my hertis eleccioun,
Most goodly fayre, without comparisoun,
I sory am thus forto write yow here.
Forwhi to say hit were me more plesere   5
Bi mouth then make this *ocupacioun*,[1]
    My love and . . .
    My recomfort . . .
Alas, alas, that y *nare*[2] to yow nere,
But what with hope endewre y the *sesoun*[3]   10
Which[4] *holt*[5] me, lo, in this opynyoun:
That to gladnes retorne wolle my *martere*,[6]
    My lvoe and . . .
    My recomfort . . .

My sole love whom I desire so,
My solace, my sweet intent,
Pretty one, unrivaled, peerless,
It displeases me to write to you.
For I would rather say it   5
In person,[7] without sending[8] it to you,
    My sole love whom I desire so,
    My solace, my sweet intent.
Alas! I can't do anything about it now[9]
But hope enables me to endure,   10
As he has promised to turn, once again,
To happiness my grievous martyrdom.[10]
    My sole love whom I desire so.

[7]Lit.: "by mouth"; hence, privately.
[8]Or: making it public as one does when one writes.
[9]He can't "contradict" his situation meaning he can't change his status.
[10]Or: "[Hope] has promised that my martyrdom will end and I will return to happiness."

XLII. (Notes)

[1]"effort."
[2]"am not."
[3]"season," "dry period," (i.e., of absence).
[4]EETS notes that this refers to *hope* in line 10.
[5]"held."
[6]"pain," "martyrdom."

43. LOGIES MOY ENTRE VOZ BRAS

Logiés moy entre voz bras
Et m'envoiez doulx baisier
Qui me viengne festier
D'aucun amoureux soulas.
Tantdis que dangier est las   5
Et le voyez sommeillier,
      Logiés . . .
      Et m'en . . .
Pour Dieu, ne l'esveilliez pas,
Ce faulx, envieux dangier;   10
Jamais ne puist s'esveillier!
Faittes tost et parlez bas:
      Logiés . . .

Rejected reading of O: 10. enuieux

XLIII. LOGGE ME DERE HERT IN YOWRE ARMYS TAYNE

Logge me, dere hert, in yowre armys *tayne*[1]
And geve me so a swete cosse, two or thre,
If it plese yow, so moche to *festen*[2] me
With lovis wele,[3] my ladi and soverayne.
But tary that to daunger, lo, be layne   5
To slepe, and that in slumbir ye him se,
      Logge me . . .
      And geve . . .
But wake him not, bewar yow that agayne,
Lete him slepe, *and that with yville the,*[4]   10
Hit hard him is of slepe awakid be,
But spekith soft and do hit playne:[5]
      Logge me . . .
      And geve . . .

Rejected readings of C: 10. lete   11. hit

86

43

Take me in your arms,[6]
And send me a sweet kiss
That will make me festive,
The source of happiness for any lover.
While Suspicion is tired out   5
And you see him sleeping [away],
    Take me in your arms,
    And send me a sweet kiss.
By God, don't wake him,
This false, envious Suspicion;   10
May he never be woken!
Act quickly and speak softly:
    Take me in your arms.

[6]Lit.: "Lodge me between your arms" in the sense of "make your arms my lodging."

XLIII. (Notes)

[1]"two."
[2]"entertain."
[3]"With the well-being love [supplies]."
[4]"and flourish with evil [so]."
[5]"It's hard to wake him from sleep, but do speak softly and be direct."

44. SE DANGIER ME TOLT LE PARLER

Se dangier me tolt le parler
A vous, mon bel amy sans per,
Par le pourchas des envieux,
Non plus qu'on toucheroit aux cieulx,
Ne me tendray de vous amer.   5
Car mon cueur m'a voulu laissier
Pour soy du tout a vous donner,
Et pour estre vostre en tous lieux,
      Se dangier . . .
      A vous . . .   10
      Par le . . .
Tout son povoir ne peut garder
Que, sur tous autres, n'aye chier
Vostre gent corps, tresgracieux,
Et se ne vous voy de mes yeulx,   15
Pour tant ne vous vueil je changier,
      Se dangier . . .

XLIV.   THOUGH DAUNGER HAVE THE SPECHE BIRAFT ME HERE

Though daunger have the speche biraft me here
Of yow, most fayre withouten any pere,
Thorugh the *purchas*[1] of cursid false envy,
Yet for no thing thei kan do, verily,
They shalle not lette me love yow fer and nere.   5
For as myn hert a hath forleft me clere[2]
To geve him silf to yow, my lady dere,
Al where[3] to serve yow to that *howre he dey,*[4]
      Though daungere . . .
      Of yow most . . .   10
      Thorugh the . . .
To lette him, lo, y kan in no manere[5]
But that in he *tath*[6] his most plesere
To thenke what vertu is in yowre body;
For though so be y se yow not with ey,   15
I love yow most for payne or displesere,
      Though daunger . . .
      Of yow most . . .
      Thorugh the . . .

44

Even if Suspicion keeps me from speaking
To you, my handsome, peerless friend,[7]
Because of the efforts of the jealous ones;
They will sooner touch the stars
Than I will stop loving you.[8]   5
For my heart has decided[9] to leave me
To give itself on its own entirely to you
And to be yours in every way.[10]
    Even if Suspicion keeps me from speaking
    To you, my handsome, peerless friend,   10
    Because of the pursuits of the jealous ones.
All its power cannot deny[11]
That, over all others, I hold dear
Your attractive, lovely body,[12]
And even if I don't see you with my eyes,   15
Nevertheless I don't want to exchange you,[13]
    Even if Suspicion keeps me from speaking.

[7]EETS notes that this chanson is addressed to a man ("mon bel amy") and suggests it is an answer to 42. In a similar vein, Guichard suggests that 44 was actually written by Charles's mistress, again as an answer to 42.

[8]Lit.: "They will no more touch ... than...." What I read as an *adynaton* Chalvet reads as "Even if they were to ... I would not be kept from."

[9]In the sense of "willed."

[10]The meaning is as much temporal as it is spatial.

[11]Or: "keep away the fact that."

[12]See Glossary.

[13]*Change* as a noun, according to Poirion, means commercial exchange, so *changier* can mean to exchange.

XLIV. (Notes)

[1]"endeavor."

[2]"For as my heart has entirely forsaken me."

[3]"everywhere."

[4]"until the hour he dies."

[5]"I can't prevent him in any way." *Lette*: "hinder," "prevent."

[6]"takes."

45. VA TOST MON AMOUREUX DESIR

Va tost, mon amoureux desir,
Sur quanque me veulx obeir,
Tout droit vers le manoir de joye.
Et pour plus abregier ta voye,
Prens ta guide, doulx souvenir.   5
Metz peine de me bien servir,
Et de ton message acomplir:
Tu congnois ce que je vouldroye,
     Va tost . . .
     Sur . . .   10
     Tout . . .
Recommandes moy a plaisir,
Et se brief ne peuz revenir,
Fay que de toy nouvelles oye
Et par bon espoir les m'envoye;   15
Ne vueilles au besoing faillir,
     Va tost . . .

XLV. GO FORTH THI WAY MY FEITHFULLE DESERVAUNCE

Go forth thi way, *my feithfulle deservaunce*,[1]
On[2] that thow *owist*[3] me thyn *obeysaunce*,[4]
Streight unto the ioyous fresshe *manere*.[5]
To shorte thi way, also, and thee to *lere*,[6]
Take to thi gide swete remembraunce.   5
To serve me welle, y trust thi governaunce,
And spede thou first thi message in substaunce,
As that knowist the *welle*[7] of my desere.
     Go forth . . .
     On that . . .   10
     Streight . . .
And recomaunde me to plesaunce
And sone to come, if thou want puysshaunce,[8]
Do so that y may tidyng of thee here,
And sende *hem*[9] me bi hope, my messangere,   15
And fayle me not for laboure nor penaunce.
     Go forth . . .
     On that . . .
     Streight . . .

45

Go swiftly, my amorous desire,
Towards whatever[10] I should obey,
Straight to the manor of joy.
And to shorten your route
Take your guide Sweet Memory.   5
Take pains to serve me well,
And carry out[11] your mission:[12]
You know what I want,
      Go swiftly, my amorous desire,
      Towards whatever I should obey,   10
      Straight to the manor of joy.
Recommend me to Delight;
And if you cannot come back soon,
Make sure I hear news of you
And send it through Good Hope: 15
Please fail me not in need,
      Go swiftly, my amorous desire.

[10]Or: "Toward all that." *Sur* is a preposition denoting
direction.
[11]Or: "accomplish."
[12]Lit.: "message."

XLV.   (Notes)

[1]"my faithful merit."
[2]"toward."
[3]"owed."
[4]"obedience."
[5]"manor house."
[6]"aid."
[7]"well-being," "source of health."
[8]"And come back soon if you need extra forces."
[9]I.e., tidings.

46. JE ME METZ EN VOSTRE MERCY

Je me metz en vostre mercy,
Tresbelle, bonne, jeune, et gente;
On m'a dit qu'estes mal contente
De moy, ne sçay s'il est ainsi.
De toute nuit je n'ay dormy, 5
Ne pensez pas que je vous mente,
    Je me . . .
    Tresbelle . . .
Pource, treshumblement vous pry,
Que vous me dittes vostre entente, 10
Car d'une chose je me vante:
Qu'en loyauté n'ay point failly.
    Je me metz . . .

XLVI. I PUT MY SILF UNTO YOWRE MERCY LO

I put my silf unto yowre mercy, lo,
Moost goodly fayre, most replete of bounte,
Hit seid me[1] is that ye are wroth with me,
Not wot y whi, nor where hit be or no,
But alle the nyght not slepen y for woo, 5
Save thenke and muse wherfore that hit shuld be.
    Y putt my . . .
    Most goodly . . .
Allas, beth not so moche to me my foo,
But yowre entent wherfore as let me se;[2] 10
For this y vaunt my silf: that y am he
That kepe his trouthe and shalle wherso y go.
    I putt my . . .
    Most goodly . . .

46

I place myself at your mercy,
Very pretty, good, young, and attractive one,
I've heard you're discontent
With me--I don't know if it's so.
All night I didn't sleep--   5
Don't think I'm lying to you--
    I place myself at your mercy,
    Very pretty, good, young, and attractive one.
And so humbly I beseech you
To tell me your thoughts,   10
For I am proud of one thing:[3]
That in faithfulness I've never slipped;
    I place myself at your mercy.

[3]Or: "For I boast of one thing."

                XLVI. (Notes)

[1]"It has come to my attention."
[2]"Alas, don't be so much my enemy; at least let me know
your reasons."

47. TROP ESTES VERS MOY ENDEBTEE

Trop estes vers moy endebtee:
Vous me devés plusieurs baisiers,
Je vouldroye moult voulentiers
Que la debte fust acquittee.
Quoy que vous soyez excusee   5
Que n'osez pour les faulx dangiers,
    Trop . . .
    Vous . . .
J'en ay bonne lettre seellee;
Paiez les, sans tenir si chiers;   10
Autrement, par les officiers
D'amours, vous serez arrestee:
    Trop estes . . .

Rejected reading of O: 3. ouldroye

XLVII. YE ARE TO MOCHE AS IN MY DETTE MADAME

Ye are to moche as in my dette, madame,
Ye owe me, swete, to many cossis dere
Which wold fulle fayne, if hit were yowr plesere,
Ye payde hem me in savyng of yowre name.
So that of dette y ought yow not to blame   5
Which dar not don me thenke hit for daungere,[1]
    Ye are to . . .
    Ye owe me . . .
Wite ye, y have a writ out for the same,[2]
To *tache*[3] yow with, y *rede*[4] yow pay hem here,   10
Lest ye be restid with an officere[5]
Of love; fy, fy, hit were to gret a shame.
    Ye are to . . .
    Ye owe me . . .

Rejected reading of C: 2. tomany   11. lest

47

You're too much in my debt:
You owe me several kisses
And I would like very eagerly
That the debt be paid.
Although you might be excused   5
For not daring because of false Suspicions,
    You're too much in my debt:
    You owe me several kisses.
I have a sealed document[6] about them;
Pay them without holding them so dear.   10
Otherwise, by the officers
Of love, you will be arrested;
    You're too much in my debt.

[6]Or: "a strong legal document." *Seellee* here means "sealed."

XLVII. (Notes)

[1]"I think you don't dare give them to me because of Suspicion."
[2]"Know that I wave a writ out for the same."
[3]"arrest."
[4]"advise."
[5]"Otherwise you'll be arrested by an officer."

48. VOSTRE BOUCHE DIT BAISIEZ MOY

Vostre bouche dit: "Baisiez moy,"
(Se m'est avis quant la regarde)
Mais dangier de trop pres la garde,
Dont mainte doleur je reçoy.
Laissiez m'avoir, par vostre foy,   5
Un doulx baisier, sans que plus tarde.
  Vostre . . .
  Se m'est . . .
Dangier me heit, ne sçay pourquoy,
Et tousjours destourbier me darde;   10
Je prie a Dieu que mal feu l'arde,
Il fust temps qu'il se tenist coy,
  Vostre bouche . . .

Rejected readings of O: 1. baisiez 11. adieu

XLVIII. YOWRE MOUTH HIT SAITH ME BAS ME BAS SWET

Yowre mouth hit saith me: "*bas*[1] me, bas swet,"
When that y yow bihold, this semeth me,
But daunger stant so nygh hit may not be[2]
Which doth me sorow gret, y yow *bihet*,[3]
But bi yowre trouth, gefe me hit now we mete:[4]   5
A pryve swet/swete cosse, two or three,
  Yowre mouth . . .
  When that y . . .
Daunger me hatith, whi y kan not *wet*[5]
And labourith, ay, my gret adversite;   10
God graunt me *onys*[6] *forbrent*[7] y may him se
That y myght stampe his asshis with my feet.
  Yowre mouth . . .
  When that y . . .

48

Your mouth says: "Kiss me"
(Or so I think when I see it).
But Suspicion guards it too closely
And so[8] I receive much pain.
Let me have, by your faith,   5
A sweet kiss, without waiting any longer;
     Your mouth says: "Kiss me"
     (Or so I think when I see it).
Suspicion hates me, I know not why,
And always vexation pricks me;   10
May he rot in hell![9]
It's time he kept silent,
     Your mouth says: "Kiss me."

[8]Or: "Because of which."
[9]Lit.: "I pray God the fire burn him badly."

XLVIII. (Notes)

[1]"kiss."
[2]"But Suspicion stands so close it [the kiss] cannot
happen."
[3]"promise."
[4]"But, by your troth, give it to me now that we have met."
[5]"understand."
[6]"soon."
[7]"burned."

49. JE NE LES PRISE PAS DEUX BLANS

Je ne les prise pas deux blans,
Tous les biens qui sont en amer,
Car il n'y a que tout amer,
Et grant foison de faulx semblans.
Pour les maulx qui y sont doublans,   5
Pires que les perilz de mer,
     Je ne . . .
     Tous . . .
Ilz ne sont a riens ressemblans,
Car un jour viennent entamer   10
Le cueur, et apres embasmer;
Ce sont amourettes tremblans.
     Je ne les . . .

XLIX. NOT OFT Y PRAYSE BUT BLAME AS IN SUBSTAUNCE

Not oft y prayse, but blame as *in substaunce*[1]
Alle the welthe of lovis paynful blis,
For every ioy with woo *enmeyntid*[2] is
Of gret *foysoun*[3] of frawde and false semblaunce.
The *wele and woo*[4] of hit doth rolle and daunce   5
As shippe in see for tempest that *veris.*[5]
     Not oft y . . .
     Al the welth . . .
This is the cause y make such resemblaunce:[6]
For as the shippe *forpossid*[7] is, this and this,   10
Right so of love the hertis *arne,*[8] ywis,
As now in wele, and now in gret penaunce,[9]
     Not oft y . . .
     Al the welth . . .

49

They're not worth two cents,[10]
All the benefits of love,
For there is only bitterness[11]
And a great abundance of deception.
For the ills involved are doubling,[12]   5
Worse than the perils of the sea.
    They're not worth two cents
    All the benefits of love.
There's nothing like them:[13]
One day they appear to entame   10
The heart, after to enshroud [it];[14]
They are fragile little flowers,[15]
    They're not worth two cents.

[10]A *blan* is worth five deniers, one *denier* is worth 1/12 of a *sou* and one *sou* is worth 1/20 of a *franc*: in short, two *blans* are worth practically nothing.

[11]On the *double entendre* of the key rhyming words, see Textual Notes.

[12]Meant in contrast to the *blans* of the first line: the benefits aren't worth a thing because there are so few of them, but the troubles, of which there are many, would be worth a lot.

[13]"They" are the *amourettes tremblans* of the last full line.

[14]The idea here is that the heart which is seemingly only calmed and caressed by love is in fact soon tamed to the point of death.

[15]Assumed by all editors, translators, and critics to refer to the flightiness of love, Michel Thom has recently shown that this phrase was a popular name for the *briza media*, a delicate flower. See Textual Notes.

XLIX. (Notes)

[1]"substantially."

[2]EETS glosses as error for *enmeynt it*: "mingled." Could be false construction created by analogy with *derkid*, e.g.

[3]"abundance."

[4]"good and bad."

[5]"changes course."

[6]"This is the reason I'm drawing this comparison."

[7]"pushed about."

[8]"burns."

[9]"Now well-off and now abject."

50. AU BESOING CONGNOIST ON L'AMY

Au besoing congnoist on l'amy
Qui loyaument aidier desire;
Pour vous je puis bien cecy dire,
Car vous ne m'avez pas failly.
Mais avez, la vostre mercy,   5
Tant fait qu'il me doit souffire.
  Au besoing . . .
  Qui . . .
Bien brief pense partir decy
Pour m'en aler vers vous de tire;   10
Loisir n'ay pas de vous escrire,
Et pour ce, plus avant ne dy.
  Au besoing . . .

Rejected reading of O: 12. pource

L. AT NEDE THE FRENDIS PREVEN WHAT THEI BE

At nede[1] the frendis preven what thei be,
In eche a werk *as stondith matere,*[2]
This say y, lo, by yow, my lady dere,
For at my nede ye have not faylid me.
But holpe me, loo, and that so moche, parde,   5
That hit contentith alle myn own desere,
  At nede . . .
  In eche a . . .
But, welaway, departen now must we,
But though it greve yow, *bere a gladsom chere,*[3]   10
For leyser more y want to write yow here,[4]
Save Ihesu graunt agayne us sone to se.[5]
  At nede the . . .
  In eche a . . .

In times of need one knows one's friends--
[Those] who loyally wish to help--
Of you I can safely say that much,
For you haven't forsaken me.[6]
On the contrary, you and your mercy have   5
Done so much that it certainly does suffice for me
    In times of need one knows one's friends--
    Those who loyally wish to help.
Very soon I'm thinking of leaving here
To go to you right away;   10
I don't have the leisure to write
And so won't say any more before I go:
    In times of need one knows one's friends.

[6]Addressed to a man, so same critical argument ensues as for 42. Chalvet claims Charles wrote this for Philippe le Bon, Guichard suggests this was written by Charles's mistress for Charles.

L. (Notes)

[1]"In times of need."
[2]EETS glosses "as the occasion arises."
[3]"put up a good front."
[4]I.e., the leisure I need to write more now is lacking, except to add the following.
[5]"Except that Jesus allow us to see each other again soon."

51.   FUYES LE TRAIT DE DOULX REGARD

Fuyés le trait de doulx regard,
Cueur, qui ne vous savez deffendre;
Veu qu'estes desarmé et tendre,
Nul ne vous doit tenir couard.
Vous serés pris, ou tost ou tard,   5
S'amour le veult bien entreprandre,
  Fuyés le . . .
  Cueur . . .
Retrayez vous soubz l'estendart
De nonchaloir, sans plus attendre;   10
S'a plaisance vous laissiez rendre,
Vous estes mort, Dieu vous en gard:
  Fuyés . . .

Rejected reading of O: 11. Sa

LI.   FLETH THE SHOTT OF SWETE REGARD

Fleth the shott of swete regard,
Myn hert, *without thou willist forto day*,[1]
Which nakid art of wepene and *aray*,[2]
For *witty*[3] flight is signe of no coward.
Abide, and thou are *tan*,[4] *maugre thi berd*,[5]   5
Without, thou cast thee unto love abay,[6]
  Fleth the . . .
  Myn hert . . .
Wherfore, withdrawith *the*[7] standard,
As of no forse, as sone as that thou may,   10
And plesaunce do thee yelde,[8] this is to say,
Thou are but deed, allas, y am *aferd*.[9]
  Fleth . . .
  Myn hert . . .

Rejected reading of C: 11. a ferd.

51.

Flee from the shaft of Sweet Look,[10]
Heart, you who know not how to defend yourself;
Seeing[11] as you are unarmed and vulnerable,
No one would call you a coward.
You'll be taken, sooner or later,   5
If love wishes to do so,
        Flee from the shaft of Sweet Look,
        Heart, you who know not how to defend yourself.
Withdraw under the standard
Of uncaring without further delay;   10
If you give yourself up to delight
You'll be dead; God protect you from it.
        Flee from the shaft of Sweet Look.

[10]I.e., the eyes.
[11]For *pourvu que*: "provided that," "given that."

LI.   (Notes)

[1]"if not, you will die."
[2]I.e., battle dress.
[3]"wise."
[4]"taken."
[5]I.e., in spite of anything you can do.
[6]"Without [retreating] you throw yourself into love's
dominion."
[7]EETS suggests inserting *under* before *the*.
[8]"If you yield yourself to delight."
[9]"afraid."

52. MON SEUL AMY MON BIEN MA JOYE

Mon seul amy, mon bien, ma joye,
Cellui que sur tous amer veulx,
Je vous pry que soiez joieux
En esperant que brief vous voye.
Car je ne fais que querir voye   5
De venir vers vous, se m'aist Dieux,
      Mon seul . . .
      Cellui . . .
Et se par souhaidier povoye
Estre empres vous un jour ou deux,   10
Pour quanqu'il a dessoubz les cieulx,
Autre rien ne souhaideroye,
      Mon seul . . .

LII. MY WELE MY IOY MY LOVE AND MY LADY

My wele, my ioy, my love, and my lady,[1]
Which y most love, and shalle wher that y go,
I pray yow to be glad, not sory, lo,
In trust that y shalle se yow hastily.
For y not bidde but seche[2] *a tyme, trewly,*   5
To come to yow, so wis God helpe me so,
      My wele . . .
      Which y . . .
For and so were[3] *bi wisshis swete that y*
Might ben with yow a day or two or mo,   10
Of alle ricches that in this world is, lo,
As had y alle my wisshis verily.[4]
      My wele . . .
      Which y . . .

My only love, my precious,[5] my pleasure,
The one whom more than anyone I adore
Please be encouraged
By the hope that[6] soon I'll see you.
For I do nothing but look for a way   5
To come to you,[7] so help me God,
     My only love, my precious, my pleasure,
     The one whom I desire above all.
And if by wishing I could
Be near you one or two days,[8]   10
For all that exists beneath the stars[9]
None of the rest would I want,
     My only love, my precious, my pleasure.

[5]See Glossary.
[6]Or: "By hoping," "in the hope that."
[7]Champion notes C[2] reads "D'a vous venir"; sense is virtually the same.
[8]Ambivalent: "for a day or two," or "in a day or two."
[9]Lit.: "heavens."

LII. (Notes)

[1]English version is addressed to a lady, French to a man.
[2]EETS paraphrases: "I ask nothing but to seek."
[3]"If it were only."
[4]"I would have all the riches in the world if all my wishes came true."

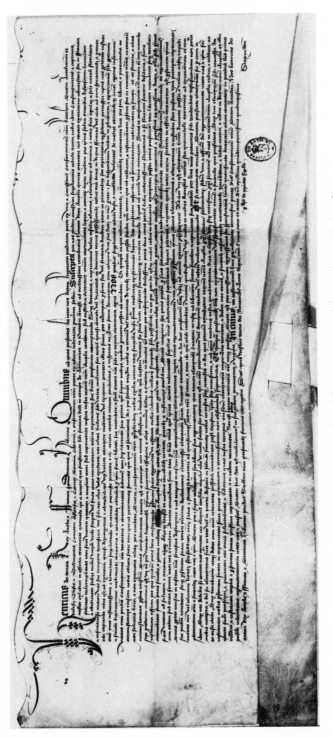

Letter of Release. Reproduced by permission of the Archives Nationales.

Fault il aveugle devenir?
N'ose l'en plus les yeulz ouvrir
Pour regarder ce qu'on desire?
Dangier est bien estrange sire,
Qui tant veult amans asservir.   5
Vous lerrez vous aneantir,
Amours, sans remede querir?
Ne peut nul dangier contredire?
    Fault il . . .
    N'ose l'en . . .   10
    Pour . . .
Les yeulz si sont fais pour servir,
Et pour raporter tout plaisir
Aux cuers, quant ilz sont en martire.
A les en garder dangier tire;   15
Est ce bien fait de le souffrir?
    Fault il . . .

Rejected reading of O: 15. Dangier

Must we then blind men be made?[1]
Do we dare no more open our eyes
To behold what we do desire?
Suspicion is certainly a strange sire
Who wishes lovers to serve in such[2] a way.   5
Will you let[3] yourselves be so unmanned,[4]
Love, without seeking some aid?
Can nothing stop[5] Suspicion?
    Must we then blind men be made?
    Do we dare no more open our eyes   10
    To behold what we do desire?
Eyes were created to serve,
And to bring back every thrill[6]
To our hearts, when they're in pain.
To keep them from that Suspicion labors;[7]   15
Is it wise to tolerate him so?
    Must we then blind men be made?

[1]Or: "Is it necessary to become blind?"
[2]Modifies either *veult* or *asservir* (as here).
[3]For *lairrez*, "you will let."
[4]Lit.: "annulled."
[5]"To contradict," but with legal and binding connotations.
[6]As in Modern French *plaisir* has sexual connotations.
[7]Lit.: "pulls."

Regardez moy sa contenance:
Lui siet il bien a soy jouer?
Certes, c'est le vray mirouer
De toute joyeuse plaisance.
Entre les parfaictes de France,   5
Se peut elle l'une advouer?
    Regardez . . .
    Lui siet . . .
Pour fol me tien, quant je m'avence
De vouloir les grans biens louer   10
Dont Dieu l'a voulue douer;
Ses fais en font la demoustrance:
    Regardez . . .

Rejected readings of O: 5. france 11. dieu

Just look at her face, will you?[1]
Isn't it well-suited to playing by itself?
Indeed, it is the true reflection
Of every joyful diversion.[2]
Of all the perfect beauties in France   5
Would you say she could be counted as one?[3]
    Just look at her face, will you?
    Isn't it well-suited to playing by itself?
Take me for a fool when I allow that[4]
I want to praise the great attractions   10
God desired to bestow on her.
The proof lies in these facts alone:[5]
    Just look at her face, will you?

[1]Difficult to translate. *Siet* comes from *seoir* which
takes an infinitive as subject; so, e.g., Ballade 9.10: "Tant
bien lui siet a la noble chanter ... qu'on...." More literally
the line could be rendered: "[You] look [for] me at her coun-
tenance." A *contenance* is a small hand mirror worn as an ac-
cessory.
[2]Extended metaphor is that of mirror with its reflection;
plaisance is difficult to translate: meaning includes connotations of trifle, game, light pleasure.
[3]Unusual reflexive use of *advouer*.
[4]Lit.: "to go out," "set out"; here perhaps in the sense
of go out on a limb?
[5]Lit.: "These facts provide the proof of it:"

Reprenez ce larron souspir
Qui s'est emblé soudainement,
Sans congié ou commandement,
Hors de la prison de desir.
Mesdisans l'ont ouy partir,   5
Dont ilz tiennent leur parlement;
  Reprenez . . .
  Qui s'est . . .
Se le meschant eust sçeu saillir
Sans noyse, tout priveement,   10
N'en peust chaloir, mais sotement
L'a fait; pour ce l'en fault pugnir:
  Reprenez . . .

Recapture that brigand sigh
That took off[1] so suddenly,
Without leave or orders,
Out of the prison of desire.
The gossips[2] all heard him go: 5
They're holding forth[3] about it now,
    Recapture that brigand sigh
    That took off so suddenly.
If the naughty one had only thought[4] to jump[5] [bail]
Without a sound,[6] quite secretly,   10
It wouldn't have mattered. But stupidly
He did it, and for this he must be punished.
    Recapture that brigand sigh.

[1]"flee," "escape," "disappear."
[2]In the poetry of the troubadours and trouvères these
figures are the spies who threaten to blow the cover of the
secret lovers.
[3]Sort of a group discussion.
[4]Past participle of *sçavoir*: "to know."
[5]Lit.: "to leap up and rush out."
[6]"commotion," "disturbance."

56. ET EUSSIEZ VOUS DANGIER CENT YEULX

Et eussiez vous, dangier, cent yeulx,
Assis et derriere et devant,
Ja n'yrez si prez regardant
Que vostre propos en soit mieulx.
Estre ne povez en tous lieux;   5
Vous prenez peine pour neant,
    Et eussiez . . .
    Assis . . .
Les fais des amoureux sont telz:
Tousjours vont en assoubtivant;   10
Jamais ne saurez faire tant
Qu'ilz ne vous trompent, se m'aist Dieux,
    Et eussiez . . .

Rejected reading of O: 12. dieux

56

Even if you had a hundred eyes, Suspicion,
Provided[1] both behind and before
You would never get close enough [in your] spying
That your intelligence[2] would improve.
You cannot be in all places at once;   5
You take such trouble for nothing.
    Even if you had a hundred eyes, Suspicion,
    Provided both behind and before.
Such is the condition of lovers,[3]
They always [do it] on the sly.[4]   10
You will never be savvy enough
That they won't trick you, so help me God,
    Even if you had a hundred eyes.

[1]"in place," "set."
[2]I use intelligence in the sense of the CIA to reinforce
the gumshoe image of Suspicion.
[3]Lit.: "Deeds of lovers are thus:"
[4]"with artifice," "with ruse."

57. D'ONC VIENT CE SOLEIL DE PLAISANCE

D'onc vient ce soleil de plaisance,
Qui ainsi m'esbluyst les yeulz?
Beauté, douceur, et encor mieulx
Y sont a trop grant abondance.
Soudainement luyst par semblance   5
Comme ung escler venant des cieulx,
    D'onc vient . . .
    Qui ainsi . . .
Il fait perdre la contenance
A toutes gens, jeunes et vielz;   10
N'il n'est eclipse, se m'aist Dieux,
Qui de l'obscurcir ait puissance;
    D'onc vient . . .

Rejected readings of O: 1. Donc   11. dieux

57

From where comes this sun of pleasure,
That so astounds my eyes?
Beauty, sweetness, and even better,[1]
Are here in too great a measure.
Suddenly lit up as if   5
From a lightning bolt coming from on high;
  From where comes this sun of pleasure,
  That so astounds my eyes?
It's a cause of anxiety[2]
To all men, young and old;   10
There is not an eclipse, so help me God,
That has the power to obscure it:
  From where comes this sun of pleasure?

[1]I.e., even more wonderful things.
[2]"It makes all men lose their composure."

Laissez moy penser a mon ayse,
Helas, donnez m'en le loisir;
Je devise avecques plaisir,
Combien que ma bouche se tayse.
Quant merencolie mauvaise   5
Me vient maintes fois assaillir,
     Laissez . . .
     Helas . . .
Car affin que mon cuer repaise,
J'appelle plaisant souvenir,   10
Qui tantost me vient resjouir,
Pource, pour Dieu, ne vous desplaise,
     Laissez . . .

Rejected reading of O: 12. dieu

Leave me to think in peace,
Alas! give me some time;
I am chatting[1] with Pleasure
Although my mouth is silent.
When wicked Loneliness comes   5
Many times to assault me,
  Leave me to think in peace,
  Alas! give me some time.
So that my heart be at ease,[2]
I call on pleasant Memory,   10
Who makes me happy as soon as he arrives;
So,[3] by God, don't let this displease you,
  Leave me to think in peace.

 [1]"gossip," "describe in detail."
 [2]"calm," "settled."
 [3]"for this reason."

Levez ces cuevrechiefs plus hault,
Qui trop cuevrent ces beaulx visages;
De riens ne servent telz umbrages
Quant il ne fait hale ne chault.
On fait a beaulté (qui tant vault)   5
De la musser, tort et oultraiges,
     Levez . . .
     Qui trop . . .
Je sçay bien qu'a dangier n'en chault,
Et pense qu'il ait donné gaiges   10
Pour entretenir telz usages,
Mais l'ordonnances rompre fault,
     Levez . . .

Rejected reading of O: 8. ui

Lift those veils[1] up higher
That cover up too much of those pretty faces;
They serve no purpose as parasols[2]
When it's neither sunny[3] nor hot.
And to hide beauty (worth such a lot)   5
Is both wrong and a grievous offense.[4]
    Lift those veils up higher
    That cover up too much of those pretty faces.
I'm sure it's Suspicion's doing,[5]
And I think he has extracted pledges[6]   10
To ensure such a custom continues,
But the ordinance must be broken:
    Lift those veils up higher.

[1]There is some debate over what these *cuevrechiefs* actually covered. Given the context it seems most likely that they were meant to be understood as veils of some sort, or scarves that covered the head and face.

[2]Lit.: "little clouds," protection from the sun.

[3]Rare word, probably comparable to Modern French *hâle*: "tanned"; here, the cause of the tanning, or the sun.

[4]Difficult to translate literally: "One does to beauty (who's worth such a lot) to hide her, wrong and grievous offense."

[5]"preoccupied with it," "involved in it."

[6]A *gaige* is, according to Poirion, a deposit given as guarantee.

60. ENTRE LES AMOUREUX FOURREZ

Entre les amoureux fourrez,
Non pas entre les decoppez
Suis, car le temps sens refroidy,
Et le cueur de moy l'est aussy.
Tel me veez, tel me prenez.   5
Jeunes gens qui amours servez,
Pour Dieu, de moy ne vous moquez,
Il est ainsi que je vous dy:
     Entre . . .
     Non pas . . .   10
     Suys . . .
Car, quant amours servy aurez
Autant que j'ay, vous devendrez
Pareillement en mon party;
Et quant vous trouverez ainsy   15
Comme je sui, lors vous serez
     Entre . . .

Rejected readins of O: 2. non   3. sans   7. dieu   16. fors

60

Among the well-dressed[1] lovers,
Not among those in rags[2]
Am I, for the weather feels cold,[3]
And my heart is just the same;
As you see me, should you take me.[4]   5
You youths who serve Love,
For God's sake don't make fun of me,
It's just as I tell you:
    Among the well-dressed lovers,
    Not among those in rags   10
    Am I, for the weather feels cold.
For when you have served Love
For as long as I have, you will become
As much a member as I am,[5]
And when you find yourselves the same   15
As I am, then you will be
    Among the well-dressed lovers.

[1]Lit.: "decked out in furs."
[2]"cut up," "in shreds."
[3]Following the emendation of *sens* for *sans* suggested by Bruneau.
[4]Or: "what you see is what you get." Possibly someone's device(?).
[5]"on my side," "in my colors."

61. DIEU VOUS CONDUIE DOUBZ PENSER

Dieu vous conduie, doubz penser,
Et vous doint faire bon voyage;
Rapportez tost joyeux messaige
Vers le cuer pour le conforter.
Ne vueillez gueres demourer,   5
Exploictez comme bon et saige;
      Dieu . . .
      Et vous . . .
Riens ne vous convient ordonner,
Les secrez savez du couraige;   10
Besongnez a son avantaige,
Et pensez de brief retourner.
      Dieu . . .

61

Godspeed, Sweet Intent,[1]
And have[2] a good trip;
Carry the joyful message
Quickly to the heart, to give it solace.
Please don't delay at all,[3]   5
Act[4] wisely and well;
    Godspeed, Sweet Intent,
    And have a good trip.
Don't let yourself be ordered about;
The secrets you know of the heart's ways,[5]   10
Use[6] to your advantage,
And try to come back soon.
    Godspeed, Sweet Intent.

[1] See Glossary.
[2] From *doner*: "give," "grant."
[3] "hardly."
[4] Lit.: "make it result in."
[5] Sentiments of the heart, including bravery.
[6] "labor," "work."

62. LES FOURRIERS D'AMOURS M'ONT LOGE

Les fourriers d'amours m'ont logé
En un lieu bien a ma plaisance;
Dont les mercy de ma puissance,
Et m'en tiens a eulx obligé.
Afin que tost soit abregé,   5
(Le mal qui me porte grevance)
    Les fourriers . . .
    En ung lieu . . .
Desja je me sens alegé,
Car acointié m'a esperance,   10
Et croy qu'amoureux n'a en France
Qui soit mieulx de moy hebergé,
    Les fourriers . . .

Rejected readings of O: 2. en; ama 6. porte porte (second
struck through) 11. france

62

The henchmen of love have lodged me
In a spot well to my liking,
For which I repay them with my will[1]
And hold myself legally bound to them.
So that soon may be lessened   5
The pain that does me wrong,
  The henchmen of love have lodged me
  In a spot well to my liking.
I feel much better already
For I have become acquainted with hope   10
And I think no lover in France
Is better cared for than I,
  The henchmen of love have lodged me.

[1] Feudal service owed by liegeman to lord.

63. QUE C'EST ESTRANGE COMPAIGNIE

Que c'est estrange compaignie,
De penser joint avec espoir!
Aidier scevent et decevoir
Ung cueur qui tout en eulx se fie.
Il ne fault ja que je le dye,   5
Chascun le peut en soy savoir
      Que c'est . . .
      De penser . . .
D'eulx me plains et ne m'en plains mye,
Car mal et bien m'ont fait avoir,   10
Manty m'ont et aussi dit voir;
Je l'aveu et si le renye
      Que c'est . . .

63

What a strange pair,[1]
Reverie joined to hope!
They know how to help and deceive
A heart who has put his faith in them.[2]
For now[3] I must say no more,   5
Everyone can find out for himself:
    What a strange pair,
    Reverie joined to hope.
Of them I do and don't complain,
For ill and good they've let me have,   10
They've lied[4] to me and also told me the truth,
I swear it and deny it too;
    What a strange pair!

    [1]"company," "group," "friendship."
    [2]Or: "that trusts itself entirely to them."
    [3]"One must not for the moment." Poirion, *Lexique*, q.v.,
cites Ballade 83.8 as example: "Il ne faut ja que plus je vous
die."
    [4]From *mentir*.

Beauté, gardez vous de mez yeulx,
Car il vous viennent assaillir;
S'il vous povoient conquerir,
Il ne demanderoyent mielx.
Vous estes seule soubz lez cieulx,   5
Le tresor de parfait plaisir,
  Beauté . . .
   Car il . . .
Congneus lez ay, jeunes et vieulx,
Qu'il ne leur chauldroit de morir,   10
Mais qu'eussent de vous leur desir;
Je vous avise qu'il sont tieulx,
  Beauté . . .

Rejected reading of O: 3. pouoient

Beauty, watch out for my eyes,
For they're coming to attack you;
If they can conquer you,
They won't ask for anything better.
You're unique under heaven,   5
The treasury of perfected pleasure;
    Beauty, watch out for my eyes,
    For they're coming to attack you.
I have known them,[1] young and old,
Who wouldn't care about dying   10
If they could have[2] their desire from you;
I warn you they are like that,
    Beauty, watch out for my eyes.

[1]Ambiguous: other eyes, other men.
[2]Lit.: "provided that."

65. BIEN VIENGNE DOULZ REGARD QUI RIT

Bien viengne, doulz regard qui rit,
Quelque bonne nouvelle porte,
Dont dangier fort se desconforte,
Et de courrous en douleur frit.
Ne peut chaloir de son despit,   5
Ne de ceulz qui sont de sa sorte,
    Bien viengne . . .
    Quelque . . .
Dangier dist: "Baille par escript
Et qu'il n'entre point en la porte."   10
Mais amour, comme la plus forte,
Veult qu'il entre sans contredit.
    Bien viengne . . .

Rejected readings of O: 2. quelque   7. ien   9. baille

65

Welcome, sweet look that laughs,
Bringing some good news
Which makes Suspicion very uncomfortable,
And, suffering, tremble[1] with anger.
One cannot concern oneself with his spite,   5
Nor with any of his ilk;
    Welcome, sweet look that laughs.
    Bringing some good news.
Suspicion says: "Get it convicted,[2]
Don't let it in the door!"   10
But Love, the stronger one,
Wants it to come in without a struggle:
    Welcome, sweet look that laughs!

[1]Burn with emotion, anger.
[2]*Baille* means to pass judgment, deliver a sentence on
someone; *en escript* implies in a binding and legal fashion.

66. EN LA PROMESSE D'ESPERANCE

En la promesse d'esperance,
Ou j'ay temps perdu et usé,
J'ay souvent conseil reffusé
Qui me povoit donner plaisance.
Las, ne suis le premier de France   5
Qui sottement s'est abusé
    En la promesse . . .
      Ou j'ay . . .
Et de ma nysse gouvernance
Devant raison, j'ay accusé   10
Mon cuer; mais il s'est excusé,
Disant que deceu l'a fiance
    En la promesse . . .

Rejected readings of O: 5. france 9. goivernance

66

With the promise of hope,[1]
Where I've spent and wasted so much time,
I've often refused the advice
That delight[2] was able to offer.   5
Alas, I'm not the first in France
Who was so foolishly abused
      With the promise of hope,
      Where I've spent and wasted so much time.
And for my stupid[3] behavior
In the face of reason I've accused   10
My heart, but he gets off
By saying confidence betrayed him
      With the promise of hope.

[1]Poirion notes that in the *Ballades* Esperance has a mystical force.
[2]Like *plaisir, plaisance* includes a sexual connotation.
[3]"negligent," "irresponsible."

67. MON CUER IL ME FAULT ESTRE MESTRE

Mon cuer, il me fault estre mestre
A ma fois, aussi bien que vous;
N'en ayés anuy ou courrous;
Certez, il couvient ainsi estre.
Trop longuement m'avez pestre,   5
Et tous jours tenu au dessous:
      Mon cuer . . .
      A ma foiz . . .
Alez a destre ou a senestre,
Priz serez, sans etre recous;   10
Passer vous fault, mon amis douls,
Ou par la, ou par la fenestre,
      Mon cuer . . .

Rejected readings of O: 7. mon   13. mon

67

My heart, I must be victorious,[1]
In my turn,[2] as well as you.
Don't be annoyed or angered by this;
Surely it has to be so.
For too long you've outfinessed me[3]   5
And each time I've wound up the loser,[4]
     My heart, I must be victorious,
     In my turn, as well as you.
Play to the right or the left
You will be beaten without a comeback[5]   10
You will have to admit, my good friend,
To either defeat or default;[6]
     My heart, I must be victorious.

[1]Lit.: "come out on top." The extended metaphor here is
that of a competition between Charles and his heart. The type
of competition is probably *savate* or *chausson*, the forerunners
of our boxing and fencing.
     [2]I.e., in turns.
     [3]"tricked": "Se vous voulez ces bordeurs croire, ilz vous
decevront et feront paistre." (*Sept Sages*, red. D, p. 40.)
     [4]Technical term for being at a disadvantage: "Et aussi
quant Picars les trovoient a leur dessoubz ils leur faisoient
assez de paine." (P. de Fenin, *Mémoires*, 1411.)
     [5]I.e., without a parting shot.
     [6]Lit.: "either that way or out of the window."

68. MES YEULZ TROP SONT BIEN RECLAMES

Mes yeulz trop sont bien reclamés
Quant ma dame si lez apelle,
Leur moustrant sa grant beauté belle;
Il reviennent comme afamés.
Maugré mesdisans (peu amés)   5
Et dangier qui tient leur querelle,
    Mes yeulz . . .
    Quant . . .
Estre devroyent diffamés,
S'il ne voloyent de bonne elle   10
Vers lez grans biens qui sont en elle;
De ce ne seront ja blasmés,
    Mes yeulz . . .

Rejected reading of O: 8. quant

68

My eyes are too easily reclaimed[1]
When my lady calls them that way[2]
Showing them her great beautiful beauty;[3]
They return starved[4] with desire.
In spite of gossips, wallflowers,[5]   5
And Suspicion who supports their view,[6]
    My eyes are too easily reclaimed
    When my lady calls them that way.
They should be ashamed[7] of themselves
If they didn't fly with a steady wing[8]   10
Toward the great treasures that are hers,
For this they will never be blamed,[9]
    My eyes are too easily reclaimed.

[1]"demanded," "invoked."
[2]"thus": adverb of manner.
[3]Redundant in French as well.
[4]"avid," "hungry."
[5]Lit.: "little-loveds." May modify *mesdisans* or be read substantively.
[6]"discussion."
[7]"dishonored."
[8]Adverbial phrase meaning "sturdy, strong wings"; *elle* equivalent to Modern French *aile*: wing.
[9]In other words, his eyes do know enough to acknowledge her great worth.

Retraiez vous, regart mal avisé,
Vous cuidez bien que nulluy ne vous voye;
Certes aguet par tous lieux vous convoie
Priveement, en habit desguisé.
De gens saichans en estes moins prisé   5
D'ainsi tousjours trotter par my la voye;
  Retraiez vous . . .
  Vous cuidez . . .
Dangier avez contre vous atisé
Quant sot maintien tellement vous forvoie,   10
Au derrenier, fauldra qu'il y pourvoye,
Il est ainsi que je l'ay devisé,
  Retraiez vous . . .

Back off, ill-directed[1] glance,
You really think no one sees you?
Certainly prying[2] leads[3] you everywhere,
Secretly, as a monk disguised.
Among those who know you're less esteemed[4]   5
When you go strutting like that in the open;
    Back off, ill-directed glance,
    You really think no one sees you?
You've alerted[5] Suspicion against you,
When stupid behavior so betrays[6] you,   10
In the end he will have to protect[7] you,
It is just as I figured--
    Back off, ill-directed glance.

[1]Both "ill-advised" and "poorly focussed."
[2]Usual meaning is "watchman" but given negative context
a "peeping-tom" is more what is meant.
[3]"accompanies," "conducts."
[4]"valued."
[5]Lit.: "stimulated."
[6]"dissembles," "goes off the beaten path."
[7]"examine," "procure."

70. REGART VOUS PRENEZ TROP DE PAINE

Regart, vous prenez trop de paine,
Tousjours courés et racourés;
Il semble qu'auz barrez jouez;
Reprenez ung peu vostre alaine.
Cuers qu'amours tient en son demaine   5
Cuident qu'assaillir les voulez,
        Regart, vous . . .
        Tousjours . . .
Au moins, une foiz la sepmaine
C'est raison que vous reposez;   10
Et affin que ne morfondez,
Il fauldra que l'en vous pourmaine,
        Regart . . .

Rejected reading of O: 3. quauzbarrez

70

Glance, you work too hard,[1]
Always running to and fro,[2]
It's as if you're in a wrestling match,[3]
Stop and catch your breath.[4]
Hearts that love holds in his power   5
Think you mean to assault them;
    Glance, you work too hard,
    Always running to and fro.
At the very least,[5] once a week
It is right that you rest;   10
And so that you don't get bored,
It will be necessary for someone to watch you.[6]
    Glance, you work too hard.

[1]Lit.: "You take too much trouble."

[2]"Racing back and forth," "going here and there"; the extended metaphor is again that of a competition, possibly wrestling.

[3]"fisticuffs": "Tout aussi tost qu'ils entrevirent, les trompettes commencerent a s'entresaluer, et luy soudain gagna en pre ou il faisoit beau jouer aux barres." (Du Villars, *Mémoires*, 8, 1557.)

[4]Lit.: "catch your breath a bit."

[5]O^2 has *Amours*, reproduced by all editors but Champion.

[6]Ambiguous: either from *parmaindre*: "to persevere," or *pormener*: "to torment."

71. LE VOULEZ VOUS

Le voulez vous
Que vostre soye?
Rendu m'octroye,
Pris ou recous.
Ung mot pour tous,   5
(Bas qu'on ne l'oye):
  Le voulez . . . Que vostre? . . .
Maugré jalous
Foy vous tendroye;
Or sa, ma joye,   10
Accordons nous--
  Le voulez . . .

Rejected reading of O: 4. recours

Do you want it
As your own?
Consider it done,[1]
By victory or default.[2]
Just tell me one thing[3]--
So low it can't be heard[4]--   5
    Do you want it As your own?[5]
In spite of the jealous,
I will keep faith,
Now try,[6] my joy,   10
Let us agree,
    You do want it.[7]

[2]"concede," "accord."
[2]"recapitulation."
[3]Lit.: "one word for all [time]."
[4]"overheard," "heard by others."
[5]Here I follow arrangement found in MS.
[6]From *essayer*. Champollion-Figeac reads "Or ça...." thus changing the sense to "Now that, ... let us agree, you want."
[7]I've taken liberties with the English word order in an attempt to communicate the word-play of the French.

Crevez moy les yeulx,
Que ne voye goutte,
Car trop je redoubte
Beaulté en tous lieulx.
Ravir jusqu'aus cieulx   5
Veult ma joye toute,
    Crevez . . . Que ne . . .
D'elle me gard Dieulx
Affin qu'en sa route
Jamais ne me boute;   10
N'esse pour le mieulx?
    Crevez . . . Que ne . . .

Rejected reading of O: 8. dieulx

Poke out my eyes
So I don't see at all,[1]
For I greatly fear
The beauty that is everywhere.
It wishes to transport to the heavens   5
My each and every joy. [2]
     Poke out my eyes So I don't see at all.
God keep me from her[3]
So that on her way[4]
I never bump[5] into her;   10
Isn't that for the best?
     Poke out my eyes. So I don't see at all.[6]

[1]*que*: for *afin que*; *ne ... goutte*: strong negative.

[2]*Joie* is very hard to translate. Frequently in Charles it stands metonymically for *joie d'espérance*. It always contains a sense of unfulfilled desire, whether spiritual or sensual.

[3]Tortured syntax: "From her keep me, God," thus stressing the importance of staying far from beauty.

[4]"path," "route."

[5]*Se bouter* can mean both "to push" as well as "to make an adulterous pass."

[6]Here, as above, following MS.

Quant je la regarde,
Elle vient ferir
Mon cueur de la darde
D'amoureus desir.

When I see her,
She succeeds in striking
My heart with the arrow
Of amorous desire.

Jeunes amoureux nouveaulx
En la nouvelle saison,
Par les rues, sans raison,
Chevauchent, faisans les saulx.
Et font saillir des carreaulx   5
Le feu, comme de cherbon,
  Jeunes . . .
Je ne sçay se leurs travaulx
Ilz emploient bien ou non,
Mais piqués de l'esperon   10
Sont autant que leurs chevaulx,
  Jeunes . . .

Young[1] new lovers,[2]
In the new season,[3]
Down the streets, carefree,
They saunter, making leaps and passes.[4]
And they make the cobblestones   5
Leap as fire does coal,[5]
      Young new lovers.
I don't know if their labors
Are well-spent or not,
But pricked by the spur   10
They are just like their horses,
      Young new lovers.

[1]Champion reads *Jennes*.(?)
[2]It's difficult to figure out which should be translated substantively.
[3]I.e., Spring.
[4]Double entendre: means both to jump like a horse and to make a pass at a woman.
[5]The sense of these lines connects the youths with the fire, cobblestones with coal.

74. GARDEZ LE TRAIT DE LA FENESTRE

Gardez le trait de la fenestre,
Amans, qui par ruez passez,
Car plus tost en serez blessez
Que de trait d'arc ou d'arbalestre.
N'alez a destre ne a senestre   5
Regardant, mais les yeulx bessez;
    Gardez . . .
Se n'avez medicin, bon maistre,
Si tost que vous serez navrez,
A Dieu soyez recommandez;   10
Mors vous tiens, demandez le prestre,
    Gardez . . .

Rejected reading of O: 10. dieu

74

Watch out for the draught[1] from the window,
You lovers who pass by on the street,
For you will be wounded faster
Than by arrow or crossbow.
Neither to the right, nor to the left   5
Let your eyes stray, but keep them downcast,
    Watch out for the draught from the window.
If you don't have a doctor, good sport,[2]
As soon as you are wounded
Give yourself up to God: 10
Death holds you; call a preacher;
    Watch out for the draught from the window.

[1]Double entendre, as "draught" in English: current of air
and path of an arrow. Refers to glance from the lady's eyes.
[2]*Maistre* frequently refers to a participant in a competition.

75. EN GIBESSANT TOUTE L'APRES DISNEE

En gibessant toute l'apres disnee,
Par my lez champs pour me desanuyer,
N'a pas long temps que faisoye, l'autr'ier,
Voler mon cueur apres mainte pensee.
L'aquilote, souvenance nommee,   5
Sourdoit deduit et savoit remerchier,
  En gibessant . . .
Gibessierre, de passe temps ouvree,
Enpli toute d'assez plaisant gibier,
Et puis je peu mon cueur, au derrenier,   10
Sur un faisant d'esperance celee,
  En gibessant . . .

Rejected reading of O: 5. La quilote

154

75

While birding[1] right after dinner,[2]
Out in the fields, to stay entertained,[3]
It wasn't long, the other day,
Till[4] I let fly my heart in chase of Deep Concern.
The bird-dog named Memory   5
Gave chase and knew how to mark,[5]
    While birding right after dinner.
The cage opened by Pastime,
Satisfied by this rather pleasant chase,
I then fed my heart, at last,   10
On the pheasant, Secret Hope.
    While birding right after dinner.

[1]From *gibier*: "birding."
[2]One of the most detailed of Charles's allegories, the extended metaphor is that of falconry, where the heart is the falcon, his prey thought or reverie and the attacking eagle memory. In the last stanza the cage is opened by diversion and the falcon re-enters to be fed the pheasant of secret hope.
[3]Lit.: "to keep from being bored."
[4]For *avant que*: "before."
[5]Technical hunting terms about which there is much debate over the exact meaning.

76. QUE FAUT IL PLUS A UNG CUER AMOUREUX

Que faut il plus a ung cuer amoureux,
Quant assiegé l'a dangier de tristesse,
Qu'avitailler tantost sa forteresse
D'assez vivres de bon espoir eureux?
Cappitaine face desir songneux   5
Qui, nuyt et jour, fera guet sans peresse;
    Que fault il plus . . .
Artillié soit d'avis avantureux,
Coulevrines, et canons a largesse,
Prestz, assortiz, et chargiez de sagesse,   10
Es boulevers et lieux avantageux;
    Que faut il plus . . .

Rejected readings of O: 7. que   12. que

76

What more needs a heart in love,
When Suspicion has besieged it with sadness,
Than to stock,[1] right away, its fortress
With enough provisions of fortunate good hope?
Let Dreaming Desire be the captain   5
Who night and day stands guard tirelessly[2]
    What more needs a heart in love?
Let Riveted Attention[3] provide the artillery,
Siege guns,[4] and cannons in abundance,
Readied, stocked,[5] and charged by wisdom   10
On the ramparts[6] and in strategic places,
    What more needs a heart in love?

[1] To provide with supplies, particularly food and munitions.
[2] Lit.: "without laziness."
[3] *Avis* means both "opinion," as in Modern French, and "attention"; *avantureux*: "bold," "sturdy."
[4] Long cannons.
[5] Often used in the context of stocking a store.
[6] For "en les boulevers."

77. DES MALEUREUX PORTE LE PRIS

Des maleureux porte le pris,
Servant dame loyalle et belle,
Qui, pour mourir en la querelle,
N'ascheve ce qu'a antrepris.
Diffamé de droit et repris   5
Par devant dame et damoiselle,
  Des maleureux . . .
Pourquoy est d'amer si espris,
Quant congnoist que son cuer chancelle
En soy donnent repreuve telle;   10
Ou a il ce mestier apris?
  Des maleureux . . .

Rejected readings of O: 6. Pardevant   7. des   12. des

77

Some[1] unlucky one wins the prize[2]
Serving a loyal and beautiful lady,
He who, to die in the struggle,
Doesn't get what he's after.
Dishonored by law and accused   5
Right in front[3] of all the women,
    Some unlucky one wins the prize.
Why is loving so esteemed[4]
When it's known her heart is willful?[5]
That by itself gives proof enough.   10
Where has he learned this trade?
    Some unlucky one wins the prize.

[1]Partitive plural for singular.
[2]Or: "pays the price."
[3]*Par*: an intensive.
[4]"valued," "esteemed."
[5]"vacillates."

78. EN AMER N'A QUE MARTIRE

En amer n'a que martire,
Nulluy ne le devroit dire
Mieulx que moy;
J'en sauroye, sur ma foy,
De ma main ung livre escripre   5
Ou amans pourroient lire,
Des yeulx larmoyans sans rire,
Je m'en croy.
Des maulx qu'on y peut eslire,
Cellui qui est le mains pire,   10
C'est anoy,
Qui n'est jamés apart soy;
Plus n'en dy bien doit souffire,
    En amer . . .

Rejected readings of O: 2. ulluy 8. En amer (written in margin)

78

In[1] loving there is only suffering;
No one ought to be able to say
This better than me.
I should know how, indeed,
To write a book on it by my own hand   5
Where lovers would be able to read,
Their laughless eyes brimming with tears,
I do believe
    [no refrain in MS]
Of the troubles that can be chosen,[2]   10
The one that is least worst
Is depression,[3]
Which is never all alone.[4]
I say no more; this should suffice:
    In loving there is only suffering.   15

[1]Denotes symbolic space, state of being.
[2]"in love."
[3]Troublesome: if read as *Anoy* (*ennui*) then active sorrow
or depression. But D'Hericault reads *Aroy*, glossed as "array"
or "court"(?); Chalvet reads *Avoy*, glossed as "groans."
[4]"on his own."

Me fauldrez vous a mon besoing,
Mon reconfort et ma fiance?
M'avez vous mis en oubliance
Pour tant se de vous je suis loing?
N'avez vous pitié de mon soing?   5
Sans vous, savez que n'ay puissance;
    Me fauldrez vous . . .
On feroit dez larmez un baing,
Qu'ay pleurées de desplaisance,
Et crie, par desesperance,   10
Ferant ma poitrine du poing,
    Me fauldrez vous . . .

Rejected reading of O: 4. Pourtant

Do you need me as I do you,
My solace and my confidante?
Or have you forgotten me
To the degree that I'm distant from you?
Have you no pity for my struggle?   5
Without you, you know, I am powerless;
  Do you need me as I do you?
One could make a bath of the tears
I have shed out of joylessness;
And I shout out of hopelessness,   10
Striking my chest with my fist:
  Do you need me as I do you?

Cueur endormy en pensee,
En transes, moitié veillant,
S'on lui va riens demandant,
Il respont a la volee,
Et parle de vois cassee,   5
Sans pourpos, ne tant ne quant,
    Cueur endormy . . .
Tout met en galimafree,
Lombart, Anglois, Alemant,
François, Picart et Normant;   10
C'est une chose faee,
    Cueur endormy . . .

Rejected readings of O: 9. anglois; alemant   10. picart;
normant

A heart hypnotized[1] by reverie,[2]
Entranced, half-awake,
If anyone asks it anything,[3]
It answers distractedly[4]
And speaks with a breaking voice,   5
Unfocussed, neither here nor there,[5]
    A heart hypnotized by reverie.
Everything is a gallimaufry--[6]
Lombard, English, German,
French, Picard, Norman.   10
It's an enchanted thing:
    A heart hypnotized by reverie.

[1]Lit.: "asleep."
[2]Like the heart, this poem seems to be half-asleep and unfocussed.
[3]Lit.: "if anyone goes asking it anything."
[4]Lit.: "on the fly."
[5]Here Charles seems to mean a more Latinate sense than usual; usually this phrase means "as little as possible."
[6]"jumbled writing."

81. IL VIT EN BONNE ESPERANCE

Il vit en bonne esperance,
Puis qu'il est vestu de gris,
Qu'il aura, a son devis,
Encore sa desirance.
Combien qu'il soit hors de France,   5
Par deça le mont Senis,
    Il vit . . .
Perdu a sa contenance,
Et tous sez jeus et ses ris;
Gaigner lui fault Paradis   10
Par force de pacience,
    Il vit . . .

Rejected readings of O: 5. france   6. senis   10. paradis

He survives on the hope alone
(And so is dressed in gray)
That he will still get his way[1]
And get what he [most] desires.
Although[2] he is outside of France,   5
On the other side of Mt. Cenis[3]
    He survives on the hope alone.
He's lost his composure[4]
And all his play and laughter;
He'll be sure to get into paradise   10
On the strength of his patience [only].
    He survives on the hope alone.

   [1]Or: "his will"; also sense of device on shield(?).

   [2]For *bien que*: "although."

   [3]Mountain in the French Alps near Charles's Italian holdings.

   [4]Calm and dignified attitude.

82. MON CUEUR PLUS NE VOLERA

Mon cueur plus ne volera,
Il est enchaperonné;
Nonchaloir l'a ordonné,
Qui ja pieça le m'osta.
Confort depuis ne lui a   5
Cure n'atirer donné
    Mon cueur . . .
Se sa gorge gettera,
Je ne sçay, car gouverné
Ne l'ay, mais abandonné   10
Soit com a venir pourra,
    Mon cueur . . .

Rejected reading of O: 11. avenir

My heart will fly[1] no more:
It has been hooded,[2]
Indifference[3] has so ordered
Who took it from me before.[4]
Ever since, it has no solace   5
Nor is any comfort[5] given it,
    My heart will fly no more.
If it refuses to eat[6]
I'm at a loss; controlled it
I haven't; abandoned rather.   10
So come what may,
    My heart will fly no more.

[1]Metaphor is again from falconry.
[2]Technical term.
[3]Loaded term for Charles; see Introduction.
[4]"formerly."
[5]"care," "concern."
[6]Difficult to translate. *Gorge* is the food given a falcon.

83. CHASCUN DIT QU'ESTEZ BONNE ET BELLE

Chascun dit qu'estez bonne et belle;
Mais mon euil jugier ne saura,
Car lignage m'avuglera,
Qui maintendra vostre querelle.
Quant on parle de demoiselle   5
Qui a largesse de biens a,
    Chascun dit . . .
A nostre assemblee nouvelle,
Verray ce qu'il m'en samblera;
Et s'ainsi est, bien me plaira,   10
Or, prenons que vous soyez telle,
    Chascun dit . . .

Rejected reading of O: 3. avoglera

83

Everyone says you're true and pretty,
But my eye will not be the judge
For lineage blinds me
Who argues on your behalf.
When one speaks of a lady   5
Who is well-endowed with riches,[1]
    Everyone says you're true and pretty.
At our latest meeting,
I'll see how it seems to me;
And if it is so, it will please me well;   10
Now let's assume you are just as
    Everyone says you're true and pretty.

    [1]Tortured syntax: understood as "qui a de biens à lar-
gesse"; for *biens* see Glossary.

84. ENCORE LUI FAIT IL GRANT BIEN

Encore lui fait il grant bien
De voir celle qu'a tant amee,
A cellui qui cueur et pensee
Avoit en elle, comme tien.
Combien qu'il n'y aye plus rien,   5
Et qu'aultre la lui ait ostee,
  Encore lui . . .
En regardant son doulz maintien
Et son fait qui moult lui agree,
S'il la peut tenir embrassee,   10
Il pense que une fois fut sien
  Encore . . .

Still it does him good
To see the one he loved so much,
For him, whose heart and dreams
She once held as his own,[1]
Even though they are no longer,[2]   5
And another has taken her from him,
     Still it does him good.
By looking at her sweet demeanor[3]
And her ways[4] that suit her so well,
He can thus hold her to him   10
And think how once she was his,
     Still;[5] it does him good.

[1]Here I follow Champollion-Figeac and D'Hericault who
read *sien*; all others read *tien*.

[2]I.e., are no longer a pair, together.

[3]"conduct," "attitude," "gestures."

[4]"actions."

[5]The sense here is that as long as he can look at her he
can still possess her to some degree. The contradiction in
the last two lines (how she once was his/Still) is, I believe,
intended; she is both a thing of the past and, to a much lesser
degree, the present.

Avugle et assourdy,
De tous poins en nonchaloir,
Je ne puis ouir ne voir
Chose dont soye esjouy.
Se desplaisant ou marry,   5
Tout m'est un, pour dire voir;
        Avugle . . .
Es escolez fu nourry
D'amours, pensant mielx valoir;
Quant plus y cuiday savoir,   10
Plus m'y trouvay rassoty,
        Avugle . . .

Rejected reading of O: 5. De

Blind and deaf
In all ways numbed
I can't hear or see
A thing I would enjoy;
Both[1] the unpleasant and the merry[2]   5
Are one to me, it's sad to say,
    Blind and deaf.
In schools I was nurtured,
On love (thinking it worth so much);
The more I thought I knew,   10
The more I found I was dumb,
    Blind and deaf.

[1]Here I follow Guichard; all others read "De desplaisant
...."
[2]Usual meaning: "sad," "angry." I read, however, as
calque from English "merry" in order to retain the pairing of
opposites found throughout the chanson.

86. SATIS SATIS PLUS QUAM SATIS

Satis, satis, plus quam satis,
N'en avez vous encor assés?
Par Dieu, vous en serés lassés
Dez folies *quas amatis.*
Cum sensibus ebetatis,   5
Sottez gens, vous les amassés
    Satis . . .
Et pour ce, *si me credatis,*
Oubliés tous lez temps passés,
Et voz meschans pensers cassés,   10
Dolendo de perpetratis
    Satis . . .

Rejected reading of O: 3. dieu

176

Enough, enough, more than enough,[1]
Haven't you had enough yet?
By God, you will be worn out
By the crazy things that you love.
With intoxicated senses   5
Stupid men, you gather them up,
        Enough, enough, more than enough.
For this reason, if you believe me,
Forget all times [in the] past,
And your naughty, broken dreams,   10
Sorrowing for the things you have done
        Enough, enough, more than enough.

[1]Underlined words in Latin in the original.

Non temptabis, tien te coy,
Regard plain d'atrayement;
Vade retro, tellement
Que point n'aproches de moy.
Probavi te, sur ma foy,   5
Je crains ton assotement,
  Non temptabis . . .
Ecce la rayson pourquoy:
Tu resveillez trop souvent
Corda; bien congnois comment   10
Presches l'amoureuse loy:
  Non temptabis . . .

Thou shalt not tempt,[1] keep to yourself,
Glance, certain of appeal.
Get back, far enough
That you don't begin to approach me.
I've tested you, by my faith;   5
I fear your stupid ways.
    Thou shalt not tempt.
Behold the reason why:
You awaken too frequently
The heart; I know well how   10
You preach the sermon of love:
    Thou shalt not tempt.

[1]Underlined words in Latin in the original.

Textual Notes

Errata

Throughout: *For* D'Hericault *read* d'Héricault

Manuscripts

A -- Bibliothèque de l'Arsenal, MS no. 2070 (15th c.)
B -- Paris, Bibl. Nationale, fr. 19139 (15th c.)
C -- London, British Library, MS Harley 682 (15th c.)
G -- Bibliothèque de Grenoble, MS no. 873 (15th c.)
M -- Bibliothèque de Carpentras, MS no. 375 (15th c.)
O -- Paris, Bibl. Nationale, fr. 25458 (15th c.)
O^2 -- Paris, Bibl. Nationale, fr. 1104 (15th c.)
H -- London, British Library, Harley 6916 (15th c.)
P -- Bibliothèque de l'Arsenal, MS no. 3457 (15th c.)
L -- London, British Library, Lansdowne 380 (15th c.)
R -- Paris, Bibl. Nationale, fr. 9223 (15th c.)
S -- Paris, Bibl. Nationale, fr. 1719 (15th c.)
C^2 -- London, British Library, Reg. 16. F. ii. (from 1500)

N.B.: I have followed Champion in the folio numbers.

1. CE MAY QU'AMOURS PAS NE SOMMEILLE

Manuscripts: O, p. 235; C, fol. 111v; G, fol. 22v; M,
fol. 44r; O², fol. 55r; H, fol. 107r; P, fol. 210r; L, fol.
224r.

Major Editions: Chalvet, p. 43; Champollion-Figeac, No.
1, p. 25; Guichard, p. 193; D'Hericault, No. 1, p. 5; Champion,
No. 1, p. 204.

Meter and rhyme: 8 ABba abAB abbaA

1, 7, 13. *May*: Champollion-Figeac does not capitalize.
1. *amours*: All editions except Guichard capitalize.
2. *esliesser*: Champollion-Figeac writes *eslieser*.
4. *pusse*: Chalvet and Champollion-figeac have *puce*.
10. *Pource*: Chalvet, Champollion-Figeac, Guichard, and
Champion write *pour ce* as two separate words.
11. *Sy*: Chalvet and Champollion-Figeac have *Cy*.

2. TIENGNE SOY D'AMER QUI POURRA

Manuscripts: O, p. 236; C, fol. 112r; G, fol. 22v; M,
fol. 34r; O², fol. 55r; H, fol. 107r; P, fol. 210r; L, fol.
224r.

Major Editions: Chalvet, p. 44; Champollion-Figeac, No.
2, p. 26; Guichard, pp. 193-4; D'Hericault, No. 2, p. 6;
Champion, No. 2, pp. 204-5.

Meter and rhyme: 8 ABba abAB abbaA

9. *devant yer*: Chalvet reads *devantier*; Champollion-
Figeac *devant'ier*.
10. *scet*: Chalvet reads *scait*.
12. *sien*: Chalvet and Champollion-Figeac read *syen*.

3. QUELQUE CHOSE QUE JE DYE

Manuscripts: O, p. 237; G, fol. 23r; M, fol. 34r; O²,
fol. 55r; H, fol. 107v; L, fol. 224 v.

Major Editions: Chalvet, p. 45; Champollion-Figeac, No.
3, pp. 26-27; Guichard, p. 194; D'Hericault, No. 3, p. 6;
Champion, No. 3, p. 205.

Meter and rhyme: 8 ABba abAB abbaA

1. *dye*: Chalvet, Champollion-Figeac and Guichard read *die*.

2. *amour*: All editions capitalize.

3. *Toutesfois*: D'Hericault and Guichard read *Touteffoiz*.

5. *acomplie*: Chalvet, and D'Hericault read *accomplie*.

4. N'EST ELLE DE TOUS BIENS GARNIE

Manuscripts: O, p. 238; C, fol. 112v; G, fol. 23r; M, fol. 34r; O^2, fol. 55r; H, fol. 107v; P, fol. 211r; L, 224v.

Major Editions: Chalvet, p. 46; Champollion-Figeac, No. 4, p. 27; Guichard, p. 194; D'Hericault, No. 4, p. 7; Champion, No. 4, p. 206.

Meter and rhyme: 8 ABba abAB abbaA

1. *biens*: Champollion-Figeac reads *bien* (singular) but retains plural in lines 7 and 12.

2. D'Hericault punctuates as "... loyaument!"

3. *serement*: D'Hericault reads *serment*.

5. *dittes*: Chalvet and Guichard read *dites*.

11. *Faictes*: D'Hericault reads *Faittes*.

12. *flaterie*: Chalvet and D'Hericault read *flatterie*.

5. QUANT J'AY NOMPAREILLE MAISTRESSE

Manuscripts: O, p. 239; C, fol. 113r; G, fol. 23v; M, fol. 34r; O^2, fol. 55r; H, fol. 108r; P, fol. 212r; L, fol. 225r.

Major Editions: Chalvet, p. 47; Champollion-Figeac, No. 5, pp. 27-28; Guichard, pp. 194-5; D'Hericault, No. 5, p. 7; Champion, No. 5, pp. 206-7.

Meter and rhyme: 8 ABba abAB abbaA

3. *joyeusement*: Champollion-Figeac reads *joieusement*.

6. DIEU QU'IL LA FAIT BON REGARDER

Manuscripts: O, p. 240; C, fol. 113v; G, fol. 23v; M, fol. 34r; O^2, fol. 35v; H, fol. 108r; P, fol. 185r; L, fol. 225r.

Major Editions: Chalvet, p. 48; Champollion-Figeac, No. 6, p. 28; Guichard, p. 195; D'Hericault, No. 6, p. 8; Champion, No. 6, p. 207.

Meter and rhyme: 8 ABba abAB abbaA

Translated by many including Ezra Pound (*Ripostes*, 1912):

God! that mad'st her well regard her,
How she is so fair and bonny
For the great charms that are upon her
Ready are all folks to reward her.
Who could part him from her borders
When spells are always renewed on her?
God! that mad'st her well regard her
How she is so fair and bonny.

From here to there to the sea's borders,
Dame nor damsel there's not any
Hath of perfect charms so many
Thought of her are of dream's order:
God! that mad'st her well regard her.

and Cedric Wallis:

How fair God made her to the eye,
How gentle graceful and how sweet,
In her such joys each other greet
As no man living could deny.
And who could tire of her beauty,
Each day renewed at Venus' feet.

On sea or land, in earth or sky,
No mistress or maiden could you meet
In each perfection all complete
To dream of whom is but to sigh.

     6. *Tousjours*: Chalvet and Champollion-Figeac read *Tous jours*.
         beauté: Chalvet, Guichard and D'Hericault read *beaulté*.
     9. Champollion-Figeac punctuates "Par deça, ne de là, la mer," while D'Hericault and Guichard read "Par deçà, ne dela la mer."
     10. Chalvet, Guichard, and D'Hericault capitalize both *dame* and *damoiselle*.
     11. *parfais*: Chalvet reads: "Qui sont en tout bien parfait telle:"; Guichard places a comma after *parfais*.
     12. *un*: Champollion-Figeac and Guichard read *ung*.
         d'y: Champollion-Figeac reads *d'i*.

7.   PAR DIEU MON PLAISANT BIEN JOYEUX

Manuscripts: O, p. 241; C, fol. 113v; G, fol. 24r; M, fol. 34r; O², fol. 55v; H, fol. 108v; P, fol. 185r; L, fol. 225v.

Major Editions: Chalvet, p. 49; Champollion-Figeac, No. 7, p. 29; Guichard, pp. 195-6; D'Hericault, No. 7, p. 8; Champion, No. 7, pp. 207-8.

Meter and rhyme: 8 ABba abAB abbaA

5.   *regard*: D'Hericault and Champion read *regart*.
       beaulx yeux: Chalvet and Champollion-Figeac read *beaulx yeulx*, D'Hericault and Champion, *beaux yeulx*.
10.   *Souventes fois*: Guichard and D'Hericault read *Souventeffoiz*.
12.   *feray*: Chalvet reads "Je n'en seray pourtant que mieulx."

8.   QUE ME CONSEILLIEZ VOUS MON CUEUR

Manuscripts: O, p. 242; C, fol. 114r; G, fol. 24r; M, fol. 34v; O², fol. 55v, H, fol. 108v; P, fol. 212r; L, fol. 225v.

Major Editions: Chalvet, p. 50; Champollion-Figeac, No. 8, p. 29; Guichard, p. 196; D'Hericault, No. 8, p. 9; Champion, No. 8, p. 208.

Meter and rhyme: 8 ABba abAB abbaA

2.   *Iray*: Guichard and D'Hericault read *Irai*.
       par: Whether used as a separate word or as a prefix, *par* has an intensifying effect: "directly."
3.   *Luy*: Guichard reads *Lui*.
       peine: Guichard and D'Hericault read *paine*.
5.   *honneur*: Champollion-Figeac reads *honneur*.
12.   *G'y*: Champollion-Figeac reads *J'y*; Guichard reads "Cy vois n'est ce pour le meilleur."
            D'Hericault punctuates "n'est ce pour le meilleur;" Chalvet reads *nesce*.

9.   OU REGARD DE VOZ BEAULX DOULX YEULX

Manuscripts: O, p. 243; C, fol. 114v; G, fol. 24v; M, fol. 34v; O², fol. 55v; H, fol. 109r; L, fol. 235v.

Major Editions: Chalvet, p. 51; Champollion-Figeac, No. 9, p. 30; Guichard, pp. 196-7; D'Hericault, No. 9, pp. 9-10; Champion, No. 9, p. 209.

Meter and rhyme: 8 ABba abAB abbaA

1. *Ou*: Chalvet reads *Au*.
    doulx: Champollion-Figeac reads *doulz*.
    Guichard and D'Hericault punctuate: "Ou regard de vos beaulx, doulx yeux,"
4. *penser*: Includes not only our thinking, but also thinking about the past, or reverie, and thinking of the future, or dreaming. In addition, *penser* can include connotations of intent and design.
6. *joyeux*: D'Hericault reads *joyeulx*; Champollion-Figeac, *joieux*.
8. Guichard punctuates with a question mark.
9. *regard*: D'Hericault reads *regart*.
12. *Pource*: Chalvet, Guichard and Champion read *Pour ce*.

10.   QUI LA REGARDE DE MES YEULX

Manuscripts: O, p. 244; C, fol. 115r; G, fol. 24v; M, fol. 34v; O^2, fol. 56r; H, fol. 109v; P, fol. 186r; L, fol. 226r.
Major Editions: Chalvet, p. 52; Champollion-Figeac, No. 10, pp. 30-31; Guichard, p. 197; D'Hericault, No. 10, p. 10; Champion, No. 10, pp. 209-210.
Meter and rhyme: 8 ABba abAB abbaA

2. *Ma dame*: Chalvet and Champollion-Figeac read *Madame*, Guichard, D'Hericault, *Ma Dame*.
6. *un*: Champollion-Figeac reads *ung*.
10. *qu'elle*: Champollion-Figeac reads *quelle*.

11.   CE MOIS DE MAY NOMPAREILLE PRINCESSE

Manuscripts: O, p. 245; C, fol. 115r; G, fol. 25r; M, fol. 34v; O^2, fol. 56r; H, fol. 109v; P, fol. 215r; L, fol. 226r.
Major Editions: Chalvet, p. 53; Champollion-Figeac, No. 11, p. 31; Guichard, p. 197; D'Hericault, No. 11, pp. 10-11; Champion, No. 11, p. 210.
Meter and rhyme: 10 ABba abAB abbaA

Champion queries whether this refers to the events of May 1415.
Le Jardin de Plaisance (*JdP*) includes a paraphrase of this chanson. Changes indicated below.

1. *May*: Champollion-Figeac and Champion read *may*.

1, 7, 13. *princesse*: Chalvet, Guichard, and D'Hericault capitalize; *JdP* reads *deesse*.

3. Chalvet omits *avez* and thus eliminates the change from second person formal (*avez*) to second person familiar (*puis*) which occurs later in the line.

4. *dame*: Chalvet capitalizes.

8. *JdP* reads "pour moster de tristesse" which fits equally well metrically and has the same meaning.

10. *povoir*: Champion reads *povair*.
   JdP reads "A mesioir ayez vostre vouloir."

11. *ayez*: Champollion-Figeac reads *aiez*.
   Chalvet glosses *m'esmayer* as "me soulager."

12. COMMANDEZ VOSTRE BON VOULOIR

Manuscripts: O, p. 246; C, fol. 115v; G, fol. 25r; M, fol. 34v; O², fol. 56r; H, fol. 109v; P, fol. 215r.

Major Editions: Chalvet, p. 54; Champollion-Figeac, No. 12, pp. 31-32; Guichard, pp. 197-8; D'Hericault, No. 12, p. 11; Champion, No. 12, pp. 210-211.

Meter and rhyme: 8 ABba abAB abbaA

1. While the French version writes of the servant in the third person, the English version uses the voice of the first person: "Comaunde me what ye wille in everi wise."

2. *treshumble*: Champollion-Figeac reads *tres humble*.

4. *povoir*: Champion reads *povair*.

6. *espargnés*: Chalvet and D'Hericault read *espargnez*.

9. *Mettez*: Guichard reads *Mectez*.

   a nonchaloir: Chalvet and Champollion-Figeac read *en nonchaloir*.

9-12. The sense of this strophe depends upon seeing the servant (the heart; see line 4) as the subject of the poem. First his qualities are described, then, in this last part, a test of these strengths and attributes is recommended.

10. *lui*: Champollion-Figeac reads *luy*.

13. BELLE SE C'EST VOSTRE PLAISIR

Manuscripts: O, p. 247; C, fol. 116r; G, fol. 25v; M, fol. 34v; O², fol. 56r; H, fol. 110r; P, fol. 216r; L, fol. 236r.

Major Editions: Chalvet, p. 55; Champollion-Figeac, No.
13, p. 32; Guichard, pp. 198-9; D'Hericault, No. 14, p. 12;
Champion, No. 13, pp. 211-212.

Meter and rhyme: 8 ABba abAB abbaA

2. *enrichir*: Champollion-Figeac reads *enrichier*.

5. *Ne me laissiez du tout*: Chalvet reads "De me laisser";
Guichard reads *dutout* as one word.

7. Guichard and D'Hericault punctuate "deuil, ne tristesse,"

15. *dolent refus*: Champollion-Figeac reads *Dolent-refus*,
thus personifying the adjective as well as the noun.

14. RAFRESCHISSEZ LE CHASTEL DE MON CUEUR

Manuscripts: O, p. 248; C, fol. 116v; G, fol. 25v; M,
fol. 35r; O^2, fol. 56v; H, fol. 110v; P, fol. 216r; L, fol.
227r.

Major Editions: Chalvet, p. 56; Champollion-Figeac, No.
14, pp. 32-33; Guichard, pp. 199-200; D'Hericault, No. 16,
p. 13; Champion, No. 14, p. 212.

Meter and rhyme: 10 ABba abAB abbaA

2. *joyeuse plaisance*: Champollion-Figeac reads *joieuse,*
D'Hericault and Champion, *Joyeuse Plaisance*.

3. *faulx dangier*: Champollion-Figeac reads *Faulx-dangier*,
D'Hericault and Champion, *Dangier*.

avec: Chalvet and Champollion-Figeac read *avecques*.

4. Chalvet and Champollion-Figeac read "L'assiégé en
tour de douleur"; Champion capitalizes *Doleur*.

6. Champollion-Figeac, Guichard and D'Hericault punctuate as "Tantost lever, ou rompre par puissance".

9. *dangier*: Champollion-Figeac, Guichard, D'Hericault,
and Champion capitalize.

12. *votre*: Champollion-Figeac reads *vostre*.

15. SE MA DOLEUR VOUS SAVIES

Manuscripts: O, p. 249; C, fol. 116v; G, fol. 26r; M,
fol. 35r; O^2, fol. 56v; H, fol. 110v; P, fol. 213r; L, fol.
226v.

Major Editions: Chalvet, p. 57; Champollion-Figeac, No.
15, p. 33; Guichard, p. 200; D'Hericault, No. 18, p. 14;
Champion, No. 15, pp. 212-213.

Meter and rhyme: 8 ABba abAB abbaA

2. *pensement*, like *penser*, includes connotations of reverie: joyous thought, preoccupation, obsession.

5. *refus*: D'Hericault and Champion capitalize.

12. *Ja*: D'Hericault reads *Jà*.

16. MA SEULE PLAISANT DOULCE JOYE

Manuscripts: O, p. 250; C, fol. 117r; G, fol. 26r; M, fol. 35r; O², fol. 57r; H, fol. 111r; P, fol. 213r; L, fol. 227r.

Major Editions: Chalvet, p. 58; Champollion-Figeac, No. 16, pp. 33-34; Guichard, p. 201; D'Hericault, No. 20, p. 14; Champion, No. 16, p. 213.

Meter and rhyme: 8 ABba abAB abbaA

Champion questions (vol. 2, p. 565) whether this chanson marks the beginning of a "roman d'amour" for one or several ladies.

Le Jardin de Plaisance offers the following paraphrase:

Mon seul plaisir, ma doulce joye,
La maistresse de mon espoir
Jay tel desir de vous veoir
Que dire ne le vous sauroie
Helas, panses que ne pourroye
Nesung bien sans vous recevoir
Mon seul plaisir . . .

Car quant desplaisir me guerroye
Souventes foiz de sa povoir
Et je vueil reconfort avoir
Esperance vers vous menvoye
Mon seul plaisir . . .

1, 7. Chalvet and Champollion-Figeac punctuate these lines without commas.

9. *desplaisir*: Champollion-Figeac, D'Hericault, and Champion capitalize.

10. *Souventesfois*: Guichard and D'Hericault read *Souventeffois*.

   povoir: Champion reads *povair*.

17. JE NE VUEIL PLUS RIENS QUE LA MORT

Manuscripts: O, p. 251; C, fol. 117v; G, fol. 26v; M, fol. 35r; O², fol. 57r; H, fol. 111r; P, fol. 214r; L, fol. 236r.

Major Editions: Chalvet, p. 59; Champollion-Figeac, No. 17, p. 34; Guichard, p. 202; D'Hericault, No. 22, p. 16; Champion, No. 17, pp. 213-214.

Structure: chanson (long)

Meter and rhyme: 8 AABba aabAAB aabbaA

2.   *voy*: Guichard reads *yoy*.

reconfort: Champollion-Figeac, D'Hericault, and Champion all capitalize.

4.   *Au meins*: Champollion-Figeac reads *Aumeins*; Chalvet and Guichard, *Au moins*.

5.   *seuffre*: Chalvet, Champollion-Figeac and D'Hericault read *souffre*.

6.   *d'espoir*: Champollion-Figeac, D'Hericault, and Champion read *d'Espoir*.

7.   *D'amours*: Chalvet, Champollion-Figeac, D'Hericault, and Champion all read *D'Amours*.

l'effort: Champollion-Figeac reads *l'esfort*.

8.   *joye*: Guichard, D'Hericault and Champion capitalize.

12.   *dieu d'amour*: Chalvet, D'Hericault and Champion read *Dieu d'Amour*; Champollion-Figeac, *dieu d'Amours*; Guichard, *dieu d'amours*.

14.   *povair*: Chalvet, Champollion-Figeac, Guichard, and D'Hericault read *povoir*.

16.   *m'y*: Champollion-Figeac reads *m'i*; Chalvet, *mi*.

18.   BELLE QUE JE CHERIS ET CRAINS

Manuscripts: O, p. 252; C, fol. 118r; G, fol. 26v, M, fol. 35r; O², fol. 57v; H, fol. 111v; P, fol. 214r.

Major Editions: Chalvet, p. 60; Champollion-Figeac, No. 18, p. 35; Guichard, p. 203; D'Hericault, No. 24, p. 17; Champion, No. 18, pp. 214-215.

Meter and rhyme: 8 ABba abAB abbaA

Champion notes (vol. 2, p. 565) that this seems to refer to the captivity of Charles d'Orléans.

3.   *dangier*: Champollion-Figeac, D'Hericault, Chalvet, and Champion capitalize.

5.   *N'il*: Chalvet reads *Nil* which he glosses as *rien*, thus changing the sense of the line to "I have nothing, of all the worldly goods, except...."

11.   *lui*: Champollion-Figeac reads *luy*.

19. MA DAME TANT QU'IL VOUS PLAIRA

Manuscripts: O, p. 253; C, fol. 118v; G, fol. 27r, M, fol. 35r; O^2, fol. 57v; H, fol. 112r; P, fol. 217r; L, fol. 238r.

Major Editions: Chalvet, p. 61; Champollion-Figeac, No. 19, p. 35; Guichard, pp. 203-4; D'Hericault, No. 26, p. 18; Champion, No. 19, p. 215.

Meter and rhyme: 8 ABba abAB abbaA

1. *Ma dame*: Chalvet and Champollion-Figeac read *Madame*; D'Hericault and Champion, *Ma Dame*.
9. *prandra*: Chalvet and Champollion-Figeac read *prendra*.
12. Champollion-Figeac punctuates: "Vostre beaute, qu'il servira".

20. DE LA REGARDER VOUS GARDEZ

Manuscripts: O, p. 254; C, fol. 119r; G, fol. 27r; M, fol. 35r; O^2, fol. 57v; H, fol. 112v; L, fol. 228r.

Major Editions: Chalvet, p. 62, Champollion-Figeac, No. 20, p. 36; Guichard, pp. 204-5; D'Hericault, No. 28, p. 19; Champion, No. 20, pp. 215-216.

Meter and rhyme: 8 ABba abAB abbaA

3. *perdrés*: Chalvet and Champollion-Figeac read *perdrez*.
5. *lui voulés*: Chalvet and Champollion-Figeac read *luy voulez*; Guichard reads *voulez*.
The sense here is that he doesn't have the power to alter his situation since sorrow has control over him. Here *maistresse* (line 6) includes the connotation of *maître*: sorrow is a female task-master.
11. Champollion-Figeac, Guichard, and D'Hericault punctuate as follows: "Sur ce, prenez avisement."
12. *vendrés*: Chalvet and Guichard read *vendrez*.

21. PUIS QUE JE NE PUIS ESCHAPPER

Manuscripts: O, p. 255; C, fol. 119r; G, fol. 27v; M, fol. 35v; O^2, fol. 58r; H, fol. 113r; P, fol. 217r; L, fol. 228r.

Major Editions: Chalvet, p. 63; Champollion-Figeac, No. 21, p. 36; Guichard, p. 205; D'Hericault, No. 30, p. 20; Champion, No. 21, p. 216.

Meter and rhyme: 8 ABba abAB abbaA

1. *Puis que*: Chalvet, Champollion-Figeac and Guichard read as one word.
2. D'Hericault and Champion capitalize *courrous*, *dueil* and *tristesse*.
3. *couvient*: Chalvet, Champollion-Figeac and D'Hericault read *convient*.
4. *vouldrés*: Chalvet, and Champollion-Figeac read *vouldrez*.
6. *doleur*: Champollion-Figeac, D'Hericault, and Champion all capitalize.
9. *penser*: D'Hericault and Champion capitalize.
10. *vuit*: Chalvet and Champollion-Figeac read *vuid*.
11. *prangne*: D'Hericault reads *prengne*; Chalvet glosses as *souffre*.
12. *lui*: Champollion-Figeac reads *luy*.

22. C'EST FAIT IL N'EN FAULT PLUS PARLER

Manuscripts: O, p. 256; C, fol. 119v; G, fol. 27v; M, fol. 35v; O², fol. 58v; H, fol. 113v; P, fol. 218r; L, fol. 228v.

Major Editions: Chalvet, p. 64; Champollion-Figeac, No. 22, p. 37; Guichard, p. 206; D'Hericault, No. 32, p. 21; Champion, No. 22, p. 217.

Meter and rhyme: 8 ABba abAB abbaA

12. *peine*: D'Hericault reads *paine*.

23. PUIS QU'AMOUR VEULT QUE BANNY SOYE

Manuscripts: O, p. 257; C, fol. 120r; G, fol. 28r; M, fol. 35v; O², fol. 58v; H, fol. 113v; P, fol. 218r; L, fol. 227r.

Major Editions: Chalvet, p. 65; Champollion-Figeac, Rondel No. 1, p. 37; Guichard, p. 207; D'Hericault, Rondeau No. 1, p. 77; Champion, No. 23, pp. 217-218.

Meter and rhyme: 8 ABba abAB abbaA

1. *Puis qu'*: Chalvet and Champollion-Figeac read *Puisqu'*.
amour: Chalvet, Champollion-Figeac, Guichard, D'Hericault, and Champion capitalize.
3. *bien*: Chalvet reads *byen*.
Chalvet and Champollion-Figeac read: "Je voy bien qu'il me fault partir." By omitting the partitive *en* the line is better able to pivot between the two disparate metaphors of the strophe.

4. *joye*: Champollion-Figeac, Guichard, D'Hericault, and Champion capitalize.

6. *mois*: Chalvet and Champollion-Figeac read *moys*.

7-8. Champion prints: "Puis qu'Amour [veult que banny soye] De son hostel, [sans revenir,]"

9. *confort*: Champollion-Figeac and D'Hericault capitalize.

11. *doulx plaisir*: Chalvet punctuates: "... de doulx plaisir?"

D'Hericault and Champion read *Doulx Plaisir*, Champollion-Figeac, *Doulx-plaisir*, Guichard, *Doulx plaisir*.

12. *desespoir*: Champollion-Figeac, D'Hericault, and Champion capitalize.

Champollion-Figeac punctuates: "Par Desespoir, qui me guerroye". Unlikely for Hopelessness to be the agent of healing.

24. POUR LE DON QUE M'AVEZ DONNE

Manuscripts: O, p. 258; C, fol. 120r; G, fol. 28r; M, fol. 35v; O², fol. 58v; H, fol. 114r; P, fol. 219r; L, fol. 227v.

Major Editions: Chalvet, p. 66; Champollion-Figeac, Rondel 2, p. 38; Guichard, p. 208; D'Hericault, Rondeau 2, pp. 77-78; Champion, No. 24, p. 218.

Meter and rhyme: 8 ABba abAB abbaA

Both EETS and Champion suggest this was written to thank the d'Armagnacs for helping Charles d'Orléans.

1. D'Hericault reads: "... que vous m'avez donné" which is supported by neither the other editions nor by the meter.

2. *tresgrant*: Champollion-Figeac reads *tres grant* (two words); Chalvet hyphenates.

6. *plaisir*: Champollion-Figeac capitalizes.

12. Champollion-Figeac and Guichard punctuate: "Vers vous, et se soit raençonné."

25. SE J'EUSSE MA PART DE TOUS BIENS

Manuscripts: O, p. 259; C, fol. 120r; G, fol. 28v; M, fol. 35v; O², fol. 58v; H, fol. 114v; P, fol. 219r; L, fol. 229r.

Major Editions: Chalvet, p. 67; Champollion-Figeac, No. 23, p. 38; Guichard, pp. 208-9; D'Hericault, No. 36, p. 23; Champion, No. 25, pp. 218-219.

Meter and rhyme: 8 ABba abAB abbaA

The reading of this poem depends in part on seeing two
of its rhyme words, *planté* (line 3) and *renté* (line 11) as
working on two different levels. While the literal reading
is, as EETS has suggested, economic, with *planté* meaning
"plenty" and *renté* "rented", the two also both have organic
connotations: *planté* can mean "plantation" and *renté, enter
de nouveau* or "grafted again."

    2. *loyauté*: Chalvet and Guichard write *loyaulté*.
    5. D'Hericault glosses this line as "Je mettrais parmi
les biens."
    6. *Ma dame*: Chalvet and Champollion-Figeac write *Madame*;
Guichard, D'Hericault and Champion, *Ma Dame*.
    10. *beauté*: Chalvet and Champollion-Figeac write *beaulté*.
    11. Chalvet writes "De l'Amour" in place of "De s'amour"
thus personifying love and making him the agent not the attri-
bute of beauty.
    12. *dangier*: champollion-Figeac, Guichard, D'Hericault,
and Champion all capitalize.

26. POUR LES GRANS BIENS DE VOSTRE RENOMMEE

Manuscripts: O, p. 260; C, fol. 121r; G, fol. 28v; M,
fol. 35v; O², fol. 59r; H, fol. 115r; P, fol. 220r; L, fol.
229r.
    Major Editions: Chalvet, p. 68; Champollion-Figeac, No.
24, p. 39; Guichard, pp. 209-10; D'Hericault, No. 37, pp. 23-
24; Champion, No. 26, p. 219.
    Meter and rhyme: 10 ABba abAB abbaA

    3. *aiez*: Guichard and D'Hericault write *ayez*.
    4. *tresloyaument*: Chalvet and Champollion-Figeac write
tres loyaument.
    9. Guichard adds a comma after *plaist*.
    10. *Du mien*: Champollion-Figeac writes *De mien*.
        melleur: Chalvet and Champollion-Figeac read
meillieur; D'Hericault, *meilleur*.
    12. *pensee*: See above, 9.4.

27. EN SONGE SOUHAID ET PENSEE

Manuscripts: O, p. 261; C, fol. 121v; G, fol. 66r; M,
fol. 36r; O², fol. 59r; H, fol. 115v; P, fol. 220r; L, fol.
229v.

Major Editions: Chalvet, omitted; Champollion-Figeac, No. 68, p. 113; Guichard, p. 210; D'Hericault, No. 39, p. 26; Champion, No. 27, p. 220.

Meter and rhyme: 8 ABba abAB abbaA

2. D'Hericault punctuates: "Vous voy, chascun jour de sepmaine".

4. D'Hericault omits the commas, thus retaining the adjectival force of *belle*.

5. *Pource*: Champollion-Figeac, Guichard, and Champion read *pour ce*.

   mieulx: Champollion-Figeac reads *myeulx*.

6. *plaisance mondaine*: Champollion-Figeac reads *Plaisance-mondaine*.

11. *dame*: Guichard and D'Hericault capitalize.

28.   DE LEAL CUEUR CONTENT DE JOYE

Manuscripts: O, p. 262; C, fol. 121v; G, fol. 66r; M, fol. 36r; O², fol. 59v; H, fol. 116r; P, fol. 221r; L, fol. 229v.

Major Editions: Chalvet, omitted; Champollion-Figeac, No. 49, pp. 113-114; Guichard, p. 211; D'Hericault, No. 40, p. 26; Champion, No. 28, pp. 220-221.

Meter and rhyme: 8 ABba abAB abbaA

10. Guichard adds comma after *honneur*.

29.   SE MON PROPOS VIENT A CONTRAIRE

Manuscripts: O, p. 263; C, fol. 122r; G, fol. 29r; M, fol. 36r; O², fol. 59v; H, fol. 116v; P, fol. 221r; L, fol. 229v.

Major Editions: Chalvet, p. 69; Champollion-Figeac, Rondel 3, p. 39; Guichard, p. 212; D'Hericault, Rondeau 3, p. 78; Champion, No. 29, p. 221.

Meter and rhyme: 8 ABba abAB abbaA

10. *sui*: Chalvet and Guichard read *suy*.

   soussy: Guichard and D'Hericault read *soucy*.

30.   PAR LE POURCHAS DU REGARD DE MES YEULX

Manuscripts: O, p. 264; G, fol. 29r; M, fol. 36r; O², fol. 59v; H, fol. 117r; P, fol. 187r; L, fol. 230r.

Major Editions: Chalvet, p. 70; Champollion-Figeac, Rondel 4, p. 40; Guichard, p. 213; D'Hericault, Rondeau 4, pp. 78-79; Champion, No. 30, pp. 221-222.

Meter and rhyme: 10 ABba abAB abbaA

Le Jardin de Plaisance (JdP) offers several interesting variations:

1. *JdP*: "Pour le pourchas."

2. *tresbelle*: Chalvet and Champollion-Figeac read *tres belle*.

4. *ennuieux*: Chalvet, Champollion-Figeac and *JdP* read *envieux* while Guichard and D'Hericault read *ennuyeux*. Both are possible given the ambivalence expressed in the preceding line; his eyes have allowed him to have pleasure and pain which could give him either cares to be pitied or envied.

5. *cellui*: Champollion-Figeac reads *celluy*; Chalvet, *celuy*.

10. *destresse*: D'Hericault capitalizes. *JdP* reads "... de fievre de destresse."

11. *bon espoir*: D'Hericault and Champion read *Bon Espoir*, Champollion-Figeac, *Bon-espoir*.

       guery: Chalvet and Champollion-Figeac read *gueri*. D'Hericault glosses this line "à l'aide de liesse."

31. POUR VOUS MOUSTRER QUE POINT NE VOUS OUBLIE

Manuscripts: O, p. 265; G, fol. 66v; M, fol. 36r; O^2, fol. 60r; H, fol. 117r; P, fol. 222r; L, fol. 230r.

Major Editions: Chalvet, omitted; Champollion-Figeac, No. 50, p. 114; Guichard, p. 214; D'Hericault, No. 44, p. 28; Champion, No. 31, p. 222.

Meter and rhyme: 10 ABba abAB abbaA

1. *oublie*: Champollion-Figeac reads *oublye*.

2. D'Hericault punctuates "Comme vostre, que suis ou que je soye,"; Guichard reads *ou* as "where."

4. *prenés*: Champollion-Figeac and D'Hericault read *prenez*.

6. *ainsi*: Champollion-Figeac reads *ainsy*.

11. *a briefz motz*: Guichard reads *en briefz motz*.

32. LOINGTAIN DE JOYEUSE SENTE

Manuscripts: O, p. 266; C, fol. 122v; G, fol. 29v; M, fol. 36r; O^2, fol. 60r; H, fol. 117v; P, fol. 222r; L, fol. 230v.

Major Editions: Chalvet, p. 71; Champollion-Figeac, No. 25, pp. 40-41; Guichard, pp. 214-15; D'Hericault, No. 46, p. 29; Champion, No. 32, p. 223.
Meter and rhyme: 8 ABba abAB abbaA

Note the simplicity of rhyme here: all A rhymes end with the morpheme -*sente*, all B rhymes with -*voir*, suggesting that the meaning of the poem turns around feeling and seeing.

4. MS O reads *sente*; editors are divided on how to read this. Chalvet and Champollion-Figeac read *sente* ("feel") while Guichard, D'Hericault and Chalvet read *s'ente* ("graft"). The latter seems more probable if only for reasons of interest and variation.
5. *Par quoy*: Chalvet and Champollion-Figeac read *Parquoy*.
   couvient: Chalvet and Champollion-Figeac read *convient*.

33. DEDENS MON SEIN PRES DE MON CUEUR

Manuscripts: O, p. 273; C, fol. 123v; G, fol. 24v; M, fol. 36r; O^2, fol. 61v; H, fol. 120r; P, fol. 208r; L, fol. 231r.
Major Editions: Chalvet, p. 72; Champollion-Figeac, No. 26, p. 41; Guichard, pp. 220-21; D'Hericault, No. 59, p. 36; Champion, No. 33, pp. 223-4.
Meter and rhyme: 8 ABba abAB abbaA

3. *dangier*: Champollion-Figeac, Guichard, D'Hericault, and Champion all capitalize.
9. *ma dame*: Chalvet and Champollion-Figeac read *Madame*; Guichard, D'Hericault and Champion, *Ma Dame*.

34. DE VOSTRE BEAUTE REGARDER

Manuscripts: O, p. 274; C, fol. 124r; G, fol. 30r; M, fol. 36v; O^2, fol. 62r; H, fol. 120r; P, fol. 188r.
Major Editions: Chalvet, p. 73; Champollion-Figeac, Rondel 5, pp. 41-42; Guichard, pp. 221-2; D'Hericault, Rondeau 6, pp. 79-80; Champion, No. 34, p. 224.
Meter and rhyme: 8 ABba abAB abbaA

4. *sauriés*: Chalvet, Champollion-Figeac and Guichard read *sauriez*.
10. *sus*: Chalvet reads *sur*; meaning is here the same.

35.   PRENEZ TOST CE BAISIER MON CUEUR

Manuscripts: O, p. 271; C, fol. 124v; G, fol. 30r; M, fol. 36v; O², fol. 61r; H, fol. 119r; P, fol. 207r; L, fol. 231v.

Major Editions: Chalvet, p. 74; Champollion-Figeac, Rondel 6, p. 42; Guichard, p. 219; D'Hericault, Rondeau 5, p. 79; Champion, No. 35, pp. 224-5.

Meter and rhyme: 8 ABba abAB abbaA

4.   *tresgrant*: Champollion-Figeac reads *très grant*, Chalvet *très-grant*.

6.   *Afin*: D'Hericault reads *Affin*.

9.   Guichard's and D'Hericault's punctuation omits commas, thus changing sense to "all night he has kept the watch, at work" rather than "all night he has labored at keeping the watch."

10.   D'Hericault reads "A fait guet, or gist en sa tente;"

12.   *Tantdis*: Chalvet and Champollion-Figeac read *Tandis*.
D'Hericault omits line altogether, no doubt an over-sight.

36.   COMMENT VOUS PUIS JE TANT AMER

Manuscripts: O, p. 272; C, fol. 125r; G, fol. 30v; M, fol. 36v; O², fol. 61v; H, fol. 119v; P, fol. 223r; L, fol. 231r.

Major Editions: Chalvet, p. 75; Champollion-Figeac, No. 27, pp. 42-43; Guichard, p. 220; D'Hericault, No. 57, p. 35; Champion, No. 36, p. 225.

Meter and rhyme: 8 ABba abAB abbaA

2.   *haïr*: Chalvet and Champollion-Figeac read *hayr*.

11.   *pour tant*: Chalvet, Champollion-Figeac and Guichard read *pourtant*.

37.   JE NE PRISE POINT TELZ BAISIERS

Manuscripts: O, p. 267; C, fol. 125r; G, fol. 30v; M, fol. 36v; O², fol. 60v; H, fol. 117v; P, fol. 203r; L, fol. 232r.

Major Editions: Chalvet, p. 76; Champollion-Figeac, No. 28, p. 43; Guichard, p. 215; D'Hericault, No. 48, p. 30; Champion, No. 37, pp. 225-226.

Meter and rhyme: 8 ABba abAB abbaA

6. *habondance*: Chalvet and Champollion-Figeac read *abondance*.

12. Chalvet glosses *festier* as *accueillir*.

38. MA SEULE AMOUR MA JOYE ET MA MAISTRESSE

Manuscripts: O, p. 268; C, fol. 125v; G, fol. 66v; M, fol. 36v; O^2, fol. 60v; H, fol. 118r; P, fol. 223r; L, fol. 232r.

Major Editions: Chalvet, omitted; Champollion-Figeac, No. 51, p. 114; Guichard, p. 216; D'Hericault, No. 50, p. 31; Champion, No. 38, p. 226.

Meter and rhyme: 10 ABba abAB abbaA

2. *demorer*: Champollion-Figeac, Guichard, and D'Hericault read *demourer*.

5-6. Subjects are hope and memory. They will relieve his distress and thus help to pass the time.

5. *espoir*: Champollion-Figeac, D'Hericault, and Champion capitalize.

6. *couvendra*: Champollion-Figeac reads *convendra*, D'Hericault *couviendra*.

39. SE DESPLAIRE NE VOUS DOUBTOYE

Manuscripts: O, p. 269; C, fol. 126r; G, fol. 31r; M, fol. 36v; O^2, fol. 60v; H, fol. 118v; P, fol. 203r; L, fol. 236v.

Major Editions: Chalvet, p. 77; Champollion-Figeac, No. 29, pp. 43-44; Guichard, p. 217; D'Hericault, No. 52, p. 32; Champion, No. 39, p. 227.

Structure: chanson (long)

Meter and rhyme: 8 AABba aabAAB aabbaA

1. Chalvet reads "Se vous desplaire" which is better grammatically, worse rhythmically.

3. *un*: Champollion-Figeac reads *ung*.

6. *dangier*: Champollion-Figeac, Guichard, D'Hericault, and Champion capitalize.

15-16. Champollion-Figeac punctuates "Car a mon cueur joyeusement, De par vous, le presenteroye,".

40. MALADE DE MAL ENNUIEUX

Manuscripts: O, p. 270; C, fol. 126v; G, fol. 67r; M, fol. 37r; O², fol. 61r; H, fol. 119r; P, fol. 205r; L, fol. 232v.

Major Editions: Chalvet, omitted; Champollion-Figeac, No. 52, p. 115; Guichard, p. 218; D'Hericault, No. 54, pp. 33-34; Champion, No. 40, pp. 227-228.

Meter and rhyme: 8 ABba abAB abbaA

1. *ennuieux*: Champollion-Figeac reads *ennuyeux*.
5. *saurez*: Champollion-Figeac reads *sçaurez*.
6. *desplaisir*: Champollion-Figeac capitalizes.
9. *peuent*: Champollion-Figeac and D'Hericault read *pevent*.

41. S'IL VOUS PLAIST VENDRE VOZ BAISIERS

Manuscripts: O, p. 279; C, fol. 126v; G, fol. 31r; M, fol. 37r; O², fol. 62v; H, fol. 122v; P, fol. 204r; L, fol. 236v.

Major Editions: Chalvet, p. 78; Champollion-Figeac, No. 30, p. 44; Guichard, pp. 225-6; D'Hericault, No. 69, p. 41; Champion, No. 41, p. 228.

Structure: chanson (long)

Meter and rhyme: 8 AABba aabAAB aabbaA

The metaphor here is that of a bargain, as the English makes clear. Paraphrased, the poem reads: "If you are selling your kisses I would happily buy some, and, in return, you would get my heart to spend as you wished. You would sell your kisses to me at a better rate because of what you're getting in return. My wish and desire are yours if, like the loyal and wise vendor [I know you are] you would reward me by putting me first."

1. Champollion-Figeac reads "Si vous plaist...."
2. *achatteray*: Guichard reads *achecteray*.
3. *aurés*: Chalvet and Champollion-Figeac read *aurez*.
   gage: Guichard reads *gaige*.
4. *feriés*: Chalvet, Champollion-Figeac and Guichard read *feriez*.
9. Chalvet reads *Mon vueil et mon desire entier*, "My wish and my whole desire" rather than "My every wish and desire."
14. *Faittes*: Chalvet, Champollion-Figeac and Guichard read *Faictes*.

15. *partage*: Guichard reads *partaige*.
16. *servy*: Chalvet and Champollion-Figeac read *servi*.

42. MA SEULE AMOUR QUE TANT DESIRE

Manuscripts: O, p. 280; C, fol. 127r; M, fol. 37r; O², fol. 63r; H, fol. 123r; P, fol. 224r; L, fol. 232v.
Major Editions: Chalvet, omitted; Champollion-Figeac, No. 53, pp. 115-116; Guichard, p. 226; D'Hericault, No. 71, p. 42; Champion, No. 42, p. 229.
Meter and rhyme: 8 ABba abAB abbaA

3. Champollion-Figeac omits first comma, thus treating *nompareille* substantively.
10. *espoir*: Champollion-Figeac, Guichard, D'Hericault, and Champion capitalize.
12. *liesse*: Champollion-Figeac writes *lyesse* and inserts a comma following, thus making "mon grief martyre" an address to her.

43. LOGIES MOY ENTRE VOZ BRAS

Manuscripts: O, p. 281; C, fol. 128r; G, fol. 31v; M, fol. 37r; O², fol. 63r; H, fol. 123v; P, fol. 224; L, fol. 233r.
Major Editions: Chalvet, p. 79; Champollion-Figeac, No. 31, p. 45; Guichard, p. 227; D'Hericault, No. 73, pp. 43-44; Champion, No. 43, pp. 229-230.
Meter and rhyme: 8 ABba abAB abbaA

2. *m'envoiez*: Chalvet and D'Hericault read *m'envoyez*.
   baisier: Champollion-Figeac reads *baisiers*, perhaps by analogy with *doulx*.
5. *dangier*: Champollion-Figeac, D'Hericault, and Champion capitalize.
6. *voyez*: Champollion-Figeac reads *voiez*.
9. *Dieu*: Champollion-Figeac reads "Pour Dieu!".
   esveillier: Champollion-Figeac reads *esveillez*.
10. *dangier*: Champollion-Figeac, D'Hericault, and Champion capitalize.
11. Chalvet and Champollion-Figeac read "Jamais ne puist-il s'esveillier" which breaks the rhythm.
12. *Faittes*: Chalvet, Champollion-Figeac and Guichard read *Faictes*.

44.   SE DANGIER ME TOLT LE PARLER

Manuscripts: O, p. 282; C, fol. 128v; G, fol. 31v; M, fol. 37r; O², fol. 63v; H, fol. 123v; P, fol. 225r; L, fol. 237r.

Major Editions: Chalvet, p. 80; Champollion-Figeac, No. 32, p. 45; Guichard, pp. 227-8; D'Hericault, No. 74, p. 44; Champion, No. 44, p. 230.

Structure: chanson (long)

Meter and rhyme: 8 AABba aabAAB aabbaA

1.   *dangier*: Champollion-Figeac, Guichard, D'Hericault, and Champion capitalize.

2.   *amy*: Champollion-Figeac reads *amis*; Guichard adds comma after *amy*.

3.   Chalvet and Champollion-Figeac punctuate as follows: "Par le pourchas des envieux;". This seems hard to justify, if *Se* introduces an "if" clause. If, however, it is read as "and so" then such punctuation is possible. See below, line 4.

4.   Chalvet and Champollion-Figeac read "Nien plus qu'on ...." which Chalvet glosses as "quand même": 'Even if he would touch the skies, I would not be kept from loving you.' Perhaps the allusion here is to Rumor in Book Four of Vergil's *Aeneid* who shrinks and grows at will.

14.   *tresgracieux*: Champollion-Figeac reads *tres gracieux*.

16.   *Pour tant*: Chalvet and Guichard read *Pourtant*.

45.   VA TOST MON AMOUREUX DESIR

Manuscripts: O, p. 277; C, fol. 129r; G, fol. 32r; M, fol. 37r; O², fol. 62v; H, fol. 121v; P, fol. 225r; L, fol. 237r.

Major Editions: Chalvet, p. 81; Champollion-Figeac, No. 33, p. 46; Guichard, pp. 223-4; D'Hericault, No. 65, p. 39; Champion, No. 45, pp. 230-231.

Structure: chanson (long)

Meter and rhyme: 8 AABba aabAAB aabbaA

1.   Chalvet and Champollion-Figeac omit comma after *tost*.

3.   *joye*: Guichard, D'Hericault and Champion capitalize.

5.   *doulx souvenir*: Champollion-Figeac reads *Doulx-souvenir*; Guichard *doulx souvenir*; D'Hericault and Champion, *Doulx Souvenir*.

7.   *message*: Chalvet and Guichard read *messaige*.
acomplir: Guichard and D'Hericault read *accomplir*.

12. *plaisir*: Champollion-Figeac, Guichard, D'Hericault, and Champion capitalize.

 Recommandes: Champollion-Figeac reads *Recommande*; Chalvet reads *Recommende-moy*.

13. *peuz*: Chalvet and Champollion-Figeac read *peux*.

15. *bon espoir*: Chalvet reads *bon Espoir*; Champollion-Figeac, *Bon-espoir*; Guichard *Bon espoir*; D'Hericault and Champion *Bon Espoir*.

46. JE ME METZ EN VOSTRE MERCY

Manuscripts: O, p. 278; C, fol. 129r; G, fol. 32r; M, fol. 37v; O^2, fol. 62v; H, fol. 122r; P, fol. 225r; L, fol. 233r.

Major Editions: Chalvet, p. 82; Champollion-Figeac, No. 34, p. 46; Guichard, p. 224; D'Hericault, No. 67, p. 40; Champion, No. 46, pp. 231-2.

Meter and rhyme: 8 ABba abAB abbaA

2. *Tresbelle*: Champollion-Figeac reads *Très belle*; Chalvet, *Très-belle*.

4. Champollion-Figeac punctuates "De moy:..."

9. *Pource*: Chalvet, Champollion-Figeac and Guichard read *Pour ce*.

47. TROP ESTES VERS MOY ENDEBTEE

Manuscripts: O, p. 275; C, fol. 130r; G, fol. 32v; M, fol. 37v; O^2, fol. 62r; H, fol. 121r; P, fol. 204r; L, fol. 233v.

Major Editions: Chalvet, p. 83; Champollion-Figeac No. 35, p. 47; Guichard, p. 222; D'Hericault, No. 62, pp. 37-38; Champion, No. 47, p. 232.

Meter and rhyme: 8 ABba abAB abbaA

2. *devés*: Chalvet and Champollion-Figeac read *devez*.

4. *fust*: Champollion-Figeac reads *feust*.

5. *Quoy que*: Champollion-Figeac reads *Quoyque*.

6. *faulx dangiers*: Champollion-Figeac reads *Faulx-dangiers*; D'Hericault and Champion, *faulx Dangiers*.

9. *seelee*: Chalvet and Champollion-Figeac read *scellee*.

12. *D'amour*: Champollion-Figeac, D'Hericault, and Champion read *D'Amours*; Chalvet reads *D'Amour*.

48. VOSTRE BOUCHE DIT BAISIEZ MOY

Manuscripts: O, p. 276; C, fol. 130v; G, fol. 32v; M, fol. 37v; O², fol. 62r; H, fol. 121v; P, fol. 207r; L, fol. 233v.

Major Editions: Chalvet, p. 84; Champollion-Figeac, No. 36, pp. 47-48; Guichard, p. 223; D'Hericault, No. 64, p. 38; Champion, No. 48, pp. 232-233.

Meter and rhyme: 8 ABba abAB abbaA

1. *Baisiez*: Chalvet, D'Hericault and Champion capitalize.
2. Champollion-Figeac inserts comma between *avis* and *quant*, thus changing the sense to "Your mouth says 'kiss me,' (or so I think) when I see it."
3. *dangier*: Champollion-Figeac, D'Hericault, and Champion capitalize.
6. *un*: Guichard reads *ung*.
   sans: Champollion-Figeac omits comma before *sans*.
9. Guichard punctuates as question.
10. *destourbier*: Guichard, D'Hericault and Champion capitalize; Chalvet reads *d'estourbier* and glosses line as "And I'm constantly overwhelmed with trouble."
12. *fust*: Chalvet and Champollion-Figeac read *feust*.

49. JE NE LES PRISE PAS DEUX BLANS

Manuscripts: O, p. 289; C, fol. 131v; G, fol. 95r; M, fol. 37v; O², fol. 64v; H, fol. 126v; P, fol. 226r; L, fol. 234r.

Major Editions: Chalvet, p. 312; Champollion-Figeac, No. 55, pp. 166-167; Guichard, pp. 232-3; D'Hericault, No. 85, p. 50; Champion, No. 49, p. 233.

Meter and rhyme: 8 ABba abAB abbaA

2-3. Note double entendre of key rhyming words *amer/amer* (love/bitter). This pun was well-known because of its use in Beroul's *Tristan* where a third pun, *la mer* (the sea) was added and the whole complex referred to the moment of infatuation for Tristan and Isolde that was also bitter and occurred at sea. This allusion may explain the otherwise gratuitous reference to the sea in line 6.
6. *Pires*: D'Hericault reads *Pire*.
11. Chalvet and Guichard add a comma after *cueur*.
12. *amourettes*: Champollion-Figeac and Guichard read *amouretes*.
   amourettes tremblans: On the meaning of this phrase, see Michel Thom, "Ce sont amourettes tremblans." Thom proves

conclusively that this phrase refers to *briza media*, (flowers (or herbs) that tremble with the slightest breath) and not, as has been assumed, to *les amours passagères*.

50.   AU BESOING CONGNOIST ON L'AMY

Manuscripts: O, p. 290; C, fol. 136r; G, fol. 33r; M, fol. 37v; O^2, fol. 65r; H, fol. 127r; P, fol. 227r; L, fol. 234r.
Major Editions: Chalvet, p. 85; Champollion-Figeac, No. 37, p. 48; Guichard, pp. 233-4; D'Hericault, No. 87, p. 51; Champion, No. 50, pp. 233-234.
Meter and rhyme: 8 ABba abAB abbaA

Addressed to a man.   Champion claims this was written for Philippe le Bon while the English, by contrast, was written to a woman.

3.   Champollion-Figeac inserts comma after *vous*, suggesting that what follows is merely parenthetical.
5.   Chalvet reads "Mais avez, en vostre mercy," which makes a lot of sense, as it changes the phrase from merely referring to the addressee of the poem to explaining in a fuller manner why he is getting this poem.
6.   Champollion-Figeac inserts a comma after *fait*; Chalvet reads: "doit bien souffire," which makes sense but does not fit as well metrically.
9.   Chalvet and Champollion-Figeac insert a comma after *brief*.
10.   *de tire*: Chalvet reads *desire*; hard to justify.

51.   FUYES LE TRAIT DE DOULX REGARD

Manuscripts: O, p. 287; C, fol. 18r; G, fol. 33v; M, fol. 37v; O^2, fol. 64r; H, fol. 116r; P, fol. 188r; L, fol. 234v.
Major Editions: Chalvet, p. 87; Champollion-Figeac, No. 39, p. 49; Guichard, p. 231; D'Hericault, No. 81, p. 48; Champion, No. 51, p. 234.
Meter and rhyme: 8 ABba abAB abbaA

1.   *doulx regard*: Champollion-Figeac reads *Doulx-regard*.
5.   Guichard punctuates: "Vous serés pris ou tost, ou tard,".
6.   *amour*: Champollion-Figeac, D'Hericault, Champion capitalize.

9. *estandart*: Champollion-Figeac reads *estendart*.

10. *nonchaloir*: Champollion-Figeac, D'Hericault, and Champion capitalize.

attendre: Champollion-Figeac and Guichard read *actendre*.

11. *plaisance*: D'Hericault and Champion capitalize.

52. MON SEUL AMY MON BIEN MA JOYE

Manuscripts: O, p. 288; C, fol. 20r; G, fol. 33r; M, fol. 37v; O², fol. 64v; H, fol. 126r; P, fol. 227r; L, fol. 234v.

Major Editions: Chalvet, p. 86; Champollion-Figeac, No. 38, p. 49; Guichard, p. 232; D'Hericault, No. 83, p. 49; Champion, No. 52, p. 235.

Meter and rhyme: 8 ABba abAB abbaA

2. *Cellui*: Champollion-Figeac reads *Celluy*.

3. *joieux*: Guichard reads *joyeux*.

5. *que querir*: Champion reads *quequerir*.

9. *souhaidier*: Chalvet and Champollion-Figeac read *souhaitier*.

11. *quanqu'il*: Champollion-Figeac reads *quant qu'il*.

12. *Autre*: D'Hericault reads *Outre*.

souhaideroye: Chalvet and Champollion-Figeac read *souhaiteroye*.

53. FAULT IL AVEUGLE DEVENIR

Manuscripts: O, p. 283; G, fol. 33v; M, fol. 37v; O², fol. 63v; H, fol. 124r; P, fol. 189r.

Major Editions: Chalvet, p. 88; Champollion-Figeac, No. 40, p. 50; Guichard, p. 228; D'Hericault, No. 75, pp. 44-45; Champion, No. 53, pp. 235-236.

Structure: chanson (long)

Meter and rhyme: 8 AABba aabAAB aabbaA

2. *yeulz*: Chalvet, Champollion-Figeac and D'Hericault read *yeulx*.

8. *dangier*: Champollion-Figeac, D'Hericault, Guichard and Champion capitalize.

12. Chalvet and Champollion-Figeac read: "Les yeulx sont fais pour servir" which lacks a foot.

14. *cuers*: Chalvet and Champollion-Figeac read *cueurs*.

15. *dangier*: Champollion-Figeac, D'Hericault, Guichard and Champion capitalize.

tire: Chalvet glosses as *s'occupe*.

15-16. Champollion-Figeac punctuates: "A les engarder;
Dangier tire, En ce bien fait de le souffrir."

54. REGARDEZ MOY SA CONTENANCE

Manuscripts: O, p. 284; G, fol. 34r; M, fol. 37v; O^2,
fol. 63v; H, fol. 124v; P, fol. 189r.
Major Editions: Chalvet, p. 89; Champollion-Figeac, No.
41, pp. 50-51; Guichard, p. 229; D'Hericault, No. 76, p. 45;
Champion, No. 54, p. 236.
Meter and rhyme: 8 ABba abAB abbaA

2. *bien*: Chalvet and Champollion-Figeac read *byen*.
5. *parfaictes*: D'Hericault reads *parfaittes*.
9. *m'avence*: D'Hericault reads *m'avance*.
11. *voulue*: Guichard reads *voulu*.
12. *fais*: Champollion-Figeac, Guichard, and D'Hericault
read *faiz*.
     demoustrance: Chalvet, Champollion-Figeac, Guichard,
and D'Hericault read *demonstrance*.

55. REPRENEZ CE LARRON SOUSPIR

Manuscripts: O, p. 285; G, fol. 34r; M, fol. 38r; O^2,
fol. 64r; H, fol. 125r; P, fol. 205r.
Major Editions: Chalvet, p. 90; Champollion-Figeac, No.
42, p. 51; Guichard, p. 230; D'Hericault, No. 79, p. 47;
Champion, No. 55, pp. 236-237.
Meter and rhyme: 8 ABba abAB abbaA

3. Chalvet and Guichard add a comma after *congié*.
4. *desir*: Champollion-Figeac, Guichard, D'Hericault and
Champion capitalize.
11. *peust*: Champollion-Figeac reads *peut*.
12. *pour ce*: Champollion-Figeac reads *pource*.

56. ET EUSSIEZ VOUS DANGIER CENT YEULX

Manuscripts: O, p. 286; G, fol. 34v; M, fol. 38r; O^2,
fol. 111v; H, fol. 125v; P, fol. 190r.
Major Editions: Chalvet, p. 91; Champollion-Figeac, No.
43, pp. 51-52; Guichard, p. 421; D'Hericault, No. 126, p. 72;
Champion, No. 56, p. 237.
Meter and rhyme: 8 ABba abAB abbaA

1. *dangier*: Champollion-Figeac, D'Hericault, Guichard and Champion capitalize.

2. *derriere*: Champollion-Figeac reads *derreriere*. Guichard adds commas after *Assis* and *derriere*.

3. *prez*: Chalvet and Champollion-Figeac read *pres*.

9. *fais*: D'Hericault reads *faiz*.

telz: Champollion-Figeac reads *tieulx*; Guichard and D'Hericault *tieux*.

10. *assoubtivant*: Chalvet reads *assoubeinant*, glossed as "furtively."

12. *Dieux*: Champollion-Figeac reads "ce m'aist Dieux"; Chalvet reads "se maist Dieux," glossed as "s'il plait à Dieu."

57. D'ONC VIENT CE SOLEIL DE PLAISANCE

Manuscripts: O, p. 295; G, fol. 34v; M, fol. 38r; O², fol. 66r; H, fol. 129v; P, fol. 190r.

Major Editions: Chalvet, p. 92; Champollion-Figeac, No. 44, p. 52; Guichard, pp. 237-8; D'Hericault, No. 96, p. 56; Champion, No. 57, p. 238.

Meter and rhyme: 8 ABba abAB abbaA

1. *D'onc*: Champollion-Figeac and D'Hericault read *D'ont*; Guichard reads *Dont*.

soleil: D'Hericault reads *souleil*.

plaisance: D'Hericault and Champion capitalize.

2. *yeulz*: Chalvet and Champollion-Figeac read *yeulx*.

3. *douceur*: Champollion-Figeac, D'Hericault, and Champion capitalize.

4. *abondance*: Guichard and D'Hericault read *habondance*.

11. *Dieux*: Champollion-Figeac reads "ce maist dieulx"; Chalvet reads "se maist Dieux."

58. LAISSEZ MOY PENSER A MON AYSE

Manuscripts: O, p. 296; G, fol. 67v; M, fol. 38r; O², fol. 66r; H, fol. 130r; P, fol. 228r.

Major Editions: Chalvet, omitted; Champollion-Figeac, No. 54, p. 116; Guichard, pp. 238-9; D'Hericault, No. 97, p. 57; Champion, No. 58, pp. 238-9.

Meter and rhyme: 8 ABba abAB abbaA

1. *Laissez*: Champollion-Figeac reads *Laissiez*.

ayse: Champollion-Figeac reads *aise*.

3. *plaisir*: Guichard, D'Hericault, and Champion capitalize.

4. *tayse*: Champollion-Figeac and D'Hericault read *taise*.

5. *merencolie*: Champollion-Figeac, D'Hericault, and Champion capitalize.

9. *affin*: Champollion-Figeac reads *afin*.

   cuer: D'Hericault reads *cueur*.

10. *plaisant souvenir*: Champollion-Figeac reads *Plaisant-souvenir*; D'Hericault and Champion, *Plaisant Souvenir*.

59. LEVEZ CES CUEVRECHIEFS PLUS HAULT

Manuscripts: O, p. 297; G, fol. 35r; M, fol. 38v; O², fol. 66v; H, fol. 130v; P, fol. 228r.

Major Editions: Chalvet, p. 93; Champollion-Figeac, No. 45, pp. 52-53; Guichard, p. 239; D'Hericault, No. 99, p. 58; Champion, No. 59, p. 239.

Meter and rhyme: 8 ABba abAB abbaA

1. Chalvet glosses *cuevrechiefs* as *bonnets*.

2. *visages*: Champollion-Figeac reads *visage*; Chalvet, *visaiges*.

3. *umbrages*: Champollion-Figeac and Guichard read *umbraiges*; Chalvet, *ombraiges*.

4. Chalvet and Guichard add a comma after *hale*.

5. *beaulté*: D'Hericault and Champion capitalize.

   Champollion-Figeac reads "En fait a beaulté, que tant vault."

6. Guichard adds a comma after *musser*.

9. *dangier*: Champollion-Figeac, Guichard, D'Hericault, and Champion capitalize.

11. *usages*: Chalvet and D'Hericault read *usaiges*.

60. ENTRE LES AMOUREUX FOURREZ

Manuscripts: O, p. 298; G, fol. 95r; M, fol. 38v; O², fol. 66v; H, fol. 130v; P, fol. 229r.

Major Editions: Chalvet, p. 313; Champollion-Figeac, No. 56, p. 167; Guichard, p. 240; D'Hericault, No. 101, p. 59; Champion, No. 60, pp. 239-240.

Structure: chanson (long)

Meter and rhyme: 8 AABba aabAAB aabbaA

2. Chalvet glosses *decoppez* as *indigents*.

6. *amours*: Champollion-Figeac, Guichard, D'Hericault, and Champion capitalize; Chalvet reads *Amour*.

211

7. Chalvet reads "Pourdieu de moy ne vous...."
    moquez: D'Hericault reads *mocquez*.
11. *suys*: Chalvet and Champion read *suis*.
12. *amours*: Champollion-Figeac, Guichard, D'Hericault, and Champion capitalize; Chalvet reads *Amour*.
16. *sui*: Champollion-Figeac reads *suy*; Chalvet and D'Hericault, *suis*.

61. DIEU VOUS CONDUIE DOUBZ PENSER

Manuscripts: O, p. 293; G, fol. 35r; M, fol. 38v; O², fol. 65v; H, fol. 128v; P, fol. 229r.
Major Editions: Chalvet, p. 94; Champollion-Figeac, No. 46, p. 53; Guichard, p. 236; D'Hericault, No. 92, p. 54; Champion, No. 61, p. 240.
Meter and rhyme: 8 ABba abAB abbaA

1. *doubz penser*: Champollion-Figeac reads *Doulx-penser*; Guichard, *Doulx penser*; D'Hericault, *Doulx Penser*; Champion, *Doubz Penser*.
4. *cuer*: Chalvet, Champollion-Figeac, Guichard, and D'Hericault read *cueur*.
5. *vueillez*: Champollion-Figeac reads *vueilliez*.
6. *Exploictez*: Chalvet, Champollion-Figeac, and D'Hericault read *Exploittez*.
    saige: Guichard reads *sage*.
10. *couraige*: Guichard reads *courage*.

62. LES FOURRIERS D'AMOURS M'ONT LOGE

Manuscripts: O, p. 294; G, fol. 35v; M, fol. 38v; O², fol. 65v; H, fol. 129r; P, fol. 230r.
Major Editions: Chalvet, p. 95; Champollion-Figeac, No. 47, pp. 53-54; Guichard, p. 237; D'Hericault, No. 94, p. 55; Champion, No. 62, p. 241.
Meter and rhyme: 8 ABba abAB abbaA

1. *amours*: Champollion-Figeac, Guichard, D'Hericault and Champion capitalize.
    m'ont: Champollion-Figeac reads *mont*.
2. *un*: Guichard reads *ung*.
10. *esperance*: Champollion-Figeac, Guichard, D'Hericault, and Champion capitalize.
12. D'Hericault reads "Qui soit mieulx que moy hebergé.

63. QUE C'EST ESTRANGE COMPAIGNIE

Manuscripts: O, p. 291; G, fol. 95v; M, fol. 38v; O², fol. 65r; H, fol. 127v; P, fol. 230r.
Major Editions: Chalvet, p. 314; Champollion-Figeac, No. 57, pp. 167-168; Guichard, p. 234; D'Hericault, No. 89, p. 52; Champion, No. 63, pp. 241-242.
Meter and rhyme: 8 ABba abAB abbaA

Like English Chanson XLIX, this chanson is based on the idea of love as a state of contraries.

2. *penser*: All editions capitalize.
   espoir: All editions capitalize.
3. *scevent*: Champollion-Figeac reads *savent*.
   Guichard adds comma after *scevent*.
6. *savoir*: Chalvet and Champollion-Figeac read *sçavoir*.
9. *mye*: Chalvet and Champollion-Figeac read *mie*.
11. *Manty*: Chalvet, Champollion-Figeac, Guichard, and D'Hericault read *menty*.
   m'ont: Guichard adds comma following.
12. *l'aveu*: Chalvet and Champollion-Figeac read *l'aveue*, (which Chalvet then glosses with *j'avoue*) suggesting either a feminine preceding direct object or a construction analogous with *renye*.

64. BEAUTE GARDEZ VOUS DE MEZ YEULX

Manuscripts: O, p. 329; G, fol. 35v; M, fol. 32v; O², fol. 69v; H, fol. 137v; P, fol. 191r.
Major Editions: Chalvet, p. 96; Champollion-Figeac, Rondel 7, p. 54; Guichard, p. 253; D'Hericault, Rondeau 20, p. 90; Champion, No. 64, p. 242.
Meter and rhyme: 8 ABba abAB abbaA

1. *mez*: Chalvet, Champollion-Figeac and D'Hericault read *mes*.
2. *il*: D'Hericault uses alternative form, *ilz*; so in lines 3 and 12.
3. *povoient*: Guichard and Champion read *pouoient*.
4. *mielx*: Chalvet, Champollion-Figeac and D'Hericault read *mieulx*.
5. *lez*: Chalvet and D'Hericault read *les*; so in line 9.
   soubz: Chalvet reads *soubs*.
9. Chalvet and Guichard omit comma after *ay*.

65. BIEN VIENGNE DOULZ REGARD QUI RIT

Manuscripts: O, p. 330; G, fol. 37r; M, fol. 32r; O², fol. 70r; H, fol. 138r; P, fol. 191r.

Major Editions: Chalvet, p. 97; Champollion-Figeac, Rondel 8, pp. 54-55; Guichard, pp. 253-254; D'Hericault, Rondeau 21, pp. 90-91; Champion, No. 65, pp. 242-243.

Meter and rhyme: 8 ABba abAB abbaA

1. *doulz*: Chalvet, Champollion-Figeac and D'Hericault read *doulx*.
3. *dangier*: All editions capitalize.
5. Guichard adds comma after *despit*.
6. *ceulz*: Champollion-Figeac reads *ceulx*.
11. *amour*: All editions capitalize.

66. EN LA PROMESSE D'ESPERANCE

Manuscripts: O, p. 331; G, fol. 95v; M, fol. 32r; O², fol. 70r; H, fol. 138v; P, fol. 243r.

Major Editions: Chalvet, p. 315; Champollion-Figeac, Rondel 29, p. 168; Guichard, pp. 254-5; D'Hericault, Rondeau 22, p. 91; Champion, No. 66, p. 243.

Meter and rhyme: 8 ABba abAB abbaA

1. *esperance*: All editions capitalize.
2. *temps*: D'Hericault reads *tant*.
3. *reffusé*: Champollion-Figeac reads *refusé*.
4. *plaisance*: D'Hericault and Champion capitalize.
9. *nysse*: Chalvet and Champollion-Figeac read *nice*.
   gouvernance: D'Hericault reads *goavernance*.
10. *raison*: Guichard, D'Hericault and Champion capitalize.
11. *cuer*: Champollion-Figeac reads *coeur*.
12. *fiance*: All editions capitalize.
    Champollion-Figeac punctuates: "Disant: que deceu l'a Fiance."

67. MON CUER IL ME FAULT ESTRE MESTRE

Manuscripts: O, p. 332; G, fol. 95v; M, fol. 32r; O², fol. 70v; H, fol. 139r; P, fol. 243r.

Major Editions: Chalvet, p. 316; Champollion-Figeac, Rondel 30, pp. 168-169; Guichard, p. 255; D'Hericault, Rondeau 23, pp. 91-92; Champion, No. 67, pp. 243-244.

Meter and rhyme: 8 ABba abAB abbaA

1. *cuer*: Chalvet, Champollion-Figeac and D'Hericault read *cueur*.

2. *fois*: D'Hericault reads *foiz*.
   aussi: Champollion-Figeac reads *aussy*.

3. *ayés*: Chalvet and Champollion-Figeac read *aiez*; D'Hericault *ayez*.
   anuy: Chalvet, Champollion-Figeac and D'Hericault read *ennuy*; Guichard reads *enuy* and adds comma following.
   courrous: Chalvet and D'Hericault read *courroux*.

5. Chalvet glosses *pestre* as *pâtir*.

6. *tous jours*: Chalvet, Champollion-Figeac and d'Hericault read *tousjours*; Guichard *toujours*.
   tenu: Guichard reads *tenir*.
   dessous: Chalvet and Champollion-Figeac read *dessoubz*; D'Hericault, *dessoue*.

9. *Alez*: D'Hericault reads *Allez*.

10. *recous*: D'Hericault reads *rescous*. Chalvet reads *recoulx* which he glosses as *secouru*.

68. MES YEULZ TROP SONT BIEN RECLAMES

Manuscripts: O, p. 333; M, fol. 32v; O², fol. 70v; H, fol. 139v; P, fol. 192r.
Major Editions: Chalvet, p. 98; Champollion-Figeac, Rondel 9, p. 55; Guichard, p. 256; D'Hericault, Rondeau 24, p. 92; Champion, No. 68, p. 244.
Meter and rhyme: 8 ABba abAB abbaA

1. *reclamés*: Champollion-Figeac reads *reclamez*.

2. *ma dame*: Champollion-Figeac reads *madame*; Guichard, D'Hericault and Champion, *ma Dame*; Chalvet, *Madame*.
   lez: Chalvet, Champollion-Figeac and Guichard read *les*.
   apelle: Chalvet and Champollion-Figeac read *appelle*.

4. *Il*: D'Hericault reads *Ilz*.
   afamés: Champollion-Figeac reads *afamez*.

5. *mesdisans*: Champollion-Figeac capitalizes.
   amés: D'Hericault reads *amez*.

6. *dangier*: Champollion-Figeac, D'Hericault, and Champion capitalize.

9. *diffamés*: Champollion-Figeac and Guichard read *diffamez*.

10. *il*: D'Hericault reads *ilz*.
    Guichard adds comma after *voloyent*.

12. *blasmés*: Champollion-Figeac reads *blasmez*.

69. RETRAIEZ VOUS REGART MAL AVISE

Manuscripts: O, p. 334; M, fol. 32v; O², fol. 70v; H,
fol. 140r; P, fol. 192r.

Major Editions: Chalvet, p. 259; Champollion-Figeac,
Rondel 16, pp. 137-138; Guichard, p. 257; D'Hericault, Rondeau
25, pp. 92-93; Champion, No. 69, pp. 244-245.

Meter and rhyme: 8 ABba abAB abbaA

3. *aguet*: Champollion-Figeac, Guichard, D'Hericault and
Champion capitalize; Chalvet reads *a guet*.
Chalvet glosses "vous convoye" as *desire* ('I want
you to...').

6. *trotter*: Guichard reads *trocter*.
par my: Chalvet and Champollion-Figeac read *parmi*.

10. *sot maintien*: Champollion-Figeac reads *Sot-maintien*;
D'Hericault and Champion: *Sot Maintien*.

70. REGART VOUS PRENEZ TROP DE PAINE

Manuscripts: O, p. 335; M, fol. 32v; O², fol. 71r; H,
fol. 140v; P, fol. 193r.

Major Editions: Chalvet, p. 260; Champollion-Figeac,
Rondel 17, p. 138; Guichard, pp. 257-8; D'Hericault, Rondeau
26, p. 93; Champion, No. 70, p. 245.

Meter and rhyme: 8 ABba abAB abbaA

2. *racourés*: D'Hericault reads *raccourus*.

5. *Cuers*: Chalvet, Guichard and D'Hericault read *Cueurs*.
amours: Champollion-Figeac, Guichard, and Champion
all capitalize; Chalvet and D'Hericault read *Amour*.

9. D'Hericault and Guichard read: "Amours, une fois la
sepmaine"; Champion claims all editors but himself reproduce
this "mauvaise lecture."

71. LE VOULEZ VOUS

Manuscripts: O, p. 336; G, fol. 75v; M, fol. 38v; O²,
fol. 71r; H, fol. 141r; P, fol. 244r.

Major Editions: Chalvet (omitted); Champollion-Figeac,
Rondel 12, p. 133; Guichard, pp. 258-9; D'Hericault, Rondeau
27, pp. 93-94; Champion, No. 71, p. 246.

Meter and rhyme: 4 ABba abAB abbaA

2. Champollion-Figeac punctuates: "Que vostre soye!"

4. *recous*: Chalvet, Champollion-Figeac and Champion read
recours.

6. *l'oye*: D'Hericault reads *loye*.
11. *Or sa*: Champollion-Figeac reads *Or, ça*.

72. CREVEZ MOY LES YEULX

Manuscripts: O, p. 337; G, fol. 75v; M, fol. 38v; O^2, fol. 71v; H, fol. 141v; P, fol. 193r.

Major Editions: Chalvet (omitted); Champollion-Figeac Rondel 3, p. 133; Guichard, p. 259; D'Hericault, No. 28, p. 94; Champion, No. 72, pp. 246-247.

Structure: chanson (anomalous: last B added)
Meter and rhyme: 5 ABba abAB abbaAB

2. *goutte*: Guichard reads *goute*.
3. *redoubte*: D'Hericault reads *redoutte*.
4. *lieulx*: Champollion-Figeac reads *lieux*.
5. *jusqu'aus*: Guichard and D'Hericault read *jusqu'aux*.
9. *Dieulx*: Champollion-Figeac prints "D'elle, me gard dieulx".
11. Guichard reads "N'est-ce pour le mieulx." Good reading.
12. Champollion-Figeac and D'Hericault omit last refrain line; Guichard and D'Hericault insert 72a as fourth strophe, D'Hericault adding a final "Crevez moy les yeulx." There seems no justification for this, as the rhyme words are entirely different. It is true, however, that 72 and 72a are the only two chansons, or fragments, with a five-beat line.

72a. [QUANT JE LA REGARDE]

Manuscripts: O, p. 337; M, fol. 38v; O^2, fol. 71v.

Major Editions: Chalvet (omitted); Champollion-Figeac (omitted); D'Hericault, No. 28, p. 94 (see above, 72.12); Guichard, pp. 259-60 (tacked onto No. 72); Champion, No. 72a, p. 247.

This fragment is considered by some an independent piece, by others a final strophe for 72. See above, 72.12.

217

N.B. From here to end rhyme scheme may be different than noted, for MS O shows no catch word for a second refrain line. Rhyme scheme may therefore be ABba abA abbaA. But, in all likelihood, these chansons are identical to those preceding.

73. JEUNES AMOUREUX NOUVEAULX

Manuscripts: O, p. 338; M, fol. 39r; O², fol. 71v; H, fol. 142r; P, fol. 244r.
Major Editions: Chalvet (omitted); Champollion-Figeac, Rondel 44, p. 261; Guichard, p. 260; D'Hericault, Rondeau 29, pp. 94-5; Champion, No. 73, p. 247.
Meter and rhyme: 8 ABba abAB abbaA

1, 7, 12. *Jeunes*: Champion reads *Jennes*.
4. Champollion-Figeac, Guichard and D'Hericault omit comma after *Chevauchent*.

74. GARDEZ LE TRAIT DE LA FENESTRE

Manuscripts: O, p. 339; G, fol. 79r; M, fol. 39r; O², fol. 72r; H, fol. 142v; P, fol. 194r.
Major Editions: Chalvet, p. 261; Champollion-Figeac, Rondel 18, pp. 138-139; Guichard, p. 261; D'Hericault, Rondeau 30, p. 95; Champion, No. 74, p. 248.
Meter and rhyme: 8 ABba abAB abbaA

Le Jardin de Plaisance offers another chanson with same refrain:

> Guardes le trait de la fenestre
> Belle, gente, amoureuse archiere
> Ne soies pas de moy meurtriere
> Je ne puys que ceste foiz estre
> Ne tire plus a lueil senestre,
> Mon cueur y est, quon ne la fiere,
> Guardes le trait!

> Je ne suys si simple ne dextre
> Se baissie neusse ma visiere
> Que une flesche dure et entiere
> Ne meust fait borgne de lueil dextre.
> Guardes le trait de la fenestre!

2. *ruez*: Chalvet and Guichard read *rues*.
4. Guichard adds comma after *d'arc*.
11. *soyez*: Guichard reads *soiez*.

75. EN GIBESSANT TOUTE L'APRES DISNEE

Manuscripts: O, p. 340; G, fol. 79v; M, fol. 38v; O², fol. 72r; P, fol. 245r.
Major Editions: Chalvet, p. 263; Champollion-Figeac, Rondel 20, pp. 138-139; Guichard, p. 262; D'Hericault, Rondeau 31, pp. 95-96; Champion, No. 75, pp. 248-249.
Meter and rhyme: 10 ABba abAB abbaA

2. *Par my*: Chalvet and Champollion-Figeac read *Parmy*. Guichard adds comma after *champs*.
3. *long temps*: Champollion-Figeac reads *longtems*; Guichard reads *longtemps*.
4. *pensee*: Champion capitalizes.
5. *L'aquilote*: Guichard reads "La quilote;" Chalvet glosses as *chien*.
    souvenance: Champollion-Figeac, D'Hericault and Champion capitalize.
6. Chalvet reads "Ourdoit deduit et sçavoit remerchier."
9. *passe temps*: D'Hericault and Champion capitalize.
11. *esperance celee*: D'Hericault and Champion capitalize; Chalvet reads *espance celee*, presumably a misreading of the abbreviation in the MS.

76. QUE FAUT IL PLUS A UNG CUER AMOUREUX

Manuscripts: O, p. 341; G, fol. 37v; M, fol. 38v; O², fol. 72r; H, fol. 143v; P, fol. 245r.
Major Editions: Chalvet, p. 99; Champollion-Figeac, Rondel 10, p. 56; Guichard, pp. 262-3; D'Hericault, Rondeau 32, p. 96; Champion, No. 76, p. 249.
Meter and rhyme: 10 ABba abAB abbaA

2. *dangier*: All editions capitalize; Guichard adds comma following.
    tristesse: D'Hericault and Champion capitalize.
4. *bon espoir*: Champollion-Figeac reads *Bon-espoir*; D'Hericault and Champion, *Bon Espoir*; Guichard, *Bon espoir*.
5. *desir songneux*: D'Hericault and Champion read *Desir Songneux*; Guichard reads *Desir songneux*.
8. *d'avis avantureux*: D'Hericault and Champion read *d'Avis Avantureux*; Guichard reads *d'Avis avantureux*.

219

9. Guichard adds comma after *canons*.

10. *sagesse*: Guichard, D'Hericault and Champion capitalize.

77. DES MALEUREUX PORTE LE PRIS

Manuscripts: O, p. 342; G, fol. 79r; M, fol. 38v; O², fol. 72v; H, fol. 144r; P, fol. 245r.

Major Editions: Chalvet, p. 262; Champollion-Figeac, Rondel 19, p. 139; Guichard, p. 263; D'Hericault, Rondeau 33, pp. 96-97; Champion, No. 77, pp. 249-250.

Meter and rhyme: 8 ABba abAB abbaA

1. *pris*: Chalvet reads *pri*.

2. *dame*: Chalvet, Guichard, D'Hericault and Champion read *Dame*.

5. Guichard adds comma after *droit*.

10. *donnent*: Chalvet, Champollion-Figeac and D'Hericault read *donnant*.

11. Guichard punctuates with a comma.
    Chalvet reads: "Où a yl".

78. EN AMER N'A QUE MARTIRE

Manuscripts: O, p. 343; G, fol. 96r; M, fol. 40r; O², fol. 72v; H, fol. 144v; P, fol. 246r.

Major Editions: Chalvet, p. 317; Champollion-Figeac, Rondel 31, p. 169; Guichard, p. 264; D'Hericault, Rondeau 34, p. 97; Champion, No. 78, p. 250.

Structure: chanson--anomalous

Meter and rhyme: 8, 8, 3, 7, 8; 8, 8, 3, (8); 8, 8, 3, 7, 8 Aabba aabA aabbaA

2. *Nulluy*: Guichard and D'Hericault read *Nully*.

6. *Pourroient* has three syllables.

7. Guichard adds comma after *larmoyans*.

9. *peut*: Champollion-Figeac reads *puet*.

11. *anoy*: Guichard, D'Hericault, and Champion capitalize.

N.B.: According to Champion, Chansons 79-87 (from here to the end) are in Charles's handwriting in MS O.

79. ME FAULDREZ VOUS A MON BESOING

Manuscripts: O, p. 344; G, fol. 67v; M, fol. 40r; O², fol. 73r; H, fol. 145r; P, fol. 247r.
Major Editions: Chalvet (omitted); Champollion-Figeac, Rondel 11, p. 116; Guichard, p. 265; D'Hericault, Rondeau 35, p. 98; Champion, No. 79, p. 251.
Meter and rhyme: 8 ABba abAB abbaA

1, 3. Guichard punctuates with question mark.
2. *reconfort*: Champollion-Figeac capitalizes.
    fiance: Champollion-Figeac capitalizes.

80. CUEUR ENDORMY EN PENSEE

Manuscripts: O, p. 345; M, fol. 40r; O², fol. 73r; H, fol. 145v; P, fol. 247r.
Major Editions: Chalvet, p. 264; Champollion-Figeac, Rondel 21, p. 140; Guichard, p. 266; D'Hericault, Rondeau 36, p. 98; Champion, No. 80, pp. 251-252.
Meter and rhyme: 8 ABba abAB abbaA

3. Champollion-Figeac reads *L'on*.
6. *pourpos*: Champollion-Figeac reads *porpos*; Chalvet, Guichard and D'Hericault, *propos*.
    tant: Guichard adds comma following.
9. *galimafree*: Chalvet reads *galimassee* which he glosses as "en galimatias."

81. IL VIT EN BONNE ESPERANCE

Manuscripts: O, p. 349; M, fol. 40v; O², fol. 74r; H, fol. 146r; P, fol. 250r.
Major Editions: Chalvet (omitted); Champollion-Figeac, Rondel 49, pp. 272-273; Guichard, p. 268; D'Hericault, Rondeau 39, p. 100; Champion, No. 81, p. 252.
Meter and rhyme: 8 ABba abAB abbaA

3. *a son devis*: Champollion-Figeac, Guichard, and D'Hericault read "a son advis."

82. MON CUEUR PLUS NE VOLERA

Manuscripts: O, p. 354; G, fol. 80r; M, fol. 41v; O², fol. 75r; H, fol. 148r; P, fol. 253r.

Major Editions: Chalvet, p. 265; Champollion-Figeac, Rondel 22, pp. 140-141; Guichard, pp. 272-3; D'Hericault, No. 124, p. 71; Champion, No. 82, pp. 252-253.

Meter and rhyme: 8 ABba abAB abbaA

4. *pieça*: Guichard reads *piaça*.

6. *Cure n'atirer*: Chalvet reads: *Cure ne atirés* which he glosses as "soin ni attirail;" Champollion-Figeac reads *ne a tirer*; Guichard and D'Hericault add a comma after *Cure* and D'Hericault adds: "on peut lire *n'a tirer*; quelques manuscrits donnent *atirée--faulx*."

12. *a venir*: Chalvet and Champollion-Figeac read *advenir;* Guichard and D'Hericault, *avenir*.

83. CHASCUN DIT QU'ESTEZ BONNE ET BELLE

Manuscripts: O, p. 355; M, fol. 41v; O², fol. 75r; H, fol. 148r; P, fol. 254r.

Major Editions: Chalvet, p. 366; Champollion-Figeac, No. 58, p. 193; Guichard, p. 273; D'Hericault, No. 125, p. 71; Champion, No. 83, p. 253.

Meter and rhyme: 8 ABba abAB abbaA

Champollion-Figeac notes that this "rondeau" seems to have been dedicated to the new duchess of Orléans, Marie de Clèves. "Ce prince renvoie à l'année suivante ouir juger si effectivement la duchesse mérite sa reputation."

1. *qu'estez*: Chalvet and Guichard read *qu'estes*.

2. *ne saura*: Chalvet and Champollion-Figeac read *n'en sera*; Guichard reads *n'e saura*.

3. *lignage*: Guichard, D'Hericault and Champion capitalize.

84. ENCORE LUI FAIT IL GRANT BIEN

Manuscripts: O, p. 356; M, fol. 41v; O², fol. 75v; H, fol. 148r; P, fol. 254r.

Major Editions: Chalvet (omitted); Champollion-Figeac, Rondel 55, pp. 277-278; Guichard, p. 274; D'Hericault, Rondeau 47, p. 105; Champion, No. 84, pp. 253-254.

Meter and rhyme: 8 ABba abAB abbaA

4. *tien*: Both Champollion-Figeac and D'Hericault read
sien at the end of the line. Champollion-Figeac has the gar-
bled "Avoit sien elle comme sien."
9. Champollion-Figeac inserts comma following *fait*.

85. AVUGLE ET ASSOURDY

Manuscripts: O, p. 357; M, fol. 42r; O², fol. 75v; H,
fol. 148v; P, fol. 194r.
Major Editions: Chalvet (omitted); Champollion-Figeac,
Rondel 56, pp. 278-279; Guichard, p. 275; D'Hericault, Rondeau
48, p. 106; Champion, No. 85, p. 254.
Meter and rhyme: 7 ABba abAB abbaA

1. D'Hericault inserts comma after *ouir*.
5. *Se*: Champion reads *De*; D'Hericault, *Soit*.
10. *amours*: Champollion-Figeac, D'Hericault, and Champion
capitalize.

Chansons Nos. 86 and 87 are very clever, for Charles
d'Orléans makes his fairly rigorous rhyme scheme work with
Latin and French combined. The Latin is more medieval than
classical; in each he uses it for a purpose: in the first the
Latin is reminiscent of that from love lyrics such as those
found in the *Carmina Burana*; in the second the Latin is church
Latin and is used to make one think of the Temptation and Dep-
osition of Christ. *Temptare*, *vade retro*, *probare*, *ecce* and
corda are all found in crucial passages in the Vulgate. This
theme is reinforced by the sentiments of lines 11 and 12.

86. SATIS SATIS PLUS QUAM SATIS

Manuscripts: O, p. 354; M, fol. 41v; O², fol. 75r.
Major Editions: Chalvet (omitted); Champollion-Figeac,
No. 128, p. 276; Guichard, p. 272; D'Hericault, No. 120, p.
69; Champion, No. 86, p. 255.
Meter and rhyme: 8 ABba abAB abbaA

2. *encor*: D'Hericault reads *pas encore* which does not
fit metrically.
6. Guichard reads: *Soctes gens vous les amassez:*
9. *pour ce*: D'Hericault reads *pource*.

87. NON TEMPTABIS TIEN TE COY

Manuscripts: O, p. 355; M, fol. 41v; O^2, fol. 75r.

Major Editions: Chalvet (omitted); Champollion-Figeac, No. 129, pp. 276-277; Guichard, p. 273; D'Hericault, No. 121, p. 69; Champion, No. 87, pp. 255-256.

Meter and rhyme: 7 ABba abAB abbaA

I.   THIS MAY THAT LOVE NOT LUSTEN FORTO SLEPE

Manuscript: C, fol. 61r.
Major Editions: Taylor, p. 137; EETS, No. 1, p. 105.
Meter and rhyme: 10 ABbaabAB abbaAB.

2. *consertis*: Taylor reads *conseitis*.

II.   NOW HOLDE HIM SILF FROM LOVE LET SE THAT MAY

Manuscript: C, fol. 61v.
Major Editions: Taylor, p. 138; EETS, No. 2, p. 105.
Meter and rhyme: 10 ABbaabAB abbaAB.

4. *And yet y not*: Taylor prints *And yet y may not*.
12. *Teys doon*: Taylor reads *Feys doon*.

III.   WHAT SO BE THAT Y SAY PARDE

Manuscript: C, fol. 62r.
Major Editions: Taylor, pp. 138-39; EETS, No. 3, p. 106.
Meter and rhyme: 8 ABbaabAB abbaAB, (except lines 11, 12
that each have an extra foot.)

11. *Yet alsolong*: Taylor reads *Yet also long*.

IV.   IS SHE NOT FULLE OF ALLE GOODLY MANERE

Manuscript: C, fol. 62v.
Major Editions: Taylor, p. 139; EETS, No. 4, p. 106.
Meter and rhyme: 10 ABbaabAB abbaAB.

6. As this idea is not in the French it seems possible
that *prise* is a subconscious calque from French "je vous en
prie" which does appear in corresponding French.

V.   SYN THAT Y HAVE A NOUNPARALLE MAYSTRES

Manuscript: C, fol. 63r.
Major Editions: Taylor, p. 139-40; EETS, No. 5, p. 107.
Meter and rhyme: 10 ABbaabAB abbaAB.

1. *nounparalle*: Taylor reads *nonparall*.
6. *stichis in my shert*: Not in the French. Probably
added to fill out metrical line.

225

VI.   O GOD HOW THAT SHE LOKITH VERRY FAYRE

Manuscript: C, fol. 63v.
Major Editions: Taylor, p. 140-41; EETS, No. 6, p. 107.
Meter and rhyme: 10 ABbaabAB abbaAB.

5.   *kouthe*: Taylor reads *konthe*.
9.   EETS points out that this probably refers to the legend of the phoenix.   Cf. Ballade 62: "For when she lyvyd she
fayrist lyvyd in dede/Right as the fenyx lyveth withouten
ayre."

VII.   BI GOD BUT OON MY VERRY PLESAUNT JAY

Manuscript: C, fol. 64r.
Major Editions: Taylor, p. 141; EETS, No. 7, p. 108.
Meter and rhyme: 10 ABbaabAB abbaAB.

1.   *Bi God but oon*: Very troublesome.   "By the one true
God"(?).
        jay: Taylor capitalizes; EETS reads *Iay*.

VIII.   NOW SAY ME LO MYN HERT WHAT IS THI REED

Manuscript: C, fol. 64v.
Major Editions: Taylor, pp. 141-42; EETS, No. 8, p. 108.
Meter and rhyme: 10 ABbaabAB abbaAB.

IX.   AS OON SWETE LOOK OF YOWRE EYEN TAYNE

Manuscript: C, fol. 65r.
Major Editions: Taylor, pp. 142-43; EETS, No. 9, pp. 108-
09.
Meter and rhyme: 10 AABbaaabAAB aabbaAAB.

X.   WHO SO BIHOLDITH WEL AS WITH MY EYE

Manuscript: C, fol. 65v.
Major Editions: Taylor, p. 143; EETS, No. 10, p. 109.
Meter and rhyme: 10 ABbaabAB abbaAB, except lines 3, 4,
6 that have an extra syllable.

3.   Taylor reads: "In hir he shall se a gret and larges"
which is closer to the French: "En elle voit a grant largesse."

226

XI.   THIS MONTHE OF MAY WITHOUTEN PERE PRINCESSE

Manuscript: C, fol. 66r.
Major Editions: Taylor, p. 143-44; EETS, No. 11, p. 110.
Meter and rhyme: 10 ABbaabAB abbaAB.

1. *May*: This refers to both the month of May and the month of "may" or possibility. See, e.g., line 3.

XII.   COMAUNDE ME WHAT YE WILLE IN EVERI WISE

Manuscript: C, fol. 66v.
Major Editions: Taylor, p. 144; EETS, No. 12, p. 110.
Meter and rhyme: 10 ABbaabAB abbaAB.

XIII.   MOST GOODLY FAYRE IF HIT WERE YOWRE PLESERE

Manuscript: C, fol. 69r.
Major Editions: Taylor, pp. 147-48; EETS, No. 17, p. 113.
Meter and rhyme: 10 AABbaaabAAB aabbaAAB.

XIV.   REFRESSHE THE CASTELLE OF MY POORE HERT

Manuscript: C, fol. 69v.
Major Editions: Taylor, pp. 148; EETS, No. 18, p. 113.
Meter and rhyme: 10 ABbaabAB abbaAB.

XV.   IF SO WERE THAT YE KNOWE MY WOO TREWLY

Manuscript: C, fol. 67r.
Major Editions: Taylor, p. 145; EETS, No. 13, p. 111.
Meter and rhyme: 10 ABbaabAB abbaAB.

1. *If so were*: For a similar use of this phrase see Chaucer, *Canterbury Tales*, "Prioress' Tale," B.1640: "I wolde demen that ye tellen sholde/ A tale next if so were that ye wolde."

XVI.   MI VERRY IOY AND MOST PARFIT PLESERE

Manuscript: C, fol. 67v.
Major Editions: Taylor, pp. 145-146; EETS, No. 14, p. 111.
Meter and rhyme: 10 ABbaabAB abbaAB.

XVII.   MORE THEN THE DETH NYS THYNG UNTO ME LEEF

Manuscript: C, fol. 68r.
Major Editions: Taylor, p. 146; EETS, No. 15, pp. 111-12.
Meter and rhyme: 10 AABbaaabAAB aabbaAAB.

XVIII.   O GOODLY FAYRE WHICH Y MOST LOVE AND DREDE

Manuscript: C, fol. 68v.
Major Editions: Taylor, p. 147; EETS, No. 16, p. 112.
Meter and rhyme: 10 ABbaabAB abbaAB.

1. *O goodly fayre*: Taylor prints *Goodly fayre*.
2. Taylor prints: "Yn seche hape and grace as have y
wonyd." This line is found in the margin to this poem in
MS C.
3-6. Here it is the beauty of the lady that keeps him
imprisoned; in the French it is the more common Suspicion.

XIX.   MADAME AS LONGE AS HIT DOTH PLESE YOW AY

Manuscript: C, fol. 71v.
Major Editions: Taylor, p. 150; EETS, No. 21, p. 115.
Meter and rhyme: 10 ABbaabAB abbaAB.

XX.   BEWAR Y REDE YOW LOKE HERE NOT UPON

Manuscript: C, fol. 72r.
Major Editions: Taylor, p. 151; EETS, No. 22, p. 115.
Meter and rhyme: 10 ABbaabAB abbaAB.

XXI.   SYN Y MAY NOT ASKAPE ME FER NOR NERE

Manuscript: C, fol. 72v.
Major Editions: Taylor, pp. 151-52; EETS, No. 23, p. 116.
Meter and rhyme: 10 ABbaabAB abbaAB.

XXII.   HIT IS DOON THER IS NO MORE TO SAY

Manuscript: C, fol. 73r.
Major Editions: Taylor, p. 152; EETS, No. 24, p. 116.
Meter and rhyme: 10 (though some lines lack a beat for
dramatic effect) ABbaabAB abbaAB.

XXIII.   SYN LOVE HATH CAST ME BANYSSHE EVERYDELLE

Manuscript: C, fol. 70r.
Major Editions: Taylor, p. 149; EETS, No. 19, p. 114.
Meter and rhyme: 10 ABbaabAB abbaAB.

XXIV.   AS FOR THE GYFT YE HAVE UNTO ME GEVE

Manuscript: C, fol. 70v.
Major Editions: Taylor, pp. 149-50; EETS, No. 20, p. 114.
Meter and rhyme: 10 ABbaabAB abbaAB.

XXV.   HAD Y AS MOCHE OF WORLDLY GOODIS

Manuscript: C, fol. 73v.
Major Editions: Taylor, p. 152-53; EETS, No. 25, p. 117.
Meter and rhyme: 8 ABbaabAB abbaAB, except lines 11-12
that have 10 syllables.

11. Very difficult to read in MS. Entire line has been
rewritten and *arent* is the least clear of the words.

XXVI.   AS FOR YOWRE PRAYES YN FAME THAT IS UPBORE

Manuscript: C, fol. 74r.
Major Editions: Taylor, p. 153; EETS, No. 26, p. 117.
Meter and rhyme: 10 ABbaabAB abbaAB.

XXVII.   IN THOUGHT IN WISSHIS AND IN DREMES SOFT

Manuscript: C, fol. 74v.
Major Editions: Taylor, p. 154; EETS, No. 27, p. 118.
Meter and rhyme: 10 ABbaabAB abbaAB.

The sense of this poem depends upon taking "see" and "say"
as paranomastic and, at least subliminally, synonomous. So,
for example, in lines 2, 5-6, 10.

XXVIII.   WITH MY TREWE HERT CONTENT OF IOY AND WELE

Manuscript: C, fol. 74r.
Major Editions: Taylor, pp. 154-55; EETS, No. 28, p. 118.
Meter and rhyme: 10 ABbaabAB abbaAB.

XXIX. AND SO BE NOW THAT Y MY PURPOS LESSE

Manuscript: C, fol. 74v.
Major Editions: Taylor, p. 155; EETS, No. 29, p. 119.
Meter and rhyme: 10 ABbaabAB abbaAB.

XXX. AS BY THE PURCHAS OF MYN EYEN TAYNE

Manuscript: C, fol. 75r.
Major Editions: Taylor, p. 156; EETS, No. 30, p. 119.
Meter and rhyme: 10 ABbaabAB abbaAb.

XXXI. TO SHEWE THAT Y HAVE NOT FORGOTEN YOW

Manuscript: C, fol. 75v.
Major Editions: Taylor, pp. 156-57; EETS, No. 31, p. 120.
Meter and rhyme: 10 ABbaabAB abbaAB.

XXXII. FORSEEK IN WOO AND FER FROM IOYOUS HELE

Manuscript: C, fol. 76r.
Major Editions: Taylor, p. 157; EETS, No. 32, p. 120
Meter and rhyme: 10 ABbaabAB abbaAB.

1. *Forseek*: Taylor prints as two words: *For seek*.

XXXIII. RIGHT NY MYN HERT WITH MY BOSOM LO

Manuscript: C, fol. 76v.
Major Editions: Taylor, pp. 157-58; EETS, No. 33, p. 121.
Meter and rhyme: 10 ABbaabAB abbaAB.

First line is missing a beat; perhaps should read: "Right
ny myn hert within my bosom lo."

XXXIV. FORTO BIHOLDE THE BEWTE AND MANERE

Manuscript: C, fol. 77r.
Major Editions: Taylor, pp. 158-59; EETS, No. 34, p. 121.
Meter and rhyme: 10 ABbaabAB abbaAB.

XXXV.   TAKE TAKE THIS COSSE ATONYS ATONYS MY HERT

Manuscript: C, fol. 77v.
Major Editions: Taylor, p. 159; EETS, No. 35, p. 122.
Meter and rhyme: 10 ABbaabAB abbaAB.

XXXVI.   WHI LOVE Y YOW SO MOCHE HOW MAY THIS BE

Manuscript: C, fol. 78r.
Major Editions: Taylor, pp. 159-60; EETS, No. 36, p. 122.
Meter and rhyme: 10 ABbaabAB abbaAB.

EETS sees this as possible support for English poems
written by an Englishman and not by Charles. The argument is
based on the difference between the French and English versions
in lines 3-4.

XXXVII.   I PRAYSE NO THING THESE COSSIS DOWCHE

Manuscript: C, fol. 78v.
Major Editions: Taylor, p. 160; EETS, No. 37, p. 123.
Meter and rhyme: 10 ABbaabAB abbaAB.

1. EETS glosses *dowche* as "German" which makes little
if any sense in the context of the poem.
7. *Ynowe*: Taylor reads as two words: *y knowe*.

XXXVIII.   MY LOVE ONLY MY IOY AND MY MAYSTRES

Manuscript: C, fol. 79r.
Major Editions: Taylor, p. 161; EETS, No. 38, p. 123.
Meter and rhyme: 10 ABbaabAB abbaAB.

XXXIX.   NAR THAT Y DREDE DISPLESEN YOW ONLY

Manuscript: C, fol. 79v.
Major Editions: Taylor, pp. 161-62; EETS, No. 39, p. 124.
Meter and rhyme: 10 AABbaaabAAB aabbaAAB.

3. *cosse*: Taylor and EETS capitalize initial *c*: MS am-
biguous: could be either a capital or lower case with a stray
line from *p* in line above.

XL. THE GRET DISESE OF SEEKFULLE ANOYAUNCE

Manuscript: C, fol. 80r.
Major Editions: Taylor, pp. 162-63; EETS, No. 40, p. 124.
Meter and rhyme: 10 ABbaabAB abbaAB.

XLI. IF HIT PLESE YOW YOWRE COSSIS FORTO SELLE

Manuscript: C, fol. 80v.
Major Editions: Taylor, p. 163; EETS, No. 41, p. 125.
Meter and rhyme: 10 AABbaaabAAB aabbaAAB.

1. *If*: Taylor prints *Iff*.

XLII. MY LOVE AND LADY WHOM Y MOST DESERE

Manuscript: C, fol. 81r.
Major Editions: Taylor, p. 164; EETS, No. 42, p. 125.
Meter and rhyme: 10 ABbaabAB abbaAB.

XLIII. LOGGE ME DERE HERT IN YOWRE ARMYS TAYNE

Manuscript: C, fol. 81v.
Major Editions: Taylor, pp. 164-65; EETS, No. 43, p. 126.
Meter and rhyme: 10 ABbaabAB abbaAB.

XLIV. THOUGH DAUNGER HAVE THE SPECHE BIRAFT ME HERE

Manuscript: C, fol. 82r.
Major Editions: Taylor, pp. 165-66; EETS, No. 44, p. 126.
Meter and rhyme: 10 AABbaaabAAB aabbaAAB.

2. *withouten any pere*: Taylor reads *without any pere.*

XLV. GO FORTH THI WAY MY FEITHFULLE DESERVAUNCE

Manuscript: C, fol. 82v.
Major Editions: Taylor, p. 166; EETS, No. 45, p. 127.
Meter and rhyme: 10 AABbaaabAAB aabbaAAB.

XLVI. I PUT MY SILF UNTO YOWRE MERCY LO

Manuscript: C, fol. 83r.
Major Editions: Taylor, p. 167; EETS, No. 46, p. 127.
Meter and rhyme: 10 ABbaabAB abbaAB.

10. *wherfore*: Taylor capitalizes initial *w*.

XLVII. YE ARE TO MOCHE AS IN MY DETTE MADAME

Manuscript: C, fol. 83v.
Major Editions: Taylor, pp. 167-68; EETS, No. 47, p. 128.
Meter and rhyme: 10 ABbaabAB abbaAB.

XLVIII. YOWRE MOUTH HIT SAITH ME BAS ME BAS SWET

Manuscript: C, fol. 84r.
Major Editions: Taylor, p. 168; EETS, No. 48, p. 128.
Meter and rhyme: 10 ABbaabAB abbaAB.

XLIX. NOT OFT Y PRAYSE BUT BLAME AS IN SUBSTAUNCE

Manuscript: C, fol. 84v.
Major Editions: Taylor, p. 169; EETS, No. 49, p. 129.
Meter and rhyme: 10 ABbaabAB abbaAB.

Unlike French, English is based on the contradictions of
love, its "odo et amo" qualities.

L. AT NEDE THE FRENDIS PREVEN WHAT THEI BE

Manuscript: C, fol. 85r.
Major Editions: Taylor, pp. 169-70; EETS, No. 50, p. 129.
Meter and rhyme: 10 ABbaabAB abbaAB, except line 2 that
is missing a syllable.

LI. FLETH THE SHOT OF SWETE REGARD

Manuscript: C, fol. 85v.
Major Editions: Taylor, p. 170; EETS, No. 51, p. 130.
Meter and rhyme: All 10 except lines 1 and 9 which have
8 beats; ABbaabAB abbaAB.

233

LI. MY WELE MY IOY MY LOVE AND MY LADY

Manuscript: C, fol. 86r.
Major Editions: Taylor, pp. 170-71; EETS, No. 52, p. 130.
Meter and rhyme: 10 ABbaabAB abbaAB.

The meanings given in the Glossaries are only those re-
flected in the chansons.

French Glossary

ABREGIER   to shorten   45.4
ACCOMPLISSEZ: ACCOMPLISSER   to carry out, accomplish   35.11
ADRESSE   direction, path, straight and narrow   5.5
AFAMES   starved   68.4
AGREE: AGREER   to suit, to be suitable for   26.9
AGUET   watchfulness; technical term for falconry   69.3
AIST: AIDIER   to help, aid   52.6, 56.12
ALEGE   relieved   62.9
ALLEGANT   soften, alleviate   38.5
AMER   to love   2.1, 19.11, 49.2
AMOURETTES   flower   49.12
ANEANTIR   to annihilate, make into nothing   53.6
ANTREPRIS   undertaking, enterprise   77.4
ANUY   pain   67.3
ASSAILLIR   to assault, attack   58.6
ASSERVIR   to serve somebody, as slave to master   53.5
ASSORTIZ   loaded (as a gun)   76.10
ASSOTEMENT   stupidity   87.6
ASSOUBTIVANT   subtly, on the sly   56.10
ATIRER   to stimulate, excite   82.6
ATRAYEMENT   daring, boldness   87.2
AUMOSNE   alms   39.14
AUTRIER   time past, at least the day before yesterday   31.6,
    75.3
AVANTUREUX   bold, hardy, brave   76.8
AVENCER   (refl.) to put forward, suggest   54.9
AVISEMENT   advice, advisement   20.11
AVITAILLER   to provide with ammunition   76.3

BAILLER   to serve a legal writ   65.9
BARREZ (JOUER AUX _____)   fisticuffs   70.3
BARRIERE   female toll-keeper, often with sexual connotations
    23.11
BESONGNEZ: BESONGNER   to fulfill a need (?)   61.10
BLANS (BLANC)   coin worth about five deniers   49.1
BOULEVERS   ramparts   76.11
BOUTER (SE BOUTER)   to push or attack fiercely, sometimes
    with a sense of harassment   72.10, 17.13

CARREAULX   paving stones, cobblestones   73.5
CELLE (CELEE): CELER   to hide   8.6, 75.11
CERTES   indeed   5.5
CHAILLE: CHALOIR   verb of necessity, comparable to Mod. Fr.
    FALLOIR,   7.11
CHANCELLE(R)   to vacillate   77.9
CHAULT: CHALOIR (see CHAILLE)   33.5, 36.3, 65.5 (CHAULDROIT
    64.10)
CHEVAUCHENT: CHEVAUCHER   to ride   73.4
CHIER (TENIR _____)   (to hold) dear   36.10, 47.10
CHIERE   face, expression   31.12
CLIGNEZ: CLIGNER   to blink   20.6
COUVENDRA: COUVENIR   verb of necessity, comparable to Mod.
    Fr. FALLOIR
COUVIENT: COUVENIR   21.3
COY   quiet   48.12

DANGIER   loaded word for Charles d'Orléans. Usually used as
    personified suspicion   14.3, 18.3, 25.12, 35.6, 35.9,
    39.6
DARDE: DARDER   to strike with an arrow   48.10   DARDE   arrow
    72a.3
DELAISSER   to abandon   34.11
DEMAINE: DEMAINER   to rule over   40.6
DEMENER   to pursue, as an idea   1.6
DEMOURER   to stay   1.11, 38.2
DEMOUSTRANCE   demonstration, proof   54.12
DERRAINEMENT   finally, most recently   9.15
DES   some; partitive plural used for singular   77.1
DESPLAISIR   lack of pleasure, displeasure   5.12
DESSERVY   deserved   29.2
DESSOUS (TENIR AU _____)   lit., to hold down; frequently used
    in context of a game meaning to be victorious over   67.6
DESTOURBER   to vex, hinder   34.9
DESTOURBIER   difficulty, trouble   48.10
DEUST (EN _____)   in pain   33.6
DOINT: DONER   to give   31.10, 61.2
DOUBLANS: DOUBLER   to double, duplicate   49.5

ELLE   wing   68.10
EMBASMER   to embalm   49.11
EMBLENT: EMBLER   to steal, steal away   20.10, 39.2, 55.2
ENCHAPERONNE(R)   hooded   82.2
ENTAMER   to calm, tame   49.10
ENTE: S'ENTER (DE)   to graft (onto)   32.4
ENTREPRANDRE   to become involved with, undertake   51.6
ES   abbreviated version of EN LES   on the   76.11
ESBATEMENT   diversion, distraction   4.10

ESCLER   lightning bolt   57.6
ESCONDIRIES: ESCONDIRE   to contradict, refuse, deny   15.12
ESCOUTER   to listen   22.12
ESLIRE   to choose   78.9
ESLIESSER   to make happy, rejoice   1.2, 17.3
ESMAYER   to trouble; to celebrate the first of May and the
    coming of Spring by crowning with green branches   11.11
ESPARGNES: ESPARGNIER   to spare   12.6, 13.8
ESPERON   spur   73.10
ESTANDART   banner, standard   51.9
ESTOIE: ESTRE   to be   18.11
ESVEILLE: ESVEILLER   to wake up   1.9, 43.9
EUIL   eye   83.2
EUREUX   lucky   76.4

FAEE   having to do with fairies, magical   80.11
FAIT   actions, deeds   84.9
FAVEUR   favoritism   4.12
FESTIER   to celebrate   37.12, 43.3
FIANCE   confidence, confidante   66.12
FIS: FAIRE   to make   31.6, 9.15
FORVOIE: FORVOYER   to go by a circuitous route; to dissemble
    69.10
FOURREZ   dressed in furs; by extension, elegant, à la mode
    60.1
FOURRIER   henchman of a royal party   62.1
FRIT: FRIRE   to tremble with desire   65.4

GAGE (GAIGE) (EN _____)   as a wager, guarantee   41.3, 59.10
GAIGE (DONNER _____)   to make a pledge, leave a deposit as
    guarantee   59.10
GALIMAFREE   galimaufry, confused discourse   80.8
GARDER (EN _____)   to watch out for   51.12
GARNIE (GARNY)   furnished, decorated   4.1, 11.12, 38.9
GIBESSIERRE   cage for falcon   75.8
GIBIER   falconry   GIBESSANT   75.1
GIST: GESIR   to lie down   35.10
GORGE (GETTER LA _____)   term from falconry meaning to offer
    food   82.9
GOUTTE (NE _____)   strong negative; not a drop   72.2
GRACIEUX   full of grace   30.12
GREIGNEUR   greater   26.11, 33.12
GREVANCE   pain, sorrow, cause of grief   62.6
GRIEF   painful   42.12
GUERDONNE: GUERDONER   to reward, recompense   18.10, 24.4,
    GUERDON   41.15
GUET   guard   35.5, 35.10

HALE   tanned   59.4
HEBERGER   lodged   62.12
HEIT: HAIR   to hate   48.9
HERITAGE   inheritance   41.4

JA (NE__)   negative of time   63.5

LARGEMENT   in abundance   5.6
LARMOYANS   tearful   78.7
LARRECIN   robbery   39.13
LAS   tired   27.12, 43.5
LAS   for HELAS   alas   29.10
LASSER   to tire out   6.5, 34.5
LEAL   loyal   28.1
LERREZ: LAISSER   to leave   53.6
LIESSE (LYESSE)   happiness   5.12, 7.2, 11.12, 13.3, 21.10,
    30.11, 34.3, 38.4, 42.12
LIGEMENT   like a liege man; absolutely, without reserve   20.2
LIGNAGE   heritage, background   83.3
LYE   joyful, gay   31.12

MAINT   many 30.4
MAINTIEN   demeanor, ways   84.8
MANDER   to command, declare   16.4
MANTY   lied   63.11 (Mod. Fr. MENTI)
MARRY   sorrowful, painful   22.6, 85.5
MARTIRE   martyrdom, suffering   42.12, 53.14, 78.1
MEINS (AU _____)   at least   17.4 (Mod. Fr. AU MOINS)
MELLEUR   better   26.10
MESDISANS   ill-speakers, gossips   55.5
MESTRE   master, victor, winner   67.1
METZ (____ PEINE)   take (pains)   45.6
MIE (NE ___)   strong negative   3.9
MILLIERS   thousands   37.5
MOIS   month, frequently shortened form of MOIS DE MAI, the
    month of May; because of this, perhaps, MOIS alone comes
    to mean naive, green   23.6
MONDAINS   earthly   18.5, MONDAINE   27.6
MORFONDEZ: MORFONDRE   to tire, get bored   70.11
MUSSER   to hide   59.6, MUSSIER   33.2

NAVREZ: NAVRER   to wound   74.9
NE   usually a negative; sometimes means "or"   3.2
NEANT   nothing   56.6
NOMPAREILLE   that which has no equal   1.12, 5.1, 11.1, 42.3
NONCHALOIR   keyword for Charles d'Orléans. Comes to mean
    emotional apathy, depression   12.9, 51.10, 82.3, 85.2
NYSSE   naive, negligent   66.9

238

OCTROYE: S'OCTROYER   to grant   71.3
ONCQUES   ever   28.3
OSTA: OSTER   to lift, remove   82.4
OSTEE: OSTER   see OSTA   84.6
OU   in addition to expected "or", can also mean "with"
    9.1
OYE: (OY) OYER   to hear   2.5, 45.14, 71.6

PARÇONNIER   participant   37.4
PAREE   decorated, ornamented   27.5
PARLEMENT   discussion, gossip session   55.6
PARTAGE   share   41.15
PASSER   to pass in the sense of not being able to play any
    more   67.11
PENEUSE   painful   40.2
PENSER   to brood, think (but with definite emphasis on a non-
    rational process)   6.12
PERESSE   laziness   76.6 (SANS _____: without a break)
PESTRE (FAIRE _____)   to trick, finesse, outthink   67.5
PEU   fed   75.10
PIEÇA   formerly   2.5
PIQUES   pricked   73.10
PLANTE   plenty; planted   25.3
POINT (NE _____)   not at all   31.1
POURCE   for this reason   11.5, 50.12, 58.12
POURCE (_____ QUE)   because   17.2 (Mod. Fr. PARCE QUE)
POURCHAS   endeavor, effort   30.1, 44.3
POURCHASSIER   to pursue   33.11   POURMAINE: POURMENER   to
    pursue, tail   70.12
POURTANT (_____ QUE)   because   7.12
POVAIR (POVOIR)   power   11.10, 12.4, 16.10
PRANGNE: PRANDRE   to take   21.11
PRESSE   crowd   10.10, 39.7
PREST   ready, prepared   6.4, 12.5, 19.3, 28.5 (Mod. Fr.
    PRETE)
PRISE: PRISER   to prize, esteem, praise   37.1, 49.1
PROPOS   stance, with emphasis on intellectual position   29.1,
    56.4
PUIST: POUVOIR   to be able   3.6
PUSSE   flea   1.4 (Mod. Fr. PUCE)

QUANQUE   all that   52.11, 11.3
QUERELLE   discussion, conversation   68.6, 77.3
QUERIR   to seek   52.5

RAENÇONNER   to ransom   18.9, 24.12
RAFRESCHISSEZ: RAFRESSCHISSER   to replenish, refurbish   14.1
RAPAISE   to become calm, be at peace   58.9

RASSOTY   stupified   85.11
RAVIR   to be ravished, swept away   72.5
RECOUS: RECOUVRER   to recoup   67.10, 71.4
REDOUBTE: REDOUBTER   to fear, to doubt   72.3
RENTE: RENTER   to rent; to graft anew   25.11
RENYE(R)   to deny   63.12
REQUIER   to seek, beseech   11.5
RETRAYEZ (-IEZ): RETRAIER   to pull back, retract   51.9, 69.1

SA: ESSAIER   to try   71.10
SCET: SÇAVOIR   to know how to do something   2.10, 10.10,
     (Mod. Fr. SAVOIR)
SEELLEE   sealed, as a letter or document   47.9
SEMBLANCE (PAR _____)   in the likeness of, just like
     57.5
SENIS (MT. _____)   mountain in French Alps   81.6
SENTE   health   32.1 (Mod. Fr. SANTE)
SENTE: SENTER   to feel   35.6
SEREMENT   oath   4.3, 5.11
SERS: SERVIR   to serve loyally   20.2
SIEGE   siege, assault   14.5   SIET (IL ____)   impersonal
     verb of suitability; takes infinitive as subject   54.2
SOMMEILLIER   to sleep   43.6
SORTE   type, ilk   65.6
SOUBTILEMENT   stealthily   20.10
SOUHAID   wish   27.1
SOUHAIDE: SOUHAIDER   to wish   9.3 (Mod. Fr. SOUHAITER)
     52.12
SOULAS   cause for rejoicing   43.4
SOURDOIT   hunting term   75.6
SOUSSIER   to worry, be concerned about   1.3
SOYE: ESTRE   to be 71.2
SUIENT: SUIVRE   to follow   10.9

TAYSE: TAIRE   to remain silent   29.9, 58.4
TELZ   such   56.9
TENIR (____ ME VEUIL)   to guard, hold, keep   5.3
TENTE   tent   35.10 (unusual in F; probably calque from E)
TIEGNE: TENIR   to hold   2.1
TIEULX   such   10.5, 64.12
TIRE (DE ____)   right away   50.10
TRAIT   draught   74.1 (includes both E. meanings of word:
     current of air and path of an arrow)
TRESORIERE   female treasurer, possible sexual connotations
     26.5

UMBRAGE   protection against the sun, parasol   59.3

VAILLANT   possession   26.11
VANTE: VANTER   to boast   46.11
VOIR   truly, accurately   12.12, 32.6, 85.6
VOLOYENT: VOLER   to fly   68.10
VUIT   empty   21.10

YER   yesterday   2.9 (Mod. Fr. HIER)

English Glossary

ABAYE(N)   to obey   LI.6
ACHERE(N)   to cheer up   XXI.9
ADVERT(EN)   to discover; make known; consider   V.11, XIV.5
AGAYNE   again   XLIII.9
ARAY   battle dress   LI.3
ARENT   to rent (?)   XXV.11
ARMYS   arms   XLIII.1
ARNE   burns   XLIX.11
ASPY(EN)   to spy on   XX.11
ASSHIS   ashes   XLVIII.12
ATONYS: ATTONES   at once   XXXV.1, XXXV.11
ATURBANCE   disturbance, particularly psychological   XL.12
AVAUNT(EN)   to boast   XII.6
AVISE(N)   to inform, advise, consider; look at   IV.3
AY   always   XXVI.2

BANDONE(N)   to abandon   XVIII.6
BAS   kiss   XLVIII.1 (F. BAISE, kiss)
BERD   beard   LI.5
BETH: BE   to be   XLI.7
BIE(N)   to buy   XXXVII.5
BIHET(E): BIHATEN   to promise   XXXIX.8, XLVIII.4
BILL(E)   any kind of written document, including poems, as
    here   XI.6
BIRAFT: BIREYVE   to deprive of   XLIV.1
BLAKE   evil, wicked   I.10
BONE   prayer   XV.9

CAYTIJF   wretch   XXXII.6
CHERE   demeanor; expression   IV.9
CONSAIT   notion   XII.9
CONSERTIS   consorts, musical groups   I.2
COSSE, -IS   kiss(es)   XXXV.1, XXXVII.1, XLVII.2
COVERT   covered   XIV.2
CROSSE   coin   XXXVII.5
CROWCHE   coin   XXXVII.5
CRY   desire, cry out   XV.9
CURRISHENES   ill-breeding   XXXV.10

DAR: DAREN   to dare   XII.6
DELE   way, aspect   XXVIII.5, XXXII.12
DERKID   darkened   XL.10
DESERE   desire   XXVIII.2, XXXVI.11, XLII.1
DESERVAUNCE   love's service   XLV.1
DEWRYNG   enduring   XXXVI.4
DEY, -AY   to die   XLIV.8, II.12
DISCURE(N)   to make known; uncover   III.10
DON: DOON   to do   XLVII.6; to make   XIX.2
DOUCHE   sweet   XXXVII.1 (F. DOUCE)
DOWTLES   beyond discussion, doubtless   V.5
DRYVE   chase   XXXI.5
DURES   hardship, oppression, duress   XIII.15
ECHON   each one   X.11
EFT   again   XXXVIII.12
ELECCIOUN   choice   XLII.2
ELLE   ells (measures of length)   XLI.6
ENDEWRE(N)   to endure   XLII.10, XIX.6
ENMEYNTID   mixed with   XLIX.3 (? false construction created
    by analogy with DERKID)
ENTIRMELLE   to mix together, intermingle   XXIII.12
EVEN   completely, equally, all the way; usually used as an
    emphatic   VII.2
EVERYDELLE   every way, wholly   XXIII.1
EYRE   heir   VI.9

FAYNE   glad, eager   XXX.12;   FAYNST   gladly   XXX.5
FELL(EN)   to feel   XXVIII.12
FESTEN   to feast, make merry   XLIII.3
FORLEFT: FORLEVEN   to forsake   XLIV.6
FLETH: FLE   to flee   LI.1
FOO   foe, enemy   XXXIII.5
FORBETITH: FORBETTEN   to batter   XIV.6
FORBRENT: FORBRENNEN   to burn   XLVIII.11
FORPOSSID   pushed about   XLIX.10
FORSLOUTH(EN)   to delay   XI.10
FORSWELL(EN)   to swell up   XLI.14
FORTORE   torn apart   XXIII.10
FOWLE   unpleasant, unkind, harsh   XIII.15
FOYSOUN   plenty   XLIX.4
FRO   away from   VIII.10
FY   term of contempt or challenge   XLI.13

GARDONYD   rewarded   XVIII.11
GANTILES   courtesy   XI.5 (F. GENTILESSE)
GEDIR   to gather   XXXIII.12
GEFE: GEVEN   to give   XX.5
GERY   capricious   XXXV.10

244

GEYN-SAY   speak against   XV.12
GOODLIHED   beauty   VIII.4
GOODLY   excellent   IV.1
GREE (IN ____)   willingly   XI.6 (F. IN GRE)
GREVE (IN ____)   in trouble   XXIV.9
GRISE   to shake   XII.9
GRUCCHYNG   complaint   XIX.4

HATITH: HATEN   to hate   XLVIII.9
HELE   health   XXXII.1
HERTIS: HERT   heart   VI.2
HEVYNES   sorrow   V.9
HOOL   whole, complete   V.2
HVUG   huge   X.3

IHESU   Jesus   L.12
IAY   joy   VII.1 (false construction from F.   JOIE by analogy
    with F. FOIE > E. FAY--so EETS).

KARFULLE   full of cares, sorrowful   XVII.2
KARIS   cares   XXXII.9
KEPE   notice   I.5
KOUTHE   to be able   VI.5

LERE(N)   to learn   XXXVI.2
LESE(N)   to lose   XX.3
LESSE   lessen   XXIX.1
LONGE (IN ____)   in length   XVIII.4
LORE   teaching   II.6
LUSTEN   to desire   I.1, XI.1; LUSTYNES   youthful energy
    LV.4
LYVE(N)   to live   XIX.2, XXII.4

MADID   was mad   XXXIII.6
MANERE   behavior   IV.1
MARTERE   martyrdom   XLII.12
MELLE   meal   XXVIII.9
MO   more   XXXIX.7
MOTE: MOTEN   to be permitted, allowed   VII.9
MOWE: MOWEN   to be strong, prevail   XIII.16
MYSBORE   misconducted   XXIX.3

NAR   were not   XXXVIII.11, XVIII.6; NARE   am not   XLII.9;
    NOLDE   would not   XXXIX.12
NAVE   have not   XXVI.10, XVI.6
NE   no, not   I.2; NIS   XVI.12
NEDE (AT ____)   in need   L.4
NELLE   will not   XLI.17

245

NEUYR   never   XXV.4
NEWE   anew   VI.4
NEWFANGILLE   fond of novelty   XXVII.12
NYS   is nothing   I.3
NYSE   nice   I.2

OBEYSHAUNT   obedient   XII.3
OCUPACION   task, labor   XLII.6
OFFICERE   minister of justice   XLVII.11
ONYS   once and for all   XXX.12
ORDEYNYD   required, ordered   XVIII.2
OWIST   owed; ought   XLIV.2

PARCAS   perchance   XXIV.12
PARDE   truly   III.1 (F. PAR DIEU)
PARSEYV(EN)   to perceive   XXXV.6
PAYRE   coin   VI.12
PERELLE   peril, danger   XLI.13
PORTAGE   error for PARTAGE   sharing   XLI.16
PRATILY   prettily   XX.10
PREEF   proof   XVII.13
PRESE   crowd   XXXIX.7
PRIKE   to prance   V.10
PURCHAS   endeavor   XXX.1
PUYSSHAUNCE   power   XLV.13

REDE(N)   to advise   XX.1, XLVII.10
REED   advice   VIII.1
REFRESSHE   replenish   XIV.1
REFUSE   refusal   XIII.15, XV.5
RESTID   arrested   XLVII.11
RIGURE   discipline, rigor   III.2

SEEKFULLE   full of sighs; sick   XL.1
SEEKLEW   sickly   XL.3
SEID   said   XLVI.3
SELY   innocent, simple   XII.2
SETT   (refl.) placed   IV.6
SEYNE   to say   IX.12
SHAPEN   planned   XVII.8
SIDIS   sides   IX.5
SITTYNG   becoming   XIII.14
SMERT   pain   V.3, XIV.4, XVII.4
SOCHE   such   XXXVII.12
SOIOWR   jaunt   XXVI.3
SONE   soon   XLI.17
SORE   pain, hurt   XXVI.12

246

SOWRE   swore   XXVI.9
SPAYNG   sparing   XII.6
STEFFEN   speech   XXIX.10
STERT: STARTEN   to start   V.10
STICHIS   stitches   V.6
SUFFIR   allow   XIV.9
SUL   sole, only   X.2
SUFFISAUNT   satisfying   XII.10
SURMOUNTYNG   surpassing; above and beyond   III.6
SWETE   sweetness   VI.1
SYN   since   V.1

TACHE   attach, arrest   XLVII.10
TAKE: TAN   taken   LI.5
TARY   slow   XLIII.5
TATH: TAKE   to take   XLIV.13
TAY(NE)   two   VII.4, IX.1, XLIII.1
TEWCHE   tush!; tut, tut!   XXII.12
TEYS   it is   II.12
THE(N)   to prosper   XLIII.10
TOFORE   before, previously   XVII.8
TOW   show reluctance   XXXI.12

UNNETHIS   scarcely   XXXIV.10
UPBORE: UPBEREN   to carry up   XXVI.1
UTTIR   to speak, utter   VIII.6

VAUNT   boast   XLVI.11
VAYLITH: VAYLEN   to avail   XV.11

WAY (ME ___)   my way, my direction   II.4
WELE   prosperity, well-being   VIII.5, XXIII.4
WELLE   well   XLV.8
WERID: WAR   to make war on   XVI.9
WERRE   war   XXXVIII.6
WIGHT   person   VI.4
WISE   manner   IV.2
WOT   know   VII.9
WRETHE   anger   XXII.5
WROFFT: WORCHE   to make, wrought   XI.6, XLI.15

YWIS   indeed   VI.6; XXIV.10; XXV.5
YVILL(E)   evil   VII.9, XLIII.10

Indexes

Index of French First Lines

Index of English First Lines